Pelican Books

The Scarman Report

Leslie George Scarman was born in 1911 and was educated at
Radley College, and Brasenose College, Oxford. He was Harms-
worth Law Scholar at the Middle Temple in 1936 and became a
barrister in the same year. He was made a Q.C. in 1957 and
between 1961 and 1973 he was a Judge of the High Court of the
Justice, Probate, Divorce and Admiralty Division, and later the
Family Division. From 1973 until 1977 he was a Lord Justice of
Appeal, since when he has been a Lord of Appeal in Ordinary. He
has been Chairman of the Law Commission, the Council of Legal
Education and the University of London Court, and was President of the Senate of Inns of Court and Bar. Since 1976 he has
been Vice-chairman of the English National Opera and was a
member of the Arts Council from 1968 until 1970 and again in
1972–3. He has been Chancellor of the University of Warwick
since 1977. In 1966 he was made an Honorary Fellow of
Brasenose College, Oxford, and in 1975 of Imperial College,
University of London, and he holds honorary doctorates in Law
from the universities of Exeter, Glasgow, London, Keele, Warwick, Bristol, Manchester and Freiburg. He received the O.B.E.
in 1944 and was knighted in 1961. Lord Scarman was made a
Privy Councillor in 1973.

He has also published *Pattern of Law Reform* (1967) and
English Law – The New Dimension (1975).

The Brixton Disorders · 10–12 April 1981

The
Scarman Report

Report of an Inquiry by the Right Honourable the

Lord Scarman, OBE

Presented to Parliament by the
Secretary of State for the Home Department
by command of Her Majesty
November 1981

Penguin Books

Penguin Books Ltd, Harmondsworth, Middlesex, England
Viking Penguin Inc., 40 West 23rd Street, New York, New York 10010, U.S.A.
Penguin Books Australia Ltd, Ringwood, Victoria, Australia
Penguin Books Canada Limited, 2801 John Street, Markham, Ontario, Canada L3R 1B4
Penguin Books (N.Z.) Ltd, 182–190 Wairau Road, Auckland 10, New Zealand

The Preface is the transcript of a talk given by Lord Scarman
in the television series *Options*, produced by Panoptic
and broadcast on Channel 4 in February 1986

Printed and bound in Great Britain by
Cox & Wyman Ltd, Reading
Set in Linotron Plantin by
Rowland Phototypesetting Ltd
Bury St Edmunds, Suffolk

WARRANT OF APPOINTMENT

In pursuance of the powers vested in me by Section 32 of the Police Act 1964, I, the Right Honourable William Whitelaw, one of Her Majesty's Principal Secretaries of State, hereby appoint the Right Honourable Lord Scarman to inquire urgently into the serious disorder in Brixton on 10 to 12 April 1981 and to report, with the power to make recommendations.

And I further appoint P. J. C. Mawer Esq. of the Home Office, to be the Secretary of the Inquiry.

And I direct, under subsection (2) of the said Section 32, that the Inquiry shall be held in public, save insofar as in the opinion of the tribunal it is expedient that any part of the Inquiry shall be held in private.

Home Office,
14 April 1981

William Whitelaw
One of Her Majesty's
Principal Secretaries of State

CONTENTS

Preface   xiii

THE REPORT

Contents

Part IV · The Police

Contents

Contents

Contents

THE PREFACE

When I was asked to report on the Brixton disorders in April 1981, some people questioned whether a judge and member of the House of Lords was the right person to carry out this investigating. What does a judge know of the conditions of life in our rundown inner cities?

But I believe that a judge does have special qualifications both for investigating disorders and for speaking about inner cities. He is a trained adjudicator between differing parties. He is a trained investigator of fact. He is by office, and should be by nature, impartial and detached.

I, myself, have had some experience of police operations and questions of public order. I headed the police inquiry into the Red Lion Square disturbances in 1974. I have some understanding of crowd problems and a considerable knowledge of police operations and police organizations. But there is one further important reason why I believe a judge can speak about inner cities. Public disorder usually arises out of a sense of injustice. A sense of injustice is not limited to people with legal or judicial training, but judges will certainly have experience in uncovering it and have an instinctive understanding of the causes and consequences of injustice. Above all, a judge has a passion for righting injustice. This is his job.

The inner city is critical for the future of the British nation. The inner cities are the testing ground where the character of Britain will be determined.

This is because of their population mix, their high rate of unemployment and their substandard physical environment. Most importantly, our fellow citizens who live there see themselves at a disadvantage compared with the rest of us, and many of them attribute their disadvantage to racial prejudice. The question the inner cities raise, therefore, is are we to become a successful, multi-racial nation or are we on a course for a revolutionary phase in our history?

This is not some future problem. It is a problem that confronts us here and now. The necessary decisions have to be made because the evidence that is emerging from the inner cities is that, unless effective action is taken very soon, the gap between the younger generation of the ethnic minority groups, who live mainly in our inner cities, and the established institutions of British society *will* widen and deepen. This gap is not yet unbridgeable. Our task as a nation is to build bridges now.

When I reported on the Brixton disturbances in 1981, there seemed to be a sense of urgency about implementing my recommendations. As far as the police reforms went, many were acted on very quickly. But when one comes to my suggestions for improving social and environmental conditions, I have to say that the government did not show the same sense of urgency until 1985, when they suddenly learned that more was needed to prevent a recurrence of Brixton than merely improving the quality of our policing. It took the Birmingham riots of 1985 to bring home the importance of implementing the social recommendations of my 1981 report. Four years of lost opportunity – lost because so much more could have been done than was in fact done.

To restore our inner cities to a healthy normality, it is necessary to understand clearly what we mean by the problem of the inner cities. As I argued in my 1981 report, the Brixton disturbances arose from a complex social, political and economic situation that was not special to Brixton but which exists in many of our inner cities. The core of the problem is this: a decaying urban structure, with its attendant evils of bad-quality and inadequate housing, and a lack of job opportunities, with its inevitable evil of high unemployment. These depressing conditions coexist with the crucial social fact that these areas have a high proportion of ethnic minority groups – blacks and Asians. And these groups believe and feel, with considerable justification, that it is the colour of their skins, and their first or second generation immigrant origins which count against them in their bid for a fair share in our society. We cannot avoid facing this important racial dimension.

It is certainly possible that if there was full employment, the racial aspect of our inner city problems would not loom large. But once you have deprivation and once minorities perceive that they are at the end of every queue, then race heats up the furnace of anger to an unbearable temperature. When you have, as we now have in our inner cities, the problems associated with un-employment and its psychological frustrations – idleness and so on – with the added factor of what is seen to be race prejudice, then the whole social situation becomes that much more bitter, the underlying tension is that much greater and tempers fly more easily.

In considering this vital racial aspect, I am deliberately concen-trating on the black community. I believe that it is specifically on this community that our efforts must be concentrated. In general, the Asian community make a very adroit use of their opportunities in this country. They fit themselves into competitive positions. They enter into professions. They manage businesses. They have a well-developed social cohesion. I would like to see black people achieving this same willingness to help themselves. But largely because of a series of historical accidents, I do not believe that they can operate as successfully as the Asian community unless they are given greater oportunities.

This brings me to what was, and is, my central contention – that we have to embark on social policies that will eradicate the multiple disadvantages that British blacks now suffer from. To pursue these policies, we must get away from the use of such horrendous terms such as 'positive discrimination' or 'preferential treatment'. Those terms seem to indicate discrimination *against* the white population of Britain. The social policies I have in mind won't be discrimina-tory in that sense at all.

It is not unjust or unfair to seek ways and means of correcting the disadvantages, even though the help requires effort and a degree of self-denial on the part of the majority. We should think of black people in our inner cities as a group that has specific needs which have to be met if they are going to have a chance to compete on a fair basis in our society. It means money and opportunities in the inner city for educational and job training. It means ensuring that when there are people of equal attainment seeking a job, the black man is not going to be number two.

Should we take it further than this? Is it right where you have two people of similar attainments – one black and one white – both applying for a job that that job should be given to the black man because he is black?

In the abstract, the answer to that question must be that he should *not* be given the job just because he is black. But the question does not always arise in this pure, abstract form. In the real world, we surely can see circumstances in which it would be desirable to give the black man the job because he is black. I am thinking, for example, of the case of a black man applying for a job in a factory where there are no, or very few, black workers; or of a black man applying for a job in the police force, where more black police officers would be so enormously helpful to the police force itself and to the rest of society.

But I am not in favour of the allocation of employment on the basis of some predetermined quota system. If you impose a quota, you will have the danger – quite apart from a white backlash – of black people seeming to form a 'second eleven' in the work-force. People would say of a black employee: 'Oh, he's only here because we have to have 40 per cent blacks in this area on the workforce.'

It is because of these kinds of undesirable consequences that we must concentrate on helping all those in our community who suffer from special disadvantages, by giving them the kind of special educational and training opportunities that will then equip them to enter into the competitive job market without the disadvantages of poor literacy, inadequate numeracy or a lack of essential work skills. Education, job training and professional and business opportunities directed to young blacks provide the key to solving the crisis in the inner cities. Our underlying social strategy should be to create ethnic minority opportunities in the universities, the professions, the civil service, the police, in politics and public life, in business activities and in industrial management.

In other words, we must create a black British middle class. This was the strategy pursued in America. As in America, so here: black and brown as well as white faces must be seen not only on the production line but also in positions of authority and influence at all levels of society. I dislike the term, 'middle class', but I think, in this context, the meaning of my remarks is clear. If we can create a black middle class, then we will also be creating a group that can exercise responsible and creative leadership in its own community and in the nation – to the benefit of all of us in Britain.

I have suggested ways in which the government should intervene to provide young blacks with a launching pad into our society. It is tempting to think that many of the social policy recommendations I set out in my report might be implemented more effectively if there was a cabinet minister specifically for the inner cities. But this would be counter-productive. The creation of a special minister is quite likely, in practice, to make the great departments of state *less*, not more, interested in their responsibilities. What is needed is a coordinated ministerial effort at cabinet level, rather than the appointment of one minister. The government, it would appear, has now accepted this view. But I would have wished to see a policy of coordination of effort started five years ago in 1981, not in 1986.

The government, over the last five years, has not tackled the core of the inner city problem – the factor of racial disadvantage. You *must* tackle racial disadvantage, and that means adjusting all government policies to this end. The government must now press ahead with racially directed social improvements on a coordinated basis.

More than mere governmental direction is, of course, needed. All of us – but particularly the business community – have a role to play in the inner cities. It is quite reasonable for a businessman to say that, if he sets up a factory or an office or workshop in an inner city area, he must have some guarantee that he can develop his business against a background of public peace and good order. So I turn now to the vital question of the role of the police in tackling the inner city crisis. Here, our strategy must be to establish a firm bond of respect and trust between the ethnic minorities and the police force.

How do I react to the accusation, which was often made to me during my investigation into the Brixton disorders, that the police are racially prejudiced?

I have studied this problem. I have had the opportunity of looking at police recruiting and I have seen that immense trouble has been taken since 1981 to supervise the attitudes and reactions of police recruits going through their initial training. Those who shows signs of racial prejudice will either have it eradicated by training, advice and leadership or they will go. I don't accept that the police force is institutionally a racially prejudiced force. But I do accept that one of the results of disorder upon police who have to deal with that disorder – often, as at Brixton, extremely violent disorder – can be bitterness against those whom they see as creating disorder. This is a problem by no means special to ethnic minority difficulties. For example, some bitterness must have arisen among the police during the miners' strike.

It is only human to feel bitter when you and your colleagues are abused, attacked and sometimes physically injured. But I believe, given the strong commitment by police leaders, that the problem will diminish.

In a number of key areas the police responded very positively to some of my recommendations. I recommended that a specific offence of racially prejudiced conduct should be included in the police's discipline code. This has now been done.

The idea of building bridges of trust is central to the recommendations which I made to create police station lay visitors. What I meant by that is that there should be a panel of independent laymen who have the right, at any time of the day or night, to visit police stations and see the conditions under which interrogations are held. I did not recommend that these lay visitors be present at actual interrogations, because that would risk them being called as witnesses for either the police or the accused. They would be cross-examined and, inevitably, their independence, which is so vital, would be compromised.

But lay visitors have wide powers. They can talk to suspects in police stations. They can examine the state of the food. They can listen to what the prisoners say. They can talk with the police officers. The result in Brixton has been a lessening of minor complaints against the police, and, of course, it is a tremendous sanction against any possible police misconduct within their own headquarters. The lay visitors have been a great success. I now urge the government to ensure that independent lay visitors are extended on a nationwide basis.

I now come to one serious omission. I recommended a far-reaching reform of the system for investigating complaints against the police. I recognize – as I said in my report – that there are difficulties in implementing this, but post-1981 experience has strengthened my view that these difficulties must be overcome.

What is needed is a system of independent investigation: in other words, the police must not investigate themselves. A police investigation which is not independently supervised is simply not good enough.

No group in our nation, not even the police, should be immune from some independent investigation. I know the immense problems involved in investigating complaints against the police. Who is competent enough to carry out such an investigation? How can this be done except with the support of the police? But the problems can be met. We have to accept that if the public, and in particular the ethnic minorities in the inner cities, are to have confidence in the police, they must not think that the police themselves are above the law.

Indeed, many police officers, and the Police Federation which represents the police force, have come to see that there is a strong case for establishing an independent investigatory system. Such a system might actually protect the rights and reputations of their own members. If an independent system establishes the innocence of police officers, this is a much stronger public affirmation of the high standards of police operations than if an internal police investigation of an alleged misconduct concludes that the police officers involved were innocent of the charges laid against them.

I must emphasize that I would not want such a formidable undertaking as a formal investigation necessarily to be carried out for every trivial complaint. That would help no one. I suggest that there should be incorporated into the system for dealing with complaints a much less formal conciliation process. This would mean that in every police station there would be an informal procedure for dealing with minor complaints. This system must ensure that a policeman does not get a mark against him every time someone lodges a minor complaint.

I want to stress here that I am speaking about the fate of real people – of fellow-citizens, of men and women I have met in Brixton. In Brixton itself the race problem between black and white people doesn't exist. They get on very well with one another. The real problem is that the people in Brixton don't think that the Establishment is doing enough for them.

The Establishment must now urgently respond to the terrible

problems faced by citizens in our inner cities. We cannot shirk this problem because it is difficult and hazardous. There is also a message for the ethnic minorities – especially for young black people in our inner cities. If the Establishment responds, so must you. Young black Britons must show a much greater determination to help themselves.

I respect them too much to regard them as passive people. They must not wait open-mouthed for the silver spoon. They must train themselves for their opportunities, which must be fairly offered them, to take part – which is their right as British citizens – in our society. To apply some words of President Lyndon Johnson to our situation, we must tackle the crisis of the inner cities, not because we are frightened of conflict, but because we are all fired by conscience and a passion for justice.

Lord Scarman
1986

THE REPORT

**Report to
the Right Honourable William Whitelaw** CH,MC,MP,
**Secretary of State for the Home Department,
on the Brixton Disorders
of 10–12 April 1981**

Part I

INTRODUCTION

A · The submission

1·1   On 14 April 1981, pursuant to Section 32 of the Police Act
1964, you appointed me to hold a local inquiry into certain matters
connected with the policing of the Brixton area of South London.
The terms of reference were: 'to inquire urgently into the serious
disorder in Brixton on 10–12 April 1981 and to report, with the
power to make recommendations'.

I now submit my report.

B · The two basic problems

1·2   During the weekend of 10–12 April (Friday, Saturday and
Sunday) the British people watched with horror and incredulity an
instant audio-visual presentation on their television sets of scenes of
violence and disorder in their capital city, the like of which had not
previously been seen in this century in Britain. In the centre of
Brixton, a few hundred young people – most, but not all of them,
black – attacked the police on the streets with stones, bricks, iron
bars and petrol bombs, demonstrating to millions of their fellow
citizens the fragile basis of the Queen's peace. The petrol bomb was
now used for the first time on the streets of Britain (the idea, no

doubt, copied from the disturbances in Northern Ireland). These young people, by their criminal behaviour – for such, whatever their grievances or frustrations, it was – brought about a temporary collapse of law and order in the centre of an inner suburb of London.

1·3   The disturbances were at their worst on the Saturday evening. For some hours the police could do no more than contain them. When the police, heavily reinforced, eventually restored order in the afflicted area, the toll of human injury and property damage was such that one observer described the scene as comparable with the aftermath of an air-raid. Fortunately no one was killed: but on that Saturday evening 279 policemen were injured, forty-five members of the public are known to have been injured (the number is almost certainly greater), a large number of police and other vehicles were damaged or destroyed (some by fire), and twenty-eight buildings were damaged or destroyed by fire. Further, the commitment of all available police to the task of quelling the riot and dispersing the rioters provided the opportunity, which many seized, of widespread looting in the shopping centre of Brixton.

1·4   Two views have been forcefully expressed in the course of the Inquiry as to the causation of the disorders. The first is: oppressive policing over a period of years, and in particular the harassment of young blacks on the streets of Brixton. On this view, it is said to be unnecessary to look more deeply for an explanation of the disorders. They were 'anti-police'. The second is that the disorders, like so many riots in British history, were a protest against society by people, deeply frustrated and deprived, who saw in a violent attack upon the forces of law and order their one opportunity of compelling public attention to their grievances. I have no doubt that each view, even if correct, would be an over-simplification of a complex situation. If either view should be true, it would not be the whole truth.

1·5   Policing policy and methods, it is obvious, reflect in part a reaction by lawfully constituted authority to the society which is being policed. A 'Section 32 inquiry' is primarily concerned with policing but, because policing methods operate in and are influenced by the social situation, it cannot stop at policing. In this Inquiry, therefore, I have sought to identify not only the policing problem specific to the disorders but the social problem of which it is necessarily part. The one cannot be understood or resolved save in the context of the other.

1·6   The policing problem is not difficult to identify: it is that of policing a multi-racial community in a deprived inner city area where unemployment, especially among young black people, is high and hopes are low. It is a problem which admits of no simple or clear-cut solution. We require of the police that they maintain and enforce the rule of law in our ethnically diverse society. Without an appreciation of the needs and aspirations of the many elements which constitute that society it is impossible to set the standards for successful policing. For good practical as well as logical reasons, therefore, it is necessary before attempting an answer to the policing problem to understand the social problem.

1·7   I identify the social problem as that of the difficulties, social and economic, which beset the ethnically diverse communities who live and work in our inner cities. These are difficulties for which the police bear no responsibility, save as citizens, like the rest of us. But, unless the police adjust their policies and operations so as to handle these difficulties with imagination as well as firmness, they will fail, and disorder will become a disease endemic in our society.

C · The Inquiry

1·8   I have conducted the Inquiry in two phases. In so doing, I have followed the precedent of my Inquiry into the Red Lion Square disorders.[1] The first phase was concerned with the course of events and the immediate causes of the disorder. It involved the taking of a substantial volume of oral evidence. It was done at Lambeth Town Hall, Brixton, beginning on 15 June 1981 and finishing on 10 July 1981. Twenty days were spent taking evidence. The second phase, on the underlying causes of the disorder, consisted of written evidence and submissions followed by a hearing at Church House, Westminster, which began on 2 September 1981 and ended on 9 September 1981. Final addresses, covering both phases, were delivered by represented parties and Counsel for the Inquiry at the

1. *Report of the Inquiry on the Red Lion Square Disorders of 15 June 1974*, HMSO, Cmnd 5919.

last stage of the second phase hearing. Appendix A gives the detail of the Inquiry.

1·9   In all, nine parties were represented before the Inquiry throughout the hearing of all the evidence:

> The Commissioner of Police of the Metropolis and his officers;
> Concern, a group of local residents;
> The Council for Community Relations in Lambeth (CCRL);
> The London Borough of Lambeth;
> ★The Brixton Neighbourhood Community Association (BNCA);
> ★The Brixton Domino and Social Club;
> ★The Melting Pot Foundation;
> The Railton Road Youth and Community Centre;
> and The Rastafarian Collective.
>
> *★Jointly represented*

In addition, the Brixton Legal Defence Group was a represented party during Phase 1 only and the Commission for Racial Equality (CRE) during Phase 2. I was greatly assisted by the representatives of the parties throughout the Inquiry and wish publicly to record my thanks to them.

1·10   Brixton provided the focus for the Inquiry, as it provided the setting for most of the public hearings. From the outset of the Inquiry, however, it was my intention to look at Brixton in a national context. This intention was given added importance by the serious disorders which occurred in other urban areas in July, including those in Southall, in Liverpool (Toxteth), in the Moss Side area of Manchester and in the West Midlands. I have not conducted a detailed investigation into those disorders: that would have been beyond my terms of reference. I have, however, invited and received evidence from a number of organizations and individuals in areas other than Brixton affected by the disorders. I have visited Birmingham, Coventry, Wolverhampton and Liverpool: and I have read the 'Hytner' report on Moss Side.[1]

1. *Report of the Moss Side Enquiry Panel to the Leader of the Greater Manchester Council* (Chairman, Mr Benet Hytner, Q C).

1·11   The visits are a feature of the Inquiry upon which I would wish to comment. Accompanied by the Secretary to the Inquiry, I have made a number of visits to Brixton as well as elsewhere to inform myself of matters which are not amenable to investigation in a forensic setting. Some were made after the conclusion of the Phase 1 hearings; and some after Phase 2. They are listed in Appendix A and noted briefly in Appendix B. I am satisfied that the visits were indispensable to a proper understanding of the background to the disturbances and of the policing problems to which they gave rise. The information they produced was general, not specific; they shed light not on events or the conduct of individuals but on policy, attitudes and beliefs. The need to make the visits is, like the written evidence received in Phase 2, an indication that a Section 32 inquiry cannot be confined within forensic limits. It is partly judicial, partly administrative in character. It must cover the social circumstances in which the police have to act.

1·12   For the reasons outlined in this introduction, I deal first, albeit briefly, with the relevant social conditions. Only then am I in a position to tell the story of the disorders or investigate the policing problem. I conclude with a discussion of proposals and recommendations for future action.

Part II
SOCIAL CONDITIONS

A · Brixton

(1) Location and environment

2·1   Brixton is an established commercial and residential centre within the inner area of South London. Administratively it forms part of the London Borough of Lambeth, one of the thirteen Inner London Boroughs, which covers an area of South London radiating out from County Hall and the South Bank Arts Centre in the north to the predominantly residential areas of Streatham and Norwood in the south. Brixton forms part of the centre of the Borough, an inner city area of mixed industrial, commercial and residential uses, with the latter predominating. Substantial local authority estates have been developed in the area, alongside streets of houses built in the nineteenth and early twentieth centuries some of which are now the subject of housing improvement programmes. Brixton Town Centre is both the main shopping centre in the Borough – with a colourful street market – and the focus of the Borough administration at the Town Hall.

2·2   Brixton was a lively and prosperous place in the late nineteenth and early twentieth centuries. The railway gave it excellent access to the centre of London: business and professional people (including members of the acting profession) lived there, some of them in large, dignified houses standing in their own grounds. Streets of small terraced houses, not unlike those which are currently fashionable in Chelsea and Islington, were built for the wage-earners who found excellent employment opportunities not only in Brixton itself but in the centre of the Metropolis. Economic decline, however, set in shortly after the First World War, and has continued to the present time.

2·3   In its appearance and amenities Brixton now shares many of the features of other decaying inner city areas, a fact which was recognized by the designation in 1977 of the inner part of the Borough of Lambeth, including Brixton, as one of seven Inner City Partnerships. Although it continues to include branches of a number of national retail chains as well as local stores, the Brixton shopping centre is declining in terms of both retail turnover and retail floorspace, a decline which, there is evidence, has accelerated since the April disorders. Since 1965 a series of plans for the redevelopment of the centre and the surrounding area have been proposed but not implemented, although the Borough Council has recently declared Brixton Town Centre a Commercial Improvement Area, so extending the Council's powers to give grants to private concerns for improvement of amenities or of commercial or industrial buildings.

2·4   To the south and east of the shopping centre lies the area of Railton and Mayall Roads. This contains some 400 dwellings, many terraced, as well as a number of shops and other commercial premises with flats above. Originally the Borough Council intended to redevelop the whole area for new housing, but in 1975 the then Secretary of State for the Environment overruled his Inspector's recommendation in favour of the Borough's plan, on the grounds that gradual renewal of the area was to be preferred to its complete clearance. The marks of the planners' indecision remain all too visible. In particular the boarded-up sites near the junction of Railton and Mayall Roads with Atlantic Road are a daily reminder of the vagaries of policy, the dangers of indecision, and the depressing effects of physical decay and economic decline.

2·5   With the rejection of its plans for comprehensive redevelopment of the Railton and Mayall Road area, the Borough Council began to turn its attention to the renovation of the properties, some 40 per cent of the total, which it owned in the area. In 1977 it declared the area a Housing Action Area, which meant that the Council could give grants for the improvement of dwellings in the area. The neatness and attractiveness of some of the properties in the streets running west of Railton Road – notably those such as Chaucer, Spenser and Shakespeare Roads at the southern end of Railton Road – are an indication of what such rehabilitation can achieve, as well as a tribute to the efforts of the local people to improve their neighbourhood.

(2) Housing

2·6   Nevertheless, the general picture of housing provision both in the Borough as a whole and in Brixton in particular is one of considerable stress. Despite a declining population, it was estimated at the time of the National Dwelling and Housing Survey (NDHS) in 1977/1978 that there was a shortage of about 20,000 dwellings in the Borough compared to the number of households requiring a separate dwelling. The local authority's waiting list alone currently numbers some 18,000 households. 37 per cent of homeless households, compared to 20 per cent of households overall in the Borough, are black. According to the NDH Survey, 10 per cent of households in the Borough are overcrowded, i.e. one or more bedrooms below standard, compared to 9 per cent for Inner London as a whole: but 13 per cent of households in Brixton are one or more bedrooms below standard. Altogether Lambeth Borough Council has estimated that some 12,000 households in the Borough live in overcrowded conditions. At the same time there is a significant number of under-occupied properties in the Borough, and 7,000 of the Borough's total of 103,620 dwellings were said to be vacant on 1 April 1980. The combination of housing shortage and unoccupied properties has led to 'squatting' in a considerable number of premises.

2·7   Over 12,000 dwellings in the Borough are defined by the local authority as unfit, and a further 8,250 lack one or more basic amenity. Some 20 per cent of the total housing stock is therefore substandard and a further 12 per cent is said to be in need of major renovation. Much of the worst housing is in Brixton, the area of the disturbances. In the Mayall/Railton Housing Action Area, only twenty-two properties were regarded by the Council in 1977 as satisfactory in terms of state of repair, housing conditions and general environmental quality. By the end of 1980, as a result of renovation work, this figure had risen to 190, but a substantial number of properties remain substandard.

2·8   22 per cent of households in the Borough own the property in which they live. About 33 per cent of households live in privately rented accommodation and the remaining 45 per cent in accommodation rented from the Borough Council, the Greater London

Council or a Housing Association. Among the council housing estates in the central part of the Borough, I have visited two – Stockwell Park and Tulse Hill. My visit to Stockwell Park confirmed that in spite of an enlightened neighbourhood management approach by the Council, the dreams of modern architects and planners do not necessarily provide any more of a setting for social harmony than do the run-down Victorian terraces in Railton and Mayall Roads. On the contrary, they give rise to problems which terraced houses avoid.

2·9 The Borough's housing problems have been summarized in written evidence presented to me by the Department of the Environment as follows:

> The Council have also been under increasing pressure to accommodate homeless families, and to provide for others in special need, including young single people and other vulnerable groups . . . The various pointers which indicate higher housing stress referred to above, with others such as shorter length of residence, proportion of heads of households born outside the United Kingdom, a tendency towards low socio-economic groups, and single-person and one-parent households, taken together provide a pattern of deprivation in Brixton and Lambeth which is severe.

The Department go on to point out that Lambeth's position is not unique and that other London Boroughs with a similar mix of ethnic groups (Brent, Hackney and Haringey) face similar and, in some respects, worse housing problems. Whether Lambeth's position is unique or not, it is clear from the evidence, and indeed to anyone who walks down the Railton and Mayall Roads, that the physical environment in which the people of Brixton live and the police have to operate is one marked by decay, and that there are in particular very serious housing problems.

(3) Leisure and recreation facilities

2·10 One other important aspect of the physical environment is the relative lack of leisure and recreation facilities in Lambeth, and in Brixton in particular. A number of public open spaces are accessible from central Lambeth, including Brockwell Park and Angell Park. In addition the efforts of the Borough Council, of the Sports Council and of local groups (including the churches) have provided a variety of sporting facilities, clubs and meeting places – such as the Railton Road Youth and Community Centre and the Mohammed Ali Sports Development Centre – to which young people can go. Grants by the Sports Council and under the Inner City Partnership and Urban Programme arrangements have helped provide new facilities. The most notable local authority project is perhaps the Brixton Recreation Centre, the development of which was begun in 1973 and is now nearing completion. At an estimated cost of £15 million, this will eventually provide a wide range of sporting and social facilities in one central location.

2·11 Nevertheless the weight of evidence I have received indicates that the provision of recreational facilities in Lambeth, particularly for young people, is at present insufficient: it remains to be seen to what extent the opening of the Recreation Centre will meet the community's needs, although there are already those who suggest, with considerable force, that it will not be a complete answer. It is clear that the exuberance of youth requires in Brixton (and other similar inner city areas) imaginative and socially acceptable opportunities for release if it is not to become frustrated or be diverted to criminal ends. It is equally clear that such opportunities do not at present exist for young people in Brixton to the extent that they ought, particularly given the enforced idleness of many youths through unemployment. The amusement arcades, the unlawful drinking clubs and, I believe, the criminal classes gain as a result. The street corners become the social centres of people, young and old, good and bad, with time on their hands and a continuing opportunity, which, doubtless, they use, to engage in endless discussion of their grievances.

B · The people of Brixton

(1) Population

2·12 Like many other inner city areas the population of Brixton is falling. The population of the Borough of Lambeth as a whole dropped by 20 per cent between the 1971 and 1981 census. It stands now at some 246,000. The major cause of this decline has not been natural change but the movement of people away from the inner city. More importantly for the health of the area, those leaving the Borough have been predominantly in the 25–60 age range, that is to say the working population, and there has been a net loss of professional and skilled workers and a net gain of clerical and manual workers. The net figures also apparently mask a high rate of population movement: the 1971 census showed that 20 per cent of Lambeth's population had moved into the Borough during the previous five years.

2·13   The population of Lambeth therefore tends to be relatively young, working-class and transient. The Borough has a higher proportion of children of school age than London as a whole, though lower than England overall, and a higher proportion of people in their twenties. Fewer Lambeth people are in professional or managerial occupations than in London as a whole, although the proportions of other non-manual, skilled or semi-skilled workers are similar. Other important features are a strikingly high figure of children in local authority care (2.3 per cent of the population aged 18 or less) and an incidence of single-parent families which, at one in six, is twice the national average. There is evidence of a higher rate of mental illness and of physical or mental handicap in the Borough than nationally. Social services expenditure by Lambeth Borough Council in 1979/1980 at £117.39 per capita was the highest in England, and over twice the average for all London Boroughs. Total revenue expenditure per capita by the local Area Health Authority in the same period was also among the highest in England at £243, compared to an average of £230 for Inner London Area Health Authorities.

2·14   The features of Lambeth's population I have mentioned are to be found accentuated in the inner area of the Borough, which includes Brixton. There is a generally higher rate of population decline than in the Borough as a whole; a higher proportion of clerical, semi-skilled and unskilled workers; a larger proportion of low income households; greater proportions of young and elderly; more one-parent families; and a higher incidence of mental illness and mental and physical handicap.

2·15   There is also in Brixton a higher proportion of black people. Overall, some 25 per cent of Lambeth's population were estimated

23

in 1978 to belong to non-white ethnic groups. West Indians were the largest black group (12.5 per cent of the Borough's population), followed by Africans (3.4 per cent), Indians, Pakistanis, Bangladeshis (2.4 per cent) and other non-white or mixed origin people (6.5 per cent). The overall percentage of non-white people in the Borough's population is similar to that in a number of other London Boroughs, such as Ealing (24 per cent), Hackney (28 per cent), Haringey (26 per cent) and Newham (23 per cent), though less than Brent (33 per cent). In Brixton – which may be considered as being made up of five wards, Ferndale, Tulse Hill, Town Hall, Angell and Herne Hill – the percentage of non-white people in the population is higher than for Lambeth as a whole, at about 36 per cent: in two wards – Ferndale and Tulse Hill – it is 49 per cent. Within the overall population of the Borough, those of non-white origin are disproportionately represented among the younger age groups. In 1978 about 39 per cent of those aged under fifteen and 29 per cent of those aged between fifteen and twenty-four belonged to non-white ethnic groups. Together the non-white groups provide more than 40 per cent of children of secondary school age. Again, in the Brixton area, the percentage of young black people is even more pronounced. In the Tulse Hill and Herne Hill wards, which provided the focus of the April disorders, black people form 30 per cent of the overall population, but 40 per cent of the 0–18-year-olds and 50 per cent of the 19–21-year-olds.

(2) The black community in Brixton

(a) The family

2·16   The older generation of black people in Brixton largely came to Britain as immigrants in the late 1940s, and in the '50s and '60s. They came in response to the demand from Britain for unskilled workers and in a search for better economic and social conditions. As immigrants to a strange country, they undoubtedly experienced problems in adjusting to a different culture and way of life, as well as, on occasion, hostility and discrimination from the host community. Their aspirations for themselves and for their children were eloquently put to me in evidence by, among others, the Brixton Domino and Social Club, as were the difficulties of adjustment they faced. One particular difficulty mentioned was that which the relatively permissive attitude of British society towards the disciplining of children presented for at least some West Indian parents in bringing up their families.

2·17   In raising their children, the older generation of black people had to do without the support of the extended network of kin which is a feature of traditional West Indian society. Though recent years have, no doubt, witnessed changes in the pattern of Caribbean society, it was, and largely remains today, the custom for women – mothers, grandmothers, and aunts – to hold the extended family together. They offered security to the young, the old, and the disabled members of the family; and they imposed a strict discipline upon the children. The role of the man was at best supportive, but seldom dominant. At worst, he was an absentee of little or no significance. It is no cause for surprise that the impact of British social conditions on the matriarchal extended-family structure of the West Indian immigrants has proved to be severe. Mothers, who in the West Indies formed the focus of the family, became in many cases wage-earners who were absent from the family home. Some idea of the destructive changes wrought in their family lives by their new circumstances can be got from a few statistics. The percentage of children in care and of single-parent families in the black community is noticeably higher than one would expect in relation to the proportion of black people in the community as a whole. 50 per cent of single-parent families in the Borough of Lambeth in 1978 were non-white. The two wards where the April disorders were centred – Tulse Hill and Herne Hill – contain some 22 per cent of all the single-parent households in Lambeth and 2.1 per cent of the 0–18 age group in those wards are in care. Of the 185 children in care in those two wards on 10 September 1980, 112 (61 per cent) were black. In addition, the Melting Pot Foundation, which provides hostel accommodation for young black people, has estimated that 200–300 young blacks are homeless, sleeping rough or squatting in the Brixton area.

(b) Education

2·18   The children of the first generation of West Indian immigrants were in many cases born in this country. They (the second generation, whether born in this country or not) and the third generation which is now emerging share, for the most part, the aspirations and expectations of other British young people. There is overwhelming evidence, however, that they have failed to benefit from our society to the extent that they might reasonably have expected. In particular, the under-achievement of West Indian children at school has been well chronicled recently in the Rampton report.[1] Though the extent and causes of their under-achievement remain a matter of controversy, I have received evidence from many organizations and individuals pointing to the failure of black youths to acquire sufficiently early the skills of language and literacy, and to the sense of disappointment and frustration which at least some black parents and children feel in the education system. But, while the existence of complaints about schooling is in no doubt, it is clear from the evidence I have received from the Inner London Education Authority, which my own visit to Tulse Hill School has confirmed, that much dedicated work is being done in the schools. The problems which have to be solved, if deprivation and alienation are to be overcome, have been identified – namely, teaching a command of the English language, a broad education in the humanities designed to help the various ethnic groups (including the 'host community') to understand each other's background and culture, and the basic training in the skills necessary to obtain work in the technological economy of the modern world; and methods, including a revolution in curriculum, to deal with these problems are being developed and put into operation. Nevertheless, it is clear that, to quote the careful words of the House of Commons Select Committee on Home Affairs in its recent report on Racial Disadvantage,[2] 'it has long been evident that we have not got ethnic minority education right . . .'[3]

(c) Unemployment

2·19   As the Select Committee in the same report wisely say, 'Disadvantage in education and employment are the two most

1. *The Interim Report of the Committee of Inquiry into the Education of Children from Ethnic Minority Groups* (Chairman: Mr Anthony Rampton, OBE), HMSO, Cmnd 8273.
2. *5th Report from the Home Affairs Committee*, Session 1980/81, H C 424–I.
3. Op. cit., paragraph 130.

crucial facets of racial disadvantage. They are closely connected. Without a decent education and the qualifications which such education alone can provide, a school-leaver is unlikely to find the sort of job to which he aspires, or indeed any job. Conversely, pupils who learn from older friends of the degree of difficulty encountered in finding employment may well be discouraged from striving to achieve at school. In other words, there is no point in getting ethnic minority education right if we do not at the same time sort out racial disadvantage in employment, and vice versa.'[1]

2·20 When the young people of Brixton leave school, many of them, white and black, face unemployment. This reflects both the general economic recession from which the country is at present suffering and the contraction in the economic and industrial base of the inner city. In early 1981, unemployment in the area of Brixton Employment Office stood at 13 per cent. For black people, the percentage is estimated to be higher. The level of ethnic minority unemployment as a proportion of total unemployment at Brixton Employment Office in May 1981 was 25.4 per cent. Over the year to February 1981, total unemployment in Great Britain increased by nearly 66 per cent, compared with 82 per cent for the ethnic minorities alone. There are indications in the evidence I have received that unemployment among members of the ethnic minorities is of longer duration than that among the white population. Most significant, blacks are without doubt over-represented among the registered and unregistered young unemployed, as a study by researchers from Liverpool University confirms.[2] In the area of the Brixton Employment Office the rate of registered unemployed among black males under 19 has been estimated at 55 per cent. According to the Manpower Services Commission:

Unemployment among young people aged 16–18 in Lambeth has risen faster over the past year than for older age groups. This is true both for total and for ethnic minority unemployment . . ., and young people form an increasing proportion of those on the unemployment register.

1. Op. cit., paragraph 126.
2. *Unregistered Youth Unemployment and Outreach Careers Work: Final Report Part 1 – Non-Registration.* K. Roberts, Jill Duggan and Maria Noble. Shortly to be published by the Department of Employment.

(d) Discrimination

2·21   The reasons for the higher level of unemployment among young black people are, no doubt, many and various. Lack of qualifications, difficulties arising from unrealistic expectations, bad time-keeping, unwillingness to travel and, most important of all, trouble with the English language are factors which, it has been suggested to me, play a part. It seems clear, however, that discrimination – by employers and at the work place – is a factor of considerable importance, and one for which the sustained efforts of the local authority, the Careers Service and the Manpower Services Commission to place young black people in work cannot easily compensate. Much of the evidence of discrimination is indirect rather than direct; but I have no doubt that it is a reality which all too often confronts the black youths of Brixton.

2·22   Discriminatory and hostile behaviour on racial grounds is not confined to the area of employment. There is evidence that it occurs not only among school children and in the street but, unintentionally no doubt, in the provision of some local authority services, principally housing. It was alleged by some of those who made representations to me that Britain is an institutionally racist society. If by that is meant that it is a society which knowingly, as a matter of policy, discriminates against black people, I reject the allegation. If, however, the suggestion being made is that practices may be adopted by public bodies as well as by private individuals which are unwittingly discriminatory against black people, then this is an allegation which deserves serious consideration, and, where proved, swift remedy.

(e) The young people of Brixton: a people of the street

2·23   Many of the young people of Brixton are therefore born and raised in insecure social and economic conditions and in an impoverished physical environment. They share the desires and expectations which our materialist society encourages. At the same time, many of them fail to achieve educational success and on leaving school face the stark prospect of unemployment. Many of these difficulties face white as well as black youngsters, but it is clear that they bear particularly heavily on young blacks. In addition, young black people face the burden of discrimination, much of it hidden and some of it unconscious and unintended. Without close parental support, with no job to go to and with few recreational facilities available, the young black person makes his life on the streets and in the seedy commercially run clubs of Brixton. There he meets criminals, who appear to have no difficulty in obtaining the benefits of a materialist society. The process was described to me in evidence by the Railton Road Youth and Community Centre as follows:

Young people around in the streets all day, with nothing to do and nowhere to go, get together in groups and the 'successful' criminal has a story to tell. So one evil has bred another, and as unemployment has grown in both older and younger generations crime has become more common-place and more acceptable. This is a vicious circle to which there is no present end in sight.

Many young black people do not of course resort to crime. Nor, recent research has suggested,[1] would it be correct to conclude that young black people are wholly alienated from British society as a result of the deprivations they suffer. But it would be surprising if they did not feel a sense of frustration and deprivation. And living much of their lives on the streets, they are brought into contact with the police who appear to them as the visible symbols of the authority of a society which has failed to bring them its benefits or do them justice.

C · Comparison with other areas

2·24 Not all of the social conditions which I have described in Brixton are reproduced in all those other parts of the country which, in the summer of 1981, suffered serious disorder. Some of the disorders occurred in areas which, by most yardsticks, could not be described as severely deprived. Nor even where there are similar-ities should it be assumed that they extend across the board; the black community of Toxteth, for example, is not one but two communities – the black Britons who have been established in the city for generations, and the new immigrants. Nor was the mix of background factors or the character of the disturbances in each area

1. 'Are Young Blacks Really Alienated?' Article by G. Gaskell and P. Smith, *New Society*, 14 May 1981.

precisely the same. Nevertheless, most of the disturbances occurred in inner city areas which share many of the features of Brixton: a high ethnic minority population, high unemployment, a declining economic base, a decaying physical environment, bad housing, lack of amenities, social problems including family breakdown, a high rate of crime and heavy policing. While I have not been empowered by my terms of reference to inquire in detail into disorders other than those in Brixton, the evidence I have received suggests that the striking feature is not the differences but the similarities between Brixton and the majority of the areas which were the focus of later trouble. Of these disorders, the ones which attracted most attention were perhaps those in Southall, Toxteth, Moss Side and the West Midlands.

(1) Southall

2·25   In *Southall*, the disorders on Friday, 3 July 1981, appear to have started as a confrontation between white skinheads and young Asians which, when the police intervened, rapidly became a confrontation between the young Asians and the police. The disorders centred on a public house in The Broadway, an area with many Asian residents and shops. The trouble began when a large group of white skinhead youths, mainly from the East End of London, who were on their way to attend a concert at the public house, began smashing shop windows in The Broadway. The disorders which ensued appear to have been a response to what the local Asian community saw as an intrusion into its area by a racially hostile group of white youths. To that extent, the circumstances of the disturbances differ from those in other areas. Nor is Southall an inner city area suffering from a high rate of street crime, although it is a pocket of relative deprivation within a generally affluent part of West London where unemployment, particularly among the ethnic minority population, is relatively high. Yet at least some of the evidence presented to me suggests that the incident was an indication not only of racial tension but of relations between Asian youths and the police which were at best characterized by lack of communication and at worst by outright hostility. It seems clear that the Asian youths were prepared to take the law into their own hands

rather than rely on the police to
got in their way, to attack them.

2·26   This leads me to make a mo
complaint about the police I have he
West Indian community is one of al
complaint of Asian leaders appears to b
sufficient to protect their community fron
members of the white community. I am a
officials have conducted into the incidence o   and I
therefore make no further comment. I do,   , note the
importance of the existence of the belief among ..ian community
leaders about police inaction – whether justified or not – in influencing the attitudes of members of that community towards the police.
Secondly, I note that the issue of racial attacks is important not
merely because of the human implications of those attacks – which
must, of course, be of paramount concern – but for what it reveals of
the attempts of extreme political groups, of both right- and left-wing
persuasion, to exploit the issue of race for their own ends. These
attempts are also revealed by the controversy which has come to
surround marches by extreme right-wing groups through areas of
high ethnic minority settlement, and the resulting opposition to
them. The impact of these marches on relations between the police
and the ethnic minority communities must not be underestimated.
The police are, of course, present at such marches not in order to
show favour to one side or the other, but because of their duty to
keep the peace. But the sight of extreme right-wing marches being
heavily escorted by columns of police has led significant numbers in
the minority communities to conclude that the police are present
purely to protect those marching and are therefore in agreement
with their political beliefs. These feelings are again important not
because they are justified – they clearly are not – but because of the
irritation they present to relations between the police and the ethnic
minority communities, an irritation which extreme political groups
are again not slow to seek to exploit. They help to bolster the
argument that the police are racially prejudiced and discriminate
against black people.

and Moss Side

Turning to Toxteth and Moss Side, while, as noted earlier, here are differences between those areas and Brixton, many of the features of deprivation and decay which characterize Brixton are there repeated. In *Toxteth*, for example, the number of unemployed registered at the Leece Street Employment Office fluctuated from 1976 to 1980 between 17,000 and 18,000, but in the twelve months from June 1980 to June 1981 the number had risen by 3,000 to over 21,000. Unemployment again appears particularly to have affected young people, and within that group, young black people. Street crime is relatively high: in 1980, of the 995 recorded offences of robbery committed within the Merseyside area, over 20 per cent were committed in one of the two police divisions which cover the Toxteth area. According to the Chief Constable of Merseyside, the area has historically been one which is difficult to police. Relations between the police and the black community in Toxteth, as was made plain to me when I visited Liverpool, are in a state of crisis. While many of the older people look to the police to protect them and wish for an increased police presence on the street, the young are alienated and bitterly hostile. Significantly, the beginning of the disorders in Toxteth on 3–6 July 1981, namely the arrest by a police traffic patrol of a youth who had been riding a motorcycle, invites comparison with the beginning of the disorders in Brixton. In each case a minor incident set off a great riot. The elements of a deprived area, unemployment, and hostility between a high proportion of the youth of the local community and the police seem well established.

2·28　Similar elements appear to have existed in *Moss Side*, though not in the same proportions. Having had the advantage of reading the 'Hytner' report,[1] I shall be brief. The area is one of the deprived parts of Manchester. Levels of unemployment are high: at the time of the National Dwelling and Housing Survey in 1977, unemployment in Moss Side was 19 per cent compared with 10 per cent for Manchester and 5 per cent for the country as a whole. In June 1981 there were 6,122 people unemployed, 22 per cent of whom were non-white. 961 young people under 20 were unemployed in April 1981 – 17 per cent of the total.

1.　Op. cit.

2·29   41 per cent of the workforce in Moss Side is low-skilled. 6 per cent of households are overcrowded and 15 per cent of households lack exclusive use of basic amenities. 10 per cent of families have a single parent. The combination of high unemployment, a relatively deprived area and of tension between the police and at least some sections of the local community, particularly the young, again seems clearly established.

(3) The West Midlands

2·30   In the *West Midlands*, the relationship between the police and the local community seems generally, though not universally, to be more favourable. Nevertheless, disorder occurred in July in a number of parts of the county, including Handsworth, Wolverhampton, Smethwick and the centre of Birmingham. Again, the areas concerned were in many cases deprived and decaying. Evidence given to me during my visits to the West Midlands suggests that the majority view in the county is that the disturbances were generally imitative of events elsewhere. Indeed it seems likely that there was a substantial 'copy-cat' element in many of the disorders which occurred during the summer, and that Brixton may have served in this respect as a model for others to follow. In some cases, it has been alleged, outsiders deliberately went into an area to foment trouble. Since I have not been empowered to conduct a detailed investigation into disturbances outside Brixton, I can make no finding on this. Nevertheless, I am unaware of any substantial body of evidence of an organized conspiracy behind the disturbances. The common strands in many of the major disorders, for which there is much evidence, are to be found in shared social conditions, in economic insecurity and perceived deprivation, in enforced idleness because of unemployment, and in the hostility of at least a section of young people to the police.

D · Conclusions

2·31   The social conditions in Brixton – many of which are to be found in other inner city areas – do not provide an excuse for disorder. They cannot justify attacks on the police in the streets, arson, or riot. All those who in the course of the disorders in Brixton and elsewhere engaged in violence against the police were guilty of grave criminal offences, which society, if it is to survive, cannot condone. Sympathy for, and understanding of, the plight of young black people, which I would expect to find in British society now that the facts are widely known, are a good reason for political, social and economic aid, and for a coordinated effort by Government to provide it, but they are no reason for releasing young black people from the responsibilities for public order which they share with the rest of us – and with the police.

2·32   Nor should it be assumed that nothing is being done for young black people in Brixton and elsewhere, or that Brixton is an area in which deprivation and decay are unrelieved by any hopeful features. It is clear from their evidence that Lambeth Borough Council are acutely aware of the problems of the community and of its black members in particular. In October 1978 they adopted a comprehensive policy to promote equal opportunities and combat racial or other disadvantage, and they also set up a Race Relations Unit within the Office of the Borough's Chief Executive to develop and advise on such matters. They have taken particular steps to improve their housing allocation and employment recruitment policies. Substantial funds have been made available by Central Government through, for example, grants pursuant to Section 11 of the Local Government Act 1966, under the Urban Programme and, most recently, through the Inner City Partnership: about £9 million of funds have, I understand, been allocated to the Partnership in the financial year 1981/82.

2·33   There is much in Brixton, and it is a tribute to its people that this is so, which is positive and creative: one only has to walk the streets to appreciate the vigour and the liveliness of its multi-racial society. Many people who live in Brixton have emphasized to me its positive features – not least the generally amicable relations between its black and white inhabitants – and their pleasure in living there.

2·34   At the same time, the disorders in Brixton cannot be fully understood unless they are seen in the context of the complex political, social and economic factors to which I have briefly referred. In analysing communal disturbances such as those in Brixton and elsewhere, to ignore the existence of these factors is to put the nation in peril.

2·35   The social and economic plight of the ethnic minorities in the United Kingdom has been researched in great depth and is now well known; and I have had the advantage of a great volume of evidence researching, exploring and explaining it. The foregoing outline (for it is no more) of the relevant conditions has drawn heavily on this evidence. Although there is evidence to suggest that the position of the ethnic minority groups has seen some improvement relative to the rest of the population in recent years,[1] overall they suffer from the same deprivations as the 'host community' (i.e. the white population), but much more acutely. Their lives are led largely in the poorer and more deprived areas of our great cities. Unemployment and poor housing bear on them very heavily: and the educational system has not adjusted itself satisfactorily to their needs. Their difficulties are intensified by the sense they have of a concealed discrimination against them, particularly in relation to job opportunities and housing. Some young blacks are driven by their despair into feeling that they are rejected by the society of which they rightly believe they are members and in which they would wish to enjoy the same opportunities and to accept the same risks as everyone else. But their experience leads them to believe that their opportunities are less and their risks are greater. Young black people feel neither socially nor economically secure.

2·36   In addition they do not feel politically secure. Their sense of rejection is not eased by the low level of black representation in our elective political institutions. Their sense of insecurity is not relieved by the liberty our law provides to those who march and demonstrate in favour of tougher immigration controls and 'repatriation' of the blacks. Rightly or wrongly, young black people do not feel politically secure, any more than they feel economically or socially secure.

2·37   The accumulation of these anxieties and frustrations and the limited opportunities of airing their grievances at national level in British society encourage them to protest on the streets. And it is

1. *Ethnic Minorities in Britain: A Study of Trends in Their Position since 1961.* Home Office Research Study No. 68, by S. Field, G. Mair, T. Rees and P. Stevens, HMSO, 1981.

regrettably also true that some are tempted by their deprivations into crime, particularly street crime – robbery, car theft and the pick-pocketing offences: in other words, some of them go 'mugging'. They live their lives on the street, having often nothing better to do; they make their protest there; and some of them live off street crime. The recipe for a clash with the police is therefore ready-mixed: and it takes little, or nothing, to persuade them that the police, representing an establishment which they see as insensitive to their plight, are their enemies. If not 'anti-police', they are against the policemen whom they see as pursuing and harassing them on the streets.

2·38   None of these features can perhaps usefully be described as a *cause* of the disorders, either in Brixton or elsewhere. Indeed, there are, undoubtedly, parts of the country which are equally deprived where disorder did not occur. But taken together, they provide a set of social *conditions* which create a predisposition towards violent protest. Where deprivation and frustration exist on the scale to be found among the young black people of Brixton, the probability of disorder must, therefore, be strong. Moreover, many of them, it is obvious, believe with justification that violence, though wrong, is a very effective means of protest: for, by attracting the attention of the mass media of communication, they get their message across to the people as a whole.

Part III
THE DISORDERS

3·1   Against the background of communal deprivation and anxieties outlined in Part II, I now consider the course and pattern of the Brixton disorders.

The area of disorder

3·2   The disorders were centred on Atlantic Road, Railton Road, Mayall Road and the surrounding streets. The shopping centre of Brixton (where much looting occurred) is near the northern end of Atlantic Road, where it enters the Brixton Road. The map (Appendix E) shows the lay-out of the streets. The width of street where Atlantic Road divides into Mayall Road and Railton Road is known locally as 'the Triangle'. Railton Road, between Atlantic Road and Leeson Road, is known as 'the Front Line'. To some, whose knowledge of these streets has come only with hindsight in the aftermath of the disorders, 'the Front Line' may seem an apt description for an area where a mob battled with the police. But, almost certainly, the term is used to describe a place where people meet on the street to talk and relax in the company of each other. Be that as it may, the Leeson Road link between Railton Road and Mayall Road was where the rioting crowd was mainly concentrated.

3·3   An important feature of the Atlantic Road/Railton Road spine is that it is bounded by the railway on the east and by a network of residential streets on the west. The railway constitutes a barrier to the escape or dispersal of a crowd from Railton or Mayall Road: for there is no way across the railway between Coldharbour Lane in the north and Shakespeare Road in the south save the Somerleyton Passage, which is opposite Leeson Road. But the network of streets to the west provide not only several escape routes from trouble in the Atlantic and Railton Roads but also an alternative route for moving north and south if, as happened on the Saturday night, those two roads are blocked. There is no doubt that the rioters used these streets for moving north and south during the riots, and ultimately for dispersal when the police became strong enough to advance against them. I turn now to trace the course of the disorders.

A · Friday, 10 April 1981

(1) The course of events

3·4   At about 6.10 p.m. on the warm evening of Friday, 10 April 1981, Police Constable Stephen Margiotta (PC 643 L) was on duty in uniform in Atlantic Road, when he noticed that traffic had come to a standstill. Crossing the road and walking towards the junction of Atlantic Road and Coldharbour Lane he saw a black youth in the road running towards him. The youth appeared to be very distressed and was apparently being pursued by two or three other black youths. PC Margiotta thought that the youth might have committed some offence and decided to try to stop him. After an initial unsuccessful attempt, the youth tripped and fell and PC Margiotta fell over him.

3·5   When PC Margiotta and the youth stood up, the officer noticed that his own arm and shirt and the back of the youth's shirt were covered in blood. The youth broke away, but stopped on the north-east corner of the junction of Atlantic Road and Coldharbour Lane where PC Margiotta, who had been joined by another officer, PC 523 L Saunders, again caught up with him. PC Saunders asked the youth what was the matter and the youth replied by taking off his shirt to reveal a wound some three or four inches long just below the centre of his back in between his shoulder blades. The wound was bleeding profusely. The youth was clearly distressed. He was also struggling to get away.

3·6   At this point the two officers became aware that they had been joined by three other black youths who were excited and shouting, 'Leave him alone.' Although PC Margiotta attempted to explain that he was not arresting the injured youth and that the youth needed urgent medical attention, the three other youths jostled the officers and the injured youth again ran off along Coldharbour Lane in the direction of Lambeth Town Hall. The officers were prevented from following him by the three youths and by a small crowd which had by now gathered.

3·7   PC Margiotta repeated that the youth who had run off was seriously injured and in need of medical treatment. He showed the blood on his clothing. The youths then appeared to calm down and one or two people helped the two officers to search nearby for the injured youth. PC Margiotta also used his personal radio to tell Brixton Police Station of the injured youth and the need to find him quickly. This message was heard by other officers in the area on their radios and they began to assist in the search for the injured youth.

3·8   The injured youth had meanwhile made his way into Rush-croft Road. He went to a house containing flats in this road and asked the white family living in one of these flats on the third floor of the building (whom he did not know) for help. The occupier of the flat put kitchen roll as a temporary dressing on the wound, which he noticed looked to have thick lumps oozing out of it. While he was doing so, he asked the youth who had been responsible for his wound. The youth replied with the one word 'Blacks'. The occupier asked a young man who was in the flat to get a cab. This arrived shortly after and the injured youth was helped downstairs and put in the back seat. The driver of the cab was asked to take the injured youth to hospital. The young man who had called the cab went with him.

3·9   The cab – a white Datsun car – drove off in the direction from which the injured youth had run, towards Vining Street. Two police officers – Police Constables 480 L Timperley and 656 L Jones – in a police transit van, who had heard PC Margiotta's radio call and were driving around the area on the look-out for the injured youth, saw the injured youth being helped into the cab and the cab drive off. They followed. When the cab was stopped by stationary traffic at the junction of Rushcroft Road and Vining Street, PC Timperley got out of the van and went up to the cab. Looking in, he saw the injured youth lying on the back seat. He opened the door of the cab and after speaking to the passenger and the driver, examined the injured youth. He thought the youth's wound looked very serious and noticed in particular that it was frothy and bubbly, as if there was air escaping from inside.

3·10   PC Timperley asked his colleague PC Jones to radio for a first-aid kit. Another officer – PC 234 L Lock – arrived with one almost immediately. PCs Timperley and Lock began to treat the injured youth's wound. They put a large sterile dressing over it and, the officers having formed the impression – because of the frothiness of the wound and because the youth complained of having difficulty in breathing – that the youth's lung might have been punctured, PC Lock pressed down on it to try to seal the wound. Meanwhile, PC Jones called over his radio for an ambulance. That call was made at 6.24 p.m.

3·11   As the officers treated the youth's wound, an inquisitive crowd of shoppers and other passers-by gathered. Some people asked why the officers were keeping the youth and whether an ambulance had been called. The officers explained that they thought it would be dangerous to move the youth because of the nature of his injury and that they had called for an ambulance.

3·12   Suddenly a crowd of thirty to forty people, mainly black youths, came running round the corner from the Atlantic Road end of Vining Street. They surrounded the car and the officers. PC Timperley heard shouts of 'What are you doing to him?', 'Look, they are killing him', and 'We will look after our own'. He explained to two youths that the officers thought the injured youth had a punctured lung and that it would be dangerous to move him. But the crowd was unreceptive. The officers were pushed aside, the injured youth was pulled from the car and he was carried off by the crowd along Vining Street and right into Atlantic Road. It was 6.31 p.m. The injured youth was then put into another car and the driver told to take him to hospital. The youth was taken to St Thomas's Hospital where he was treated for his injuries and from where he discharged himself on 13 April 1981. The arrival of the injured youth was regarded as an isolated incident by the hospital: contrary to a rumour, the hospital authorities were not warned by the police of expected trouble in Brixton that weekend and did not know of any until the hospital was placed on stand-by by the London Ambulance Service at about 7.00 p.m. on the Saturday.

Disorder breaks out

3·13   When the crowd of black youths had first appeared on the scene, PC Jones had called for assistance from other officers. Officers who had responded to this call and other officers who had been in the area following PC Margiotta's earlier call looking for the injured youth, pursued the crowd as it disappeared into Atlantic Road. Some of these officers were in plain clothes, most were in uniform. The crowd ran south along Atlantic Road to its junction with Railton and Mayall Roads, the area known as 'the Triangle'. As they ran south, PC Margiotta, who had washed the injured youth's blood from his hands in a nearby shop and was now responding to the call for urgent assistance, ran north towards them. As he passed through the crowd, which he estimated as numbering at least forty to fifty black youths, some of the youths threw bricks and bottles at him. PC Margiotta ran through the crowd and joined his colleagues. The time was now 6.35 p.m. More bricks and bottles were thrown at the officers. A man was arrested in Railton Road for threatening behaviour.

3·14   A police van carrying four officers with three shields on board responded to the call for assistance. It arived on the scene at 6.36 p.m. The Duty Officer from Brixton Police Station, Inspector Scotchford, arrived at the same time. He saw officers moving north along Railton Road being stoned by a crowd of predominantly black youths. Inspector Scotchford immediately took charge, ordering the officers to deploy the shields and to disperse the crowd. He estimated that the crowd now numbered about 100; some thirty to forty officers were present. These officers advanced south down Railton Road to the junction with Leeson Road. In the course of this manoeuvre, three people were arrested and six officers received relatively minor injuries. When they reached that junction the stone throwing stopped. At 6.41 p.m. Inspector Scotchford called over his radio for further assistance and ordered his officers, who included two with dogs, to disperse the crowd which was facing them. He asked, however, for those answering his call for assistance not to attend the scene but to wait in reserve. Some units were held in the Brockwell Park area, others outside Lambeth Town Hall.

3·15   At 6.42 p.m. the windscreen of a police transit van in Leeson Road was broken by a missile and as a result an officer was injured.

The person responsible was not arrested but he was seen by police. At about this time the Chief Superintendent in charge of the Brixton Division, Mr Marsh, arrived on the scene. He reported the situation to the Acting Commander of 'L' District, Chief Superintendent Nicholson. (The Commander of 'L' District, Commander Fairbairn, was away attending a course.) There was in fact something of a lull. The crowd facing the police had broken up into small groups, although these did not disperse. At 6.44 p.m. Inspector Scotchford ordered all police units who were not engaged to leave the immediate area and go to the positions where other units were being held in reserve. At 7.06 p.m. Chief Superintendent Marsh ordered the removal of police dog vans from the scene.

3·16   The lull ended some four minutes later when the person who had thrown the missile which had smashed the windscreen of the police transit van in Leeson Road was again seen there and arrested. Another black youth jumped onto the roof of the police van into which the first youth had been put, damaging it in the process. The van – its driver perhaps afraid it was about to be overtaken by the crowd – drove away with the second youth still clinging to it. When, after a short distance, he dropped off, he too was arrested.

3·17   Immediately following these arrests there was further missile-throwing by the crowd at the police and a police 'Panda' car was damaged. The police again deployed their protective shields. The missile-throwing, however, soon slackened and stopped and the crowd began to disperse. At 7.15 p.m. Chief Superintendent Marsh ordered all but six of his reserve mobile units to return to their normal duties. By 7.30 p.m. the incident was over. Altogether, six people had been arrested, six police officers injured and four police vehicles damaged. Twenty uniformed officers patrolling on foot in pairs were left in the Railton Road/Mayall Road area to ensure that disorder did not break out again.

Four crucial police decisions

3·18   Later that evening Chief Superintendent Nicholson took a number of important decisions about the policing of the area in the light of the day's events. First he arranged for four additional serials of officers (in the Metropolitan Police a serial consists of an Inspector, three Sergeants and twenty Constables) to be posted to Brixton until further notice. Secondly, he decided to reduce the number of mobile units in the Brixton area to three van patrols but to increase the number of foot patrols to twenty-eight officers patrolling in pairs. This pattern was put into effect at 11 p.m. and continued throughout Friday night and into Saturday. The remaining officers from the four serials were held in reserve at Brixton Police Station. Thirdly, he discussed with Detective Chief Superintendent Plowman (Head of CID in 'L' District) whether Operation 'Swamp', a plain-clothes police operation aimed at street crime which involved extensive use of the power to stop and search (see paragraphs 4·37–4·40, infra), should continue on Friday evening and on Saturday. He decided that it should, although he instructed that there should be no 'unnecessary covert operations' in the Railton Road/ Mayall Road area.

3·19   Finally, concerned at the rumours about the incident involving the injured youth which had rapidly begun to circulate in Brixton, Chief Superintendent Nicholson decided to call in several leaders of the community to put to them the police account of the incident and to seek their help in stilling those rumours. Among the rumours were that the police had deliberately prevented the youth going to hospital, that the police had refused to call an ambulance and that the police had themselves caused the youth's injury. There were also rumours about police brutality in handling the crowds which had built up during the incident and in making arrests. Before the meeting took place, Mr Nicholson reported the general situation and his intention to call in the community leaders to Commander Fairbairn over the telephone: the Commander approved his deputy's decisions.

Meeting with community leaders

3·20   The meeting began at 9 p.m. It was conducted by Commander Ferguson, the Head of A7, the Community Relations Branch of the Metropolitan Police. He had heard at about 7 p.m. of the trouble in Brixton following the incident with the injured youth and, knowing the sensitivity of the area, had gone to the police station to offer his services to the District Commander. Chief Superintendent Nicholson had seen Mr Rene Webb, Director of the Melting Pot Foundation, before Commander Ferguson arrived. Together with members of his staff and Inspector Oliver, the Assistant Community Liaison Officer on 'L' District (Superintendent MacLennan, the District Community Liaison Officer, was absent on leave), Commander Ferguson saw at Brixton Police Station between 9 p.m. and 1 a.m.:

> Mr George Greaves, the Principal Community Relations Officer of the Council for Community Relations in Lambeth;
> Mr Tony Phillips, deputy to Mr Greaves;
> The Reverend Graham Kent, Minister of Railton Road Methodist Church;
> Mr and Mrs Ivan Madray, youth workers at the Railton Road Youth and Community Centre;
> and Mr Courtney Laws, Director of the Brixton Neighbourhood Association.

3·21   The police gave those who attended an account of the day's events and asked them to assist in dispelling rumours within the community. They also told the community leaders of their intention to increase the number of police in the area. For their part, the leaders were already conscious of the tension in the area following the incidents earlier in the day. A number had heard anger and concern expressed by people in the area because it was alleged the police had detained and questioned the injured youth instead of getting him to hospital. Moreover, on their arrival at the police station they had had to make their way through a group of anxious relatives and friends of those arrested earlier. Some of the leaders advised Commander Ferguson to send an officer to see and calm this group. They also expressed concern about police tactics and the number of police deployed in the area, and advised that the police presence in Railton Road, particularly of motorized patrols, should be reduced.

3·22   Commander Ferguson understood this latter request, which was made by Mr Madray, to be a request for motorized patrols in the area of the Railton Road Youth and Community Centre to be removed or reduced when members were leaving the youth club that evening. In turn, he asked Mr Madray to request the members of the club to go home in small groups. Mr Madray agreed and left the police station at about 10.30 p.m. in order to see that this was done. When the other community leaders left the police station later that night, they had undertaken to do what they could to dispel rumours and to calm the situation. In the next few hours, and on Saturday, they told those they met what they had learned from the police of the Friday incidents and generally sought to ease tension. Although some of them were uneasy about the future, neither they nor the police foresaw the extent of the trouble that lay ahead.

(2) Comment and findings

3·23   Nothing that happened on Friday could have taken the police by surprise – until they were stoned. Tension between the police and black youths was, and remains, a fact of life in Brixton. Young black people, as well as many local people of all ages and colours, lacked confidence in the police. The worst construction was frequently put upon police action, even when it was lawful, appropriate and sensible. PC Margiotta acted properly – but I doubt if he was surprised when the stabbed youth, whom I am satisfied he wanted when he knew he was injured to help, treated him as an enemy from whom to escape. PCs Timperley, Jones and Lock acted, I am also satisfied, in what they believed to be the best interests of the wounded man. Their decision, which was to apply first-aid (which PC Lock did expertly) and then to wait for the ambulance, which they had requested over the radio, has been heavily criticized in the Inquiry. It has been said that they should have allowed the car, in which the youth was being conveyed, to proceed with all speed to a hospital. I reject the criticism. The officers could properly and reasonably reach the view that it was better to await the ambulance. They had to exercise judgement in a difficult situation. They cannot be faulted in what they did: indeed, I believe they acted correctly.

3·24   The crowd, however, thought otherwise. I doubt if this caused the officers any surprise. Distrust of police action on the streets was too common a phenomenon of life in Brixton. Had the crowd dispersed after making their protest, the sad little incident of the injured youth, its detail forgotten or distorted, would have followed many others into that limbo of the half-remembered and the half-imagined from which popular attitudes and beliefs are wont to derive their strength. The legend of police hostility and indifference to black youths would have been marginally strengthened: but no more.

3·25 ˙ But unfortunately the incident ended with a sinister twist. When the crowd seized the wounded man and the police radioed for assistance, the incident suddenly acquired the makings of a serious disturbance involving a conflict between young black people and the police. A substantial number of police answered the call for assistance. As they came running to the scene, the crowd of black youths felt, with some reason, that they were being pursued. They turned and fought. Their action was criminal, and is not to be condoned. It was not, however, planned. It was a spontaneous act of defiant aggression by young men who felt themselves hunted by a hostile police force.

3·26 I am satisfied that Chief Superintendent Nicholson (for whose decisions Commander Fairbairn, who was kept informed, accepted full responsibility) saw the dangers and took decisions, which, with one significant exception, were appropriate in the situation which had developed. The four additional serials were a necessary reinforcement: the increased foot patrols (twenty-eight officers patrolling in pairs) were a wise precaution, even though when Saturday dawned their presence on the streets must have heightened tension to some degree. The risk had to be taken, if the precarious tranquility achieved on Friday evening was to be preserved (bearing in mind the rumours which had spread, and continued on the Saturday to flourish). The decision to invite community leaders to a meeting at the police station was good imaginative policing: and it was excellent that Commander Ferguson came from Scotland Yard to conduct the discussions.

3·27 But the decision to continue with Operation 'Swamp' on Friday evening and Saturday was unwise. That a stop and search operation was in progress on the streets of Brixton, though not its unhappy code-name, was well known to the young blacks: for it was upon them that it had a direct and unwelcome impact. And they were the very people whose conflict with the police on that Friday evening had led to the situation then under review at the police station. I am satisfied that the senior police officers concerned considered all aspects of the situation before they took the decision, which Commander Fairbairn approved and for which he accepts full responsibility. I understand why it was decided to continue with the operation: street crime was a grave matter in Brixton, upon which the silent law-abiding majority of residents felt very strongly. But I am bound to say that the wise course would have been to have discontinued the operation. And we now know that it was an arrest by two 'Swamp' officers which set off the Saturday disorders. Subject to that one comment, I find that the police met the challenge of the Friday incident appropriately and sensibly, and with a genuine regard for the views of leaders of the community directly affected by the disturbance.

B · Saturday, 11 April 1981

(1) The course of events

3·28   Saturday began as an apparently normal, busy day in Brixton. The weather was again fine and the streets and market were crowded with shoppers. Two things were different, however. First, there was the increased police presence in the area. Whereas normally there would have been about eight police constables on foot patrol throughout the Brixton Division, an additional twenty-eight constables operating in pairs patrolled Railton Road, Mayall Road and the surrounding area. There were also three mobile van patrols and other officers were held in reserve at Brixton Police Station. Many of those who came into Brixton to shop in the course of Saturday remarked on the heavier police presence in the area.

3·29   The other special feature of Saturday was the rumours which, in spite of the efforts of police (including the local home beat officers) and community leaders, were continuing to circulate in the area about the incident of the day before. By Saturday afternoon it was even rumoured that the injured youth was dead. All of the rumours had in common the criticism that the police had failed to take sufficiently swift action to deal with the youth's serious injury. Tension was apparent to a number of people in Brixton that day, to police officers as well as to members of the public.

The S & M incident

3·30   At 2 p.m. the 112 officers in 'L' District engaged in Operation Swamp (paragraphs 4·37–4·40, infra) came on duty, forty-eight of them in the Brixton area. Squad 7, consisting of twelve officers, had been operating in plain clothes throughout the week in Railton Road and Mayall Road and the surrounding area. At about 4.40 p.m. two of the officers from this squad – PC 248 L Cameron (aged 20) and PC 752 L Thornton (aged 24) – were walking back to Brixton Police Station from Dulwich Road via Kellett Road and Atlantic Road when they saw a blue Datsun car parked outside No. 82 Atlantic Road, the office of S & M Car Hire. As the two officers passed the car, they looked in and saw the driver placing what appeared to be pieces of folded paper in his right sock. Having in mind the reputation of the area for drug trading, they thought that the pieces of paper might contain drugs and decided to investigate.

3·31   The officers approached the driver and questioned him about what he had in his socks. They explained that they thought he might be in possession of drugs and asked if they could search him. The driver laughed and told them that as a mini-cab driver it was his practice to put his money in his socks for safe-keeping. He agreed to be searched. PC Cameron searched him and found nothing incriminating. The pieces of paper proved, as the cab driver had said, to be bank notes. While PC Cameron was searching the cab driver a crowd of some thirty, mainly black, youths had begun to assemble on the pavement outside the S & M Car Hire Office. Some of them had come from the All-Star Takeaway next door. The officers noticed this and that the crowd was hostile; they decided, however, to continue their investigation. They thought that the money the cab driver had could have been the proceeds of drug trafficking. There is dispute about whether they asked the driver's permission to do so, but one of them (PC Thornton) began to search the car. When the driver objected that the officer might be going to plant something incriminating in the car, he stopped, however, and got out. Meanwhile the crowd had continued to grow. Its hostility to the police officers was plain. People were shouting abuse at the officers and alleging that they were harassing the cab driver.

3·32   PC Cameron then went with the cab driver to the rear of the car where he began to take down the driver's particulars. PC

Thornton walked round the front of the car to check the Road Fund licence and then began to walk down the outside of the pavement in front of the S & M Car Hire Office, between the kerb and a row of concrete bollards which are set in the pavement there. As well as the crowd on the pavement, the officer noticed some six or seven black people on the flat roof of the All-Star Takeaway, a few of whom were carrying cameras. The people on the roof and others at the windows of the Takeaway Service were joining the crowd in shouting abuse at the two officers. There is dispute about what precisely happened. According to PC Thornton, as he attempted to rejoin his colleague, he found his way blocked by a young black man who was leaning against the side of the blue Datsun. The officer asked the young man to move but the latter simply abused him. The officer alleges that the young man then pushed him in the chest with both hands. According to the young man, the officer threatened him and trod on his foot, causing him to react and push the officer. According to the cab driver, the young man did no more than say persistently to the police officers, 'Leave him alone' (i.e. the cab driver). Other witnesses say PC Thornton was aggressive in his manner towards the crowd and the young man in particular.

3.33 Whatever the circumstances, it is clear that at this point the young black man was arrested by PC Thornton for obstructing a police officer in the execution of his duty. It is alleged by the officer that when he took hold of the young man, the latter became extremely violent. A police van, for which the officers had made a radio request, arrived at 4.48 p.m. With the help of uniformed officers who had been attracted to the scene by the noise of the crowd, PC Thornton put the young man in the back of the van. By this time the crowd outside the S & M Office had grown to about 150. Its members had closed in around the police officers and were angry at what many saw as a further example of police harassment. People were spilling onto the road as well as occupying the pavement. The traffic in Atlantic Road had come to a stop.

The outbreak of disorder

3.34 As the police van drew away with PCs Cameron and Thornton and the young man in it, the crowd around the van rocked it. A missile was thrown, smashing the window of the nearside rear door and flinging the van door open. The van stopped momentarily when PC Cameron saw a uniformed officer stagger out of the crowd holding his stomach and got out to assist him. The officers in the van thought that this officer had been stabbed, although he had in fact been hit by a missile and winded. They reported their belief over the radio. The van with PC Thornton and the young man in it then left the scene. PC Cameron and the winded officer walked back towards the crowd, and, as they did so, bottles and other missiles were thrown at them.

3·35   Inspector Scotchford, who was again Duty Inspector at Brixton Police Station, received a radio call at 4.52 p.m. that a person had been stabbed near the S & M Car Hire Office. He went immediately to the scene. On his arrival, he saw a large crowd, a number of police officers, some in uniform and others in plain clothes, and several police vans and a police dog van parked just north of the Triangle, the apex of Railton and Mayall Roads. Traffic in Atlantic Road had come to a standstill. Inspector Scotchford realized at once that the situation was serious. He asked over his radio for the two senior officers on duty at Brixton Police Station that Saturday – Chief Superintendent Boyling and Chief Inspector Benn – to come to the scene. He also told the officers present to move the crowd back onto the pavement in order to allow the traffic to clear. But the crowd would not move. They continued to abuse the police, alleging harassment. Missiles were still being thrown and some arrests had been made. A number of people, some of them white, were taking photographs of incidents between the crowd and the police.

3·36   While Inspector Scotchford was trying to get traffic moving again, a number of black people came up to him with a plastic carrier bag. During the scuffle with the young man he had arrested earlier, PC Thornton had lost hold of a plastic carrier bag, in which, so he says, he was carrying his truncheon, his police personal radio and a black cotton bomber jacket: the bag had been snatched by someone in the crowd outside the S & M Office and had disappeared. The people who now approached Inspector Scotchford were demanding that he look in the bag and into those held by other plain clothes officers at the scene. They said that the bags contained iron bars. The Inspector said that he would listen to their complaints when order was restored and the traffic was flowing again. But this was not good enough for the crowd. They became very angry and started to jostle the Inspector. A number of people were taking photographs of the exchange.

3·37   When, a few moments later, Chief Superintendent Boyling and Chief Inspector Benn arrived separately on the scene, they too were immediately surrounded by a large and hostile crowd. It was about 5.10 p.m. The crowd was complaining about the earlier arrests, about police harassment and alleging that some police officers had been wearing National Front badges. Inspector Scotchford briefed his senior officers on the situation, but it was obvious to them that the air was electric. A young black man, Mr Tony Morgan, who was on the scene and had witnessed the initial incident, warned Chief Superintendent Boyling that if he did not get his officers out of the area, there would be a riot. Mr Boyling did not take this advice literally. But he did take steps to try to diffuse the situation. He asked Mr Morgan to stay with him to liaise between himself and the crowd. He had a message put out asking all police R/T cars (i.e. all obvious police vehicles) not to attend the incident because he was concerned that their horns and flashing lights might be thought provocative. He also told two plain-clothes officers who were alleged by the crowd to have worn National Front badges to go back to Brixton Police Station.

3·38   Mr Boyling walked around the crowd and spoke to as many people as he could. The general criticism was of the number of police officers present. By this time about fifty to sixty officers were in the area. They had come in response to calls for assistance. Not all of them were immediately visible: some were in vans parked in Mayall Road near the Triangle; most had gathered in that area. The Chief Superintendent judged the crowd as numbering not less than 200. It was mainly to the north of the police officers, in Atlantic Road towards Coldharbour Lane.

Serious disorder begins

3·39   Mr Boyling was standing talking to Mr Morgan about what should be done when he noticed that the crowd in Atlantic Road was covering the full width of the road. Suddenly there was a cry of 'Look out'. Looking up, the Chief Superintendent saw bricks and stones coming through the air towards him. The missiles hit the police dog van parked across the apex of the Triangle, smashing its windows. The police officers in Mayall Road took cover, some behind the vans, some inside them. Those not in Mayall Road, including Chief Superintendent Boyling, ran to join their colleagues. The missiles were coming over thick and fast as the crowd ran towards the police officers. Several officers were hit by missiles and fell.

3·40   The crowd surged up to the dog van and turned it on its side. A young black man set it alight. A police car nearby was also set alight. Chief Superintendent Boyling saw that he was confronted by a serious breakdown of law and order. He took two decisions. He called for urgent assistance from all over the Metropolitan Police District. He also ordered the officers with him to draw their truncheons and to charge the crowd to the north in Atlantic Road, so as to disperse them.

3·41   The charge achieved its objective. The crowd ran away pursued by the police. Some of the crowd ran into the side streets off Atlantic Road. The main body ran north up Atlantic Road and into Coldharbour Lane. The majority of the police stopped when they reached the junction of Atlantic Road and Coldharbour Lane, although a few officers pursued the crowd into Coldharbour Lane and the side streets off Atlantic Road. One of the consequences of the charge was that some of the crowd used the side streets to make their way south to join the crowd in the Leeson Road area.

3·42   Having cleared Atlantic Road, Chief Superintendent Boyling then took steps to secure it against the possibility that the crowd might return. With the relatively small number of officers he had available, he organized as best he could cordons of officers across the junction of Atlantic Road and Coldharbour Lane and at the mouth of each of the three side streets off the southern part of Atlantic Road, namely Kellett Road, Saltoun Road and Vining Street. He also tried to find out whether anyone had been injured in the charge and he called over his radio for further urgent police assistance and for an ambulance and the fire brigade. He also asked for his senior officer, the Acting Commander, Chief Superintendent Nicholson, to come to the scene. The time was 5.27 p.m.

3·43   When Chief Superintendent Nicholson arrived in response to

Chief Superintendent Boyling's call he took charge at the scene, continuing the process Mr Boyling had begun of securing Atlantic Road while summoning reinforcements. While he stood briefing Mr Nicholson shortly after his arrival, Chief Superintendent Boyling was aware from his personal radio of calls for assistance because of shop windows being broken and looting in the main shopping area of Brixton Road, Coldharbour Lane, Electric Avenue and Atlantic Road north of the police cordon. The time was now about 6 p.m.

3·44   Looking south down Railton Road as they conversed, Chief Superintendent Nicholson and Chief Superintendent Boyling could see a crowd in Railton Road at the junction with Leeson Road. Chief Superintendent Boyling tried to gather enough officers together to go south down Railton Road and join with Inspector Scotchford, who had gone down Mayall Road to Leeson Road, in dispersing the crowd. With about four officers, he went south a short way down Railton Road, but he soon realized that the number of officers he had was wholly insufficient. Leaving the officers at the junction of Railton Road and Atlantic Road, he walked down Mayall Road to the junction with Leeson Road to join Inspector Scotchford.

Leeson Road

3·45   Not all the police officers in Mayall Road had joined Chief Superintendent Boyling in the charge north up Atlantic Road. While Mr Boyling was attending to the crowd in the north, Inspector Scotchford had gone south down Mayall Road to the junction with Leeson Road by the Windsor Castle Public House. He was aware that there was another crowd, mainly of black youths, numbering he later judged about 100 to 150, which was gathering in Leeson Road.

3·46   As Inspector Scotchford and his officers – about twenty in number – turned right into Leeson Road, they saw that the Road was packed with people and were met by a hail of bricks, bottles and other missiles including broken lengths of metal railing. Without protective shields, the officers took what shelter they could behind parked vehicles and in the angle of the Windsor Castle at the junction of Mayall and Leeson Roads. Some officers commandeered dustbin lids. They subsequently made a number of attempts to advance into Leeson Road but each time the barrage of missiles forced them back. Police casualties were heavy. Inspector Scotchford called for urgent assistance and for protective shields. A privately owned vehicle was turned over and set on fire. It was here in Leeson Road that, at about 5.45 p.m., the first petrol bombs were thrown at the police.

3.47 While they were held at the corner by the Windsor Castle, Inspector Scotchford and his officers were joined first by Chief Inspector Benn and then by Chief Superintendent Boyling. Some time after his arrival, Mr Boyling was approached by a white woman who had come from the crowd in Railton Road. Speaking with an American accent, the woman told the Chief Superintendent that she lived in Railton Road and had been asked to act as spokeswoman for the crowd. The woman said the police presence was provocative. She asked Mr Boyling to go with her to speak to the crowd. Debating with himself whether to do so, Mr Boyling stepped into the road with the woman, but as soon as he did so the hail of missiles from the crowd, which had temporarily almost ceased, started again. The Chief Superintendent refused to go with the woman. He told her that if she wished she could tell the crowd that they must disperse and that the police would not withdraw. After a short while, the woman returned to the crowd.

3.48 A police tender with shields on board arrived in Mayall Road in response to calls from Chief Superintendent Boyling and Inspector Scotchford at about 6.18 p.m. Having equipped their officers with shields, Chief Superintendent Boyling and Inspector Scotchford made another attempt to clear Leeson Road. Many officers were injured in this push, three as a result of petrol bombs. The officers found that petrol ran under the shields and their clothing caught fire. Half of Inspector Scotchford's own relief of fourteen officers were hurt, most of them with head injuries. The officers again withdrew to the junction of Mayall Road and Leeson Road. Inspector Scotchford began to fear for the safety of his party of officers.

3.49 Shortly after, some reinforcements arrived in the shape of a half-serial of officers from the Special Patrol Group. With this assistance, the officers made a final but again unsuccessful attempt to advance into Leeson Road. The crowd had also been reinforced by the arrival of people who had been cleared from Atlantic Road by

Chief Superintendent Boyling's charge. More police officers were injured. Indeed, so great was the pressure of missiles from the crowd and of the crowd itself on the police that Chief Superintendent Boyling ordered his men to withdraw northwards up Mayall Road. As they withdrew leaving behind a police van, the crowd pursued the officers, throwing everything that came to hand. They overturned the van and set it alight, along with two other cars in Leeson Road. It was now that members of the crowd set fire to the Windsor Castle Public House.

3·50   The burning of the vehicles and of the Windsor Castle briefly relieved the pressure on the police. The crowd fell back allowing the police, who had been in danger of being overrun and were also being stoned from the side, to regroup and continue an orderly withdrawal up Mayall Road to its junction with Railton Road at the Triangle. Here they formed a cordon facing south across the mouth of Mayall Road.

3·51   When Chief Superintendent Boyling, Inspector Scotchford and their officers arrived at the Triangle at about 6.45 p.m., they found that the police were still consolidating their control of the southern portion of Atlantic Road from the junction with Coldharbour Lane to the Triangle. With the arrival of Mr Boyling and his officers, an extended cordon was formed across the mouths of Railton and Mayall Roads. In effect, therefore, the police now held a base which extended the length of Atlantic Road from Coldharbour Lane to the Triangle. South of the Triangle, Railton and Mayall Roads were held by the crowd.

The Triangle

3·52   While Chief Superintendent Boyling and Inspector Scotchford had been pinned down by the crowd at the junction of Mayall and Leeson Roads, the thin cordon of officers Mr Boyling had left at the junction of Railton and Atlantic Roads had itself come under attack. At about 5.55 p.m. a No. 2 Bus on its normal route from Herne Hill north up Railton Road to Atlantic Road had been commandeered by people in the crowd about the Leeson Road/Railton Road junction. The Conductor was assaulted and robbed of his takings. While this was going on a crowd of about sixty youths throwing missiles advanced up Railton Road towards the dozen or

55

so police officers who formed a line at the junction of Railton and Atlantic Roads, but retreated when the officers drew their truncheons and advanced towards the crowd. After an unsuccessful attempt to overturn the bus in Railton Road, a member of the crowd drove it, with other people from the crowd on board, north up Railton Road towards the police line at the junction with Atlantic Road. Other people in the crowd followed it, shouting and throwing bricks and pieces of wood at the officers who, at that time, were without shields. Seeing the bus and the crowd coming towards the police line with the apparent intention of breaking it, one of the officers threw a brick at the windscreen of the bus. The windscreen smashed, the man driving the bus jumped out and it veered to the right of the police line, eventually coming to rest against a wall at the top of Railton Road near the junction with Kellett Road. The bus incident illustrated the aggressive spirit of the crowd and the defensive posture imposed upon the police by the lack of adequate reinforcements.

3·53   After a relatively brief lull in which the bus was driven away and the police line was slowly reinforced, the crowd in Railton Road began a concerted attack on the police line. A white man and a black youth appeared to one officer present to be directing operations. A car in Railton Road was overturned. The crowd tore down the corrugated iron sheeting in front of sites on the west of Railton Road where houses had been demolished. With the access this gave them to a virtually unlimited reserve of ammunition, and protected in part by the corrugated sheeting, the crowd were able to keep up a heavy bombardment of missiles on the police cordon. Many officers were injured.

3·54   It was into this scene of riot that the Commander of 'L' District, Commander Fairbairn, had arrived at about 6.15 p.m. He had phoned Brixton Police Station from home at about 5.20 p.m., was told of the disorder and made his way at once to Brixton. On his arrival, the Commander found that only some of the officers in the cordon across Railton Road had shields, but that many had no protection against the barrage of missiles, now including petrol bombs, which were being thrown at them. Looking down Railton Road, he could see fires on his left; a vehicle in the road was also on fire. He immediately asked for more shields to be supplied and for a helicopter to be sent to assist him by overseeing the movement of the crowd. The helicopter could not be made available because of lack of crew, but shortly afterwards a tender arrived with shields on board which were distributed to the officers in the cordon.

3·55 Commander Fairbairn saw at once that he had insufficient officers to disperse the crowd facing him. He decided that the best he could do was to try to contain the situation until he had sufficient officers to move forward and clear the area. He envisaged doing this by a pincer movement from both ends of Railton Road. This approach was confirmed by Deputy Assistant Commissioner Walker, responsible for Number 4 Area of the Metropolitan Police of which 'L' District is part, when he arrived on the scene at about 6.30 p.m., and it remained the basis of police strategy throughout the rest of the evening. After a brief conference, Mr Walker went back to Brixton Police Station to organize and deploy the police reinforcements that were beginning to come in, leaving Commander Fairbairn in charge of operations at the Triangle.

3·56 Chief Superintendent Boyling and Inspector Scotchford having withdrawn from Mayall and Leeson Roads, the police consolidated their hold across the junction of Railton and Mayall Roads with Atlantic Road at the Triangle. Gradually a double cordon was put across Railton Road facing south, with a single cordon across Mayall Road facing south and another single cordon at the junction of Kellett and Talma Roads. The crowd meanwhile were maintaining their attack on the Railton Road cordon. In addition to the bricks and petrol bombs, members of the crowd were hurling iron railings and lengths of wood at and over the police shields and even pouring various liquids (in one case a bottle of whisky) over the shields. Several officers were injured as burning petrol ran down their shields and the foam padding on the back of the shields as well as the officers' clothing caught fire. Commander Fairbairn encouraged his officers as best he could to withstand this attack until further reinforcements arrived.

An attempt at mediation

3·57 At about 7 p.m. the Commander was approached by four people in a determined attempt to mediate between the police and the crowd. Of the four, two were members of Lambeth Borough

Council, Councillors John Boyle and Stewart Lansley, one was the Anglican Vicar of St Matthew's Church, Brixton, the Reverend Robert Nind, and the other was Mr Tony Morgan, who had remained in the area since he had been asked to do so by Mr Boyling. The four explained to the Commander that in their view the only way to reduce tension was for the police to withdraw from the area and allow the crowd to disperse. Commander Fairbairn replied that in view of the disorder he would not withdraw and risk the possibility of the disturbances spreading. Some minutes later the four offered to go and speak to the crowd and invited the Commander to go with them. He refused but agreed to find the four a loud-hailer. The four moved forward, missiles being thrown towards them, and three of them – the two Councillors and Mr Morgan – passed beyond the police lines and the cars overturned by the crowd. Mr Nind made his way by side streets round the back of the crowd.

3·58 Once they passed behind the upturned vehicles, the mediators were seized by some of the crowd who told them their terms for dispersing. They wanted the police to withdraw, they wanted an end to police harassment and they wanted those arrested to be released. The crowd also complained that they felt surrounded by the police. After returning to the police lines, the mediators relayed these messages to Commander Fairbairn. The Commander, however, did not believe that those who had said they would disperse if the police withdrew could, even if they wished, enforce their view on others in the crowd. He maintained his refusal to withdraw.

3·59 At this point Mr Boyle said that the crowd had another demand: they wanted to put their case to the media. Mr John Clare, Community Affairs and Education Correspondent of the BBC, who was on the scene recording the exchange with Commander Fairbairn, went forward behind the barrier of cars and interviewed one of the crowd. But missiles again began to be thrown at the police. So ended the most significant attempt at mediation between the police and the crowd in the course of the evening.

3·60 The attack by the crowd on the police cordon in Railton Road continued from now until 8.45 p.m. when the police were at last sufficiently reinforced to be able to move forward. Petrol bombs and other missiles were continually hurled at the line of police shields. At one point a car was pushed to within a few feet of the police line. Shortly after, the police saw a black man pour liquid from a jerry can across Railton Road and beckon them to come forward. In spite of the constant attacks, the police under Commander Fairbairn continued to hold their line while gradually reinforcements were brought into the area. During this critical phase the officers in the line, supported by their Commander's leadership and encouraged by the comradeship of their colleagues, displayed exemplary steadiness and courage. Some, it is clear, picked up stones or other missiles which had been thrown at them, and flung them back. It may not have been lawful: but it was understandable, and excusable, when in self-defence.

The looting and arson

3·61 While the centre of the disorder was Leeson Road and the northern end of Railton Road, its effects were being felt over a wide area of central Brixton. In the commercial area of Brixton Road, the northern half of Atlantic Road, Electric Avenue and Coldharbour Lane, widespread looting had developed since about 6 p.m. Both whites and blacks – some of them very young – were involved. To several witnesses, the whites appeared to be generally older, and more systematic in their methods. It also appears that the looters were, in the main, quite different from the people who were attacking the police in Railton Road. Several witnesses had the impression that many of the looters came from outside Brixton, and were simply taking advantage of the disorders for their own criminal purposes. Small groups of police officers who ventured into the area were attacked. With the number of police inadequate both to control the looting and to deal with the disorder in Railton Road, the commercial centre of Brixton north and west of the concentration of police near the Triangle had effectively been given up to the looters. Many premises were damaged and entered on this Saturday evening and substantial quantities of goods and other property were stolen from them.

3·62 The other major area in which the police were absent lay, of course, south of the police lines at the Triangle, in Mayall and Railton Roads and in the streets to the west of there. This was territory effectively held by the rioters. In one of the most disturbing aspects of the disorders, ambulances and fire engines responding to calls for help in this area were attacked and an ambulanceman and several fire officers injured. Altogether on Saturday evening one ambulanceman and fourteen fire officers were reported injured and four ambulances and nine fire appliances were damaged. Four fire appliances were temporarily abandoned by their crews in the face of the hostility of the crowd, a turntable ladder was stolen and set alight, and a considerable quantity of Fire Brigade equipment was stolen or damaged. The crowd in Railton Road, which consisted mainly of black people but with some white people present, had begun to move south down Railton Road, entering commercial and other premises, including a number of private houses, stealing their contents and in some cases setting fire to the buildings. The premises attacked in this way included two public houses (the George and the Hamilton Arms), a plumbers merchants, as well as shops and other premises. Several people were assaulted in these attacks: some lost not merely their possessions but their homes and their livelihoods as a result of them. The destruction, quite apart from the financial loss, was devastating in human terms, as more than one hapless victim testified in the Inquiry.

Effra Parade

3·63   The main concentration of fires in Railton Road lay near the junction with Effra Parade. The fire brigade had been unable to deal with them because of the hostility of the crowd, and the presence of two serials of police under Chief Inspector Delaney had not proved sufficient to overcome this. Shortly after 8 p.m. Chief Superintendent Robinson was directed by Mr Walker to take two further serials to Effra Parade to assist the Fire Brigade. As they drove along Brixton Road they were stoned by small groups of youths, but they continued to the junction of Effra Parade and Dulwich Road where they joined Chief Inspector Delaney's two serials and a further serial which shortly afterwards arrived to assist. Looking along Effra Parade to Railton Road, Mr Robinson could see that not only were several vehicles on fire at the Railton Road end of Effra Parade but also the George Public House on the north side of Effra Parade.

3·64   With the courage and decisiveness which were to prove characteristic of his conduct that evening, Chief Superintendent Robinson decided to advance along Effra Parade with four of his serials equipped with shields, so as to clear the way for the fire appliances to tackle the fire. The fifth serial was left to protect the fire appliances in the rear. As he was making his arrangements, the fire appliances were instructed by their control to leave the scene due to the hostility of the crowd, but they agreed to await the outcome of the police action.

3·65 Chief Superintendent Robinson then led about sixty to seventy officers behind a single line of shields along Effra Parade towards the junction with Railton Road. As the officers neared the junction they could see a large crowd numbering perhaps 300 to 400 in Railton Road, which soon began to direct a heavy barrage of missiles at them. The police cordon stopped briefly just short of the junction while Mr Robinson surveyed the many fires in Railton Road – which were well advanced – and agreed a course of action with his senior officers. This was to clear the junction by splitting the cordon, one half of which, with Mr Robinson in command, turned north into Railton Road and the other, under Mr Delaney, south. Both cordons were immediately attacked ferociously by the crowd, and the northern cordon stopped facing north across Railton Road under a hail of bricks, bottles, tiles, pieces of wood, milk crates, scaffold poles and petrol bombs. The southern cordon was similarly subjected to a fierce barrage of missiles including petrol bombs and a new weapon, spinning plates. In spite of this the southern cordon managed to advance slowly as far as the northern edge of the junction of Railton Road and Chaucer Road, where they were halted by the sustained bombardment from the crowd.

3·66 Chief Superintendent Robinson radioed for ambulances and for police assistance. He also summoned the fire appliances to begin to tackle the fires around the junction of Effra Parade and Railton Road. He then went south to the cordon at Chaucer Road. Once there he decided that his officers would have to extend their control over the whole of the junction with Chaucer Road in order to avoid being attacked, as they now were, from the sides. Under the sustained assaults of the crowd – at one point a car was pushed as a battering ram into the police line – the officers succeeded in establishing a new cordon in Railton Road at the south side of the junction with Chaucer Road, as well as cordons across the flanks of Chaucer Road itself, thus securing the whole of the junction.

3·67   At this point, Chief Superintendent Robinson was himself hit and partially stunned by a missile thrown from the crowd. Recovering himself, he made his way back to the northern cordon which, again under heavy attack, succeeded in advancing a further twenty yards or so north up Railton Road. A few reinforcements arrived in response to the Chief Superintendent's increasingly urgent calls for assistance, and about six fire appliances. The fire officers fought with great determination the fires around them, in spite of the danger from collapsing buildings and the missiles of the crowd, and under the difficulty that their hoses were being cut by the glass and other sharp objects which were strewn around the ground. Many police officers were injured, some seriously: ambulances were ferrying them from a house in Effra Parade, the occupants of which had offered to help and who rapidly found themselves in charge of a casualty clearing station. As the number of police officers injured rose steadily, Chief Superintendent Robinson's calls for assistance became increasingly insistent.

The police advance

3·68   Although he did not know it, the police were at last beginning to marshal sufficient officers to disperse the crowds of whose anger the Chief Superintendent and his men were the target. At about 8.30 p.m. Commander Adams (at the time of the disturbances in charge of the Traffic Division of the Metropolitan Police, but Commander Fairbairn's predecessor as Commander of 'L' District) had arrived at Brixton Police Station and had been directed by Mr Walker to take the reserves available at that time (numbering about 150 officers, of whom about 100 were members of the Special Patrol Group) to the southern end of Railton Road, and move north, while Commander Fairbairn moved south with the object of dispersing the crowd westwards into the side streets off Railton Road, so relieving Mr Robinson. Commander Fairbairn was himself injured at about 8.30 p.m., but about fifteen minutes later he gave the order for officers in the cordon at the northern end of Railton Road to begin their advance south, at the same time sending other officers under Chief Superintendent Boyling south down Mayall Road to cover his flank. Under a continuing hail of missiles and petrol bombs the officers in Railton Road then began to pick their way slowly south round both burning and burnt-out vehicles, clearing the remnants of the crowd behind the demolition site on the west side of Railton Road. Once beyond the vehicles, the officers re-formed in a line and moved towards Dexter and Leeson Roads, the crowd dispersing in front of them as they did so.

3.69   Commander Adams and his serials reached the Herne Hill end of Railton Road and at about 8.52 p.m. they began to move north up Railton Road. At its junction with Mayall Road, the group of officers divided, Commander Adams leading about fifty officers behind a line of shields north up Mayall Road, the remaining officers under Chief Superintendent Sillence continuing north up Railton Road. A crowd of several hundred youths threw some missiles at the officers in Railton and Mayall Roads, but again they dispersed as the officers advanced.

3.70   However, the effect of this advance from north and south into Railton Road was, temporarily at least, to put great pressure on Chief Superintendent Robinson's cordons in Railton Road north and south of Effra Parade. At about 9 p.m. Mr Robinson's north cordon was temporarily overwhelmed by the crowd attacking it. Many officers were injured, some of them seriously and some police shields were captured by the crowd. The officers (now some twenty-five to thirty in number with about ten to twelve shields between them) fell back to the north side of the junction with Effra Parade where they managed to reform a line. This meant, however, that the cordon and the crowd were virtually on top of the fire appliances and firemen. A fire officer said to the Chief Superintendent that he and his officers would have to withdraw. Chief Superintendent Robinson told the fire officer that reinforcements were on the way and asked him to remain a little longer, to which he agreed. But considering the situation, it seemed to Mr Robinson that extra-ordinary measures were necessary if he was to save the position and prevent his officers or the firemen being further injured or even killed. He took a hose from a fireman, ordered other officers to do likewise and turned the jets on the crowd. The action achieved the effect Mr Robinson desired. The crowd fell back and the firemen were able to continue to fight the fires.

3·71   At about this time Chief Superintendent Robinson was struck for a second time on the face by a missile thrown from the crowd. When, a few minutes later, he recovered, he was approached by a senior fire officer who told him that the fire hoses should not be used for crowd control. The Chief Superintendent replied that their use had been and remained necessary in his view if the police and firemen were not to be overrun. Shortly after this, Mr Robinson received a message that his southern cordon was under very heavy pressure and unable to hold its position for very much longer. He told his officers that reinforcements were coming; meanwhile, they must continue to hold their position.

The disorder diminishes

3·72   Reinforcements arrived via Effra Parade at about 9.30 p.m. in the shape of three serials of officers (some with shields) under Chief Superintendent Skinner. These officers took over the northern cordon and began to move northwards. It was about this time that they began to see Commander Fairbairn's men approaching with shields from the north. The crowd between the lines of officers dispersed, mainly west along Barnwell Road but some to the east along Leeson Road and the Somerleyton Passage. The fire hoses being used against the crowd were stopped and Chief Superintendent Robinson reinforced his southern cordon which, under the pressure of the crowd, had had to withdraw to the northern side of the junction with Chaucer Road. Shortly afterwards, Mr Robinson saw the crowd in front of the southern cordon disperse, many escaping along Spenser Road, as the officers under Commander Adams and Chief Superintendent Sillence came into view. Within about ten minutes the area had become quiet. Commander Adams had moved from Mayall Road through Chaucer Road to join up with Mr Sillence, and since some missiles were being thrown towards his officers by the crowd dispersing up Spenser Road he took most of his officers west along Spenser Road to Dulwich Road. The police in Railton Road were left to consolidate their cordons so as to continue to protect the Fire Brigade fighting the fires in Railton Road.

3·73   By about 10.00–10.15 p.m. the main disorders in the Railton Road/Mayall Road area were over, and the police were able to re-establish an effective presence throughout Brixton, including the commercial area around Brixton Road, Electric Avenue and Cold-harbour Lane. Commander Adams and his officers moved north up Dulwich Road and, hearing of continuing trouble in Brixton Road, made their way up Effra Road to the area outside Lambeth Town Hall. Here they assisted other officers in dispersing crowds along Brixton Road, and in Coldharbour Lane. By about 11 p.m., apart from isolated incidents, order had been restored to Brixton.

Taking stock

3·74   Both the police and the community were now able to take stock of what had happened. In cold statistical terms, eighty-two people had been arrested, 279 police officers injured, forty-five members of the public injured (there were probably more), sixty-one private vehicles and fifty-six police vehicles damaged or destroyed, and 145 premises damaged, twenty-eight of them by fire. As important, however, was the effect of what had happened on the attitudes and feelings of those involved. The police had undergone an experience, till then unparalleled on the mainland of the United Kingdom. Within the community there were some who felt elated because, as they saw it, the community had taken a stand against the police; and there were some who saw disorder as an opportunity for publicized protest; but many more were saddened and uncertain at the implications of the events. It was clear to all, however, that the scars of what had happened would linger in Brixton, and particularly in the relationship between the police and public, for a long time to come.

(2) Comment and findings

3·75   The incident which sparked off the disorder on Saturday was nothing unusual on the streets of Brixton – two plain-clothes police officers questioning a suspect, a hostile crowd gathering and complaining of police harassment, an arrest, and a final violent protest as the police sought to remove the arrested man. Usually, however, such an incident would end there: the protesting crowd would, after a little while, disperse and normality would return. Why, on this occasion, did the incident escalate into a major disorder culminating in arson and a full-scale battle against the police?

3·76   The inference is irresistible that many young people, and especially many young black people, were spoiling for a row as a result of their frustrations, fancied or real, and of their beliefs as to what happened on Friday. The young people who crowded the streets believed Friday's events to be yet another typical instance of police harassment of young blacks. And many of them were deceived by rumour into thinking that police callousness on the Friday had actually led to the death of the wounded man. The tinder for a major conflagration was there: the arrest outside the S & M Car Hire Office was the spark which set it ablaze.

3·77   There is no need to probe deeper for the immediate cause of the Saturday riot. I have heard no evidence to suggest that there was any prior organization or conspiracy. There was no plan, no 'D-day' or 'H-hour'. But many young people were itching to have a go. The spirit of defiance and aggression was in them. Many observers noted their elation as events developed to the disadvantage of the police. They were enjoying themselves. Deeper causes undoubtedly existed, and must be probed; but the immediate cause of Saturday's events was a spontaneous combustion set off by the spark of one single incident.

3·78   The raw material of the explosion was the spirit of angry young men; the spark was their anger at a piece of police action of no great consequence in itself. Much criticism was levelled during the Inquiry at the two officers who conducted the search of the mini-cab driver outside the S & M Car Hire Office. It was alleged that they acted contrary to the directions of their senior officers and unreasonably, even unlawfully, in searching the mini-cab driver in the first place, even more so in subsequently searching his car after the wads of paper they had seen the driver stuffing into his sock turned out to be bank notes, as he had asserted, and did not contain drugs, as they suspected. It was suggested that they acted rashly in remaining at the scene to take the driver's particulars and that one officer in particular acted provocatively and aggressively in the incident with the growing crowd of onlookers which led to the arrest of the young black man. In defence of the officers, it was suggested that they would not have been carrying out their duty to enforce the law if they had acted otherwise and that they behaved lawfully and reasonably. It was pointed out that, according to the two officers, they had, before searching the car, obtained the consent of the mini-cab driver to do so, and that Section 23 of the Misuse of Drugs Act 1971 provides a statutory power for a constable to stop and search not only anyone reasonably suspected of being in possession of drugs, but also any vehicle in which it is reasonably suspected there might be such drugs.

3·79   I find that the conduct of the two young officers in searching the mini-cab driver, and subsequently his car, was not unlawful. Once they had seen the driver acting, as they thought, in a suspicious manner, the two officers behaved within their legal powers. Where in my view they can rightly be criticized is that in handling what was plainly a tense situation they acted without the discretion and judgement which maturer years might have brought. Perhaps they had become inured by their experience of the hostility which police action could arouse in Brixton to the point where they failed to recognize real danger signals or to strike the correct balance between enforcing the law and keeping the peace. The important question which has to be answered is not whether two young police officers acted foolishly or brashly or even unlawfully in persisting with their questions and search of a cab-driver or in arresting a protesting bystander, but why the incident set off a riot. I consider that question later.

3·80   I do not set out here my findings on the police handling of the Saturday disturbances. They will be found in Part IV, where I consider two of the main criticisms of the police, namely 'overreaction' to the disorders and the opposite allegation of 'delay and lack of vigour' in suppressing them.

C · Sunday, 12 April 1981

(1) The course of events

3·81   The scars left by the disturbances of Saturday were visible in a very real sense when the following day dawned. Throughout the Saturday night the police had maintained a strong presence in Brixton in order to protect the emergency services and damaged property and to prevent a recurrence of the looting and disorder.

That presence was gradually increased in the course of Sunday. Two cordons of police were established in Brixton on Sunday: one, the outer cordon – the line of which ran along Dulwich Road, Effra Road, Brixton Water Lane, Brixton Road, Gresham Road, Coldharbour Lane and the railway line between East Brixton Station and Herne Hill Station – prevented unnecessary traffic entering the area; the other, inner cordon – which ran along Coldharbour Lane, Effra Road, Brixton Water Lane, Trelawn Road, Barnwell Road, Leeson Road and the area bordering the railway line to Coldharbour Lane – prevented unnecessary pedestrian movement into the heart of the 'Front Line' area. Partly to cut down the movement of people into the area, Brixton Underground Station remained closed all day. Within the cordons, the police and other emergency services, including those of the local authority, began the task of assessing the damage and of clearing it up. The area within the inner cordon was policed, initially at least, by about 100 officers on foot; between the inner and outer cordons, mobile as well as some foot patrols were operating. Gradually the people of Brixton began moving about the streets and journalists and sightseers came to survey the scene of the troubles.

3·82 Apart from a number of hoax calls to the police alleging a build-up of black or skinhead youths, the morning of Sunday was generally quiet and trouble-free. Rumours, including one that the National Front proposed to descend on the area, continued, however, and the police were prepared for the possibility of disorder later in the day. At 3 p.m., Deputy Assistant Commissioner Walker resumed overall command of the police in the area, and between 3 p.m. and 4 p.m. forty-six serials of officers (including eight SPG serials) moved into the area. Most were used to relieve officers on duty; others were kept in reserve at Brixton Police Station. At about this time, the police noted that groups of youths, mainly black, were beginning to gather; two people were arrested at 3.25 p.m. in Wiltshire Road, one for throwing a missile at a police officer. At 3.56 p.m. the police received a report that Lambeth Town Hall was to be attacked that night. At 4 p.m. you yourself visited the centre of Brixton accompanied by the Commissioner of Police of the Metropolis, Sir David McNee. The visiting party was booed and jeered as it inspected the area.

Disorder re-starts

3·83   Trouble broke out again at about 4.27 p.m. when police outside the burnt-out shell of The George Public House in Railton Road were attacked by youths throwing missiles. Three officers were injured, but reinforcements were rapidly called in and the incident soon subsided. At 4.40 p.m. the police were deployed to deal with reports of looting in Electric Avenue. So the pattern of the disorders of Sunday began to emerge, with the police responding to relatively isolated incidents of trouble occurring over a wide area of Brixton.

3·84   At 4.45 p.m. another meeting of community leaders chaired by Commander Ferguson took place at Brixton Police Station to discuss the situation. There were present at the meeting a number of the community leaders who had first met the Commander on Friday evening, including Mr Courtney Laws and Mr and Mrs Madray, as well as Mr Ricky Cadogan, the Chairman of the Council for Community Relations in Lambeth, and Mr Peter Strick, a member of the Council. Mr Timothy Raison MP, Minister of State at the Home Office, was also present.

3·85   While the meeting was in progress, however, serious disorder developed in various parts of Brixton. The general pattern of the incidents of that evening was of groups of youths, smaller in number than those of the previous day, throwing missiles at the police and, in many cases, looting. Although there were more of them, the intensity of these attacks was generally less than those on Saturday (although a total of 122 police officers were injured on this day) and, again unlike Saturday, there were no serious instances of arson.

3·86   This pattern of incidents developed at about 5 p.m. when an attempt by police officers to arrest a youth for obstruction in Coldharbour Lane resulted in other youths stoning the police. Four officers were injured before reinforcements arrived and order was restored. Meanwhile groups of youths had gathered outside Lambeth Town Hall and in the Railton Road area. Stones were thrown at the police at both these locations. At 5.13 p.m. two shield serials were sent to the junction of Effra Road and Rushcroft Road, where missiles were being thrown at the police. A police van in Brixton Road was stoned and a large crowd moved towards the Town Hall stoning the police. When Commander Fairbairn arrived outside the

Town Hall in his car at 5.15 p.m., many young people threw stones at the car. Reinforcements, including a shield serial, were deployed there. Brixton Police Station also came under threat when, at about 5.30 p.m., a large crowd of black youths ran along Pope's Road towards the Station. Mounted officers on reserve were posted in that road and five of them were deployed across the road facing the crowd. When the crowd saw these officers draw their truncheons, they turned and withdrew. This was the only occasion throughout the disturbances when mounted officers were actively involved in the events.

3·87 Pressure continued meanwhile on the police around the Town Hall and at 5.35 p.m. No. 4 Unit of the Special Patrol Group was sent there to assist. Police vehicles were damaged by missiles here and in Stockwell Road, and a number of arrests were made. The police began to try to remove the rubble which lay in the streets to prevent it being re-used against them. There were reports of stoning and damage to property in Brixton Road, Ferndale Road, Railton Road, Atlantic Road and Mayall Road. At 6.05 p.m. police were sent to protect Brixton Fire Station in Gresham Road. Looting was reported in Electric Avenue at 6.20 p.m., and disorder in the Stockwell Park Road area at 6.26 p.m. and shortly afterwards in Effra Road. Coaches carrying police serials had been stoned from flats in the Stockwell Park Road and at 5.56 p.m. police vehicles had been ordered not to use the road in order to prevent further damage and injury. At about 6.45 p.m., serious disorder took place in Barnwell Road when a large crowd of youths, mainly black, stoned the police. Many officers – including four-fifths of one shield serial – were injured before the crowd dispersed. Shortly afterwards Commander Fairbairn found a police coach at the junction of Barnwell Road and Railton Road, all the windows of which had been smashed as a result of an attack on it by people with iron bars.

3·88 Sporadic attacks on the police and attempts at looting continued throughout the Brixton area over the next three to four hours. The Town Hall remained a particular focus. At one point, youths moved up Brixton Hill towards St Matthew's Church and on reaching the Church pulled down the hoardings to use as a barricade against the police. Eventually these were removed by the police and the youths dispersed, but by 7.50 p.m. disorder had again erupted in Brixton Road outside the Town Hall. There was also stone throwing in the Railton Road and Atlantic Road area and reinforcements were sent to help the police clear Atlantic Road. Shop windows were broken in Brixton Hill; at 9.08 p.m. a shop in Clapham High Street was looted, and looting was also reported at about the same time in Stockwell Road. There were further reports of looting in Brixton Hill at 9.23 p.m. and in Arodene Road at 9.35 p.m.

3·89   At about 9.30 p.m. Chief Superintendent Sillence, the officer in charge of the Special Patrol Group (SPG), arrived at Stockwell Park Walk where he was told that the road had been closed to police vehicles because of stoning from the balconies of the flats in the Stockwell Park Estate. Mr Sillence summoned No. 7 Unit of the SPG to clear away crowds sitting on the walls on either side of Brixton Road. At first this went well, but the officers then began to be stoned both from the crowd and from the flats. In spite of this the officers dispersed the crowd, and then with two other SPG Units Mr Sillence ran across to the Estate to clear the balconies from which the stoning had come. Once this had been achieved the SPG Units withdrew, leaving a serial of uniformed officers patrolling the balconies to prevent any recurrence of the problem. (There had been previous incursions by police officers into the Estate late on Saturday evening and earlier on Sunday.) A similar incident occurred at about 10.30 p.m. at the Loughborough Estate, which the police handled in a similar way.

3·90   At about the same time, a crowd gathered outside Brixton Police Station. Three serials of officers were deployed to protect the Station and clear the area. The frequency of incidents was now diminishing, although looting and disturbances were reported from Electric Avenue, Streatham Hill, Brixton Hill and Acre Lane. Odd groups of youths were still stoning the police and their vehicles. Gradually, however, the disorder ceased. By 1 a.m. on Monday, 13 April, Brixton was quiet again.

3·91   In the course of the disorders on Sunday a total of 165 people were arrested. 122 police officers and three members of the public were reported injured, and sixty-one police vehicles and twenty-six other vehicles damaged or destroyed. Altogether, over 2,500 police officers had been deployed in controlling the disorders of the day.

(2) Comment and findings

3·92   Sunday was a day of aftermath. The disorders were serious and inflicted heavy casualties on the police. But they lacked the intensity of Saturday. They were, however, more widespread. Outsiders, some no doubt attracted by media coverage of Saturday's events, were more in evidence: there was more systematic and opportunistic looting: and the rumours which continued to run rife throughout the day undoubtedly fuelled the tension and violence in the streets. The police presence was heavy, as could have been expected following the events of the previous day, and in my view was fully justified. But perhaps because of this and the number of sightseers, there are more allegations of aggressive behaviour and misconduct by the police in relation to the disorders of Sunday than to those of the previous two days.

3·93   Sunday was for some, mostly young and black, a day to taunt, annoy and defy the police whom they believed they had for a time successfully fought on the Saturday. For some, it was an occasion to stand and stare at the evidence of the previous day's disorders and to watch the skirmishes between the police and their attackers. For others – the great majority – who said nothing, did nothing and stayed at home, it was a day of shock, as they contemplated the implications of the night before.

Postscript

3·94   Although they lie strictly outside my terms of reference, I should add that there were some disturbances (relatively minor) in Brixton on the evening of Monday, 13 April 1981. In incidents in which bricks and other missiles were thrown at the police and vehicles set on fire, twenty-nine arrests were made and one member of the public and eight police officers were injured. One police vehicle was damaged and two privately owned vehicles were destroyed. But by 11.30 p.m., those disorders too were over.

D · The nature of the disorders

3·95   I conclude this account of the disorders in Brixton with some comments on their nature and their causation.

(1) Were the disorders a riot?

3·96   I have reached the conclusion that it is necessary to express my opinion on this question. I understand that nobody has been prosecuted for riot in Brixton. But I see no reason why an expression of my opinion on the general behaviour of the disorderly crowds should pre-judge the trial of any individual accused of riot (if any there be): for in such a trial the question will be whether the accused himself participated in the riot. But if, following upon my expression of opinion, it should be considered unjust to proceed against any person for riot arising from the Brixton disorders, it is better that no such proceedings should be taken than that this Report should be silent on the question. I am required to report on the disorders. A Report which omitted to indicate my view of the nature of the disorders would be an incomplete diagnosis of the social ills with which I am concerned and an unsure foundation upon which to make proposals and recommendations for their remedy.

3·97   Riot is a tumultuous disturbance of the peace by three or more persons assembled together with an intent mutually to assist one another by force, if necessary, against anyone who opposes them in the execution of a common purpose, and who execute or begin to execute that purpose in a violent manner so as to alarm at least one person of reasonable firmness and courage.[1]

Friday, 10 April

3·98   The disorder was not initially a riot. But it had become a riot by 6.36 p.m. when Inspector Scotchford arrived on the scene. The critical moment was when the crowd turned and stoned the police. This was violent crowd action in which members of the crowd were mutually assisting each other in the execution of a common purpose, namely an attack upon the police. It was dangerous and alarming.

1. Halsbury, *Laws of England*, 4th Edition, paragraph 861.

Saturday, 11 April

3·99   The evidence of a tumultuous, violent crowd determined to execute and executing a common purpose to attack the police with alarming and very dangerous missiles is too plain to be challenged. And nobody who gave evidence – certainly none of the respected local leaders who gave evidence – challenged either the alarming use of force by the crowd or the existence of a common purpose to attack the police. Certainly a riot had begun by the time the crowd attacked the police in 'the Triangle' about 5.15 p.m. (paragraph 3·39, supra).

Sunday, 12 April

3·100   The nature of the Sunday disturbances differed from those on Friday and Saturday. But their widespread, sporadic character put an even greater strain on the police; and the toll of police casualties was high. No one who gave evidence doubted that Sunday's crowds had a common purpose to attack the police; and the means they used were violent, frightening, and dangerous. I conclude, therefore, that there was rioting on the Sunday.

(2) Were the disorders organized?

3·101   Two linked questions have now to be considered. Were the disorders premeditated or planned? Did 'outsiders' instigate or participate in them? The evidence I have heard indicates that the disorders originated as a spontaneous crowd reaction to police action which, rightly or wrongly, the crowd believed to be harassment of black people. The disorders were not, I am satisfied, premeditated. But, once they had begun, an element of leadership and direction did emerge; and strangers were observed participating in the disorders. Though the evidence of leadership and of 'outsider participation' is slight, it is persuasive, and has not been controverted. I have in mind the course of events on Saturday: the particular incident of the woman with the American accent (paragraph 3·47, supra); the presence of the white man and black youth apparently directing operations in Railton Road after the bus incident (paragraph 3·53, supra); the terms offered by the rioters to the two councillors and Mr Morgan (paragraph 3·58, supra); and three further pieces of evidence to which I shall now refer. Though the evidence is too slight to amount to proof in a court of law, it indicates plainly enough not only that there was a degree of direction but also that, after the disorders had begun, some strangers participated in the attack upon the police, some leaders emerged and some used the disorders for the deliberate commission of criminal offences. I now turn to mention briefly three pieces of evidence which cast some light in this shadowy area.

The George

3·102 The Vicar of St Jude's gave evidence of what may well have been the initial break into the public house. He saw a 'grimly determined' group of black men, armed with bricks and an iron bar, come running up from the Dulwich Road and break into the public house: they then turned their attention to the newsagent's shop opposite, smashing it up. When he protested, they replied that 'the police had been harassing the black and homosexual communities and that they could stand it no longer'. The George had a reputation (whether justified or not I do not know) of having in the past discriminated against black people, and the newsagent was alleged to have refused to serve homosexuals, a group of whom were residents in Railton Road.

Strangers

3·103 An indication of the presence of outsiders is to be found in the evidence of a police constable. He gave evidence that many of the black people opposing him and his colleagues in Railton Road were strangers (i.e. he did not recognize them as Brixton people). And there were other witnesses who spoke of unfamiliar faces in the crowds.

Petrol bombs

3·104 The evidence does suggest that a sinister contribution was made by strangers in making and distributing petrol bombs. Indeed, it is possible, though the evidence is not sufficient to warrant a finding, that without the guidance and help of certain white people the young blacks, who were the great majority of the rioting crowds, would not have used the bombs. Be that as it may – and I have to leave it as an open question – clear and credible evidence was given to me in private session by two witnesses who reside in streets adjacent to Railton Road that they saw white men making, stacking and distributing petrol bombs in the Railton Road/Leeson Road area on Saturday.

3·105   There is no doubt from the evidence that the materials to make petrol bombs were readily available to the rioters, both white and black – bottles looted from shops and public houses, petrol siphoned from the tanks of commandeered vehicles, and wicks from rags and other materials to hand. It is unlikely therefore that the use of petrol bombs is evidence of any premeditation in the conduct of the disorders. But the bombs indicate the existence of a degree of organization among the rioters once the disorders began. There is convincing evidence of the existence of at least one makeshift 'factory' in which petrol bombs were made for use by the rioters in Brixton on the Saturday.

The Rastafarians

3·106   It is convenient to consider at this point whether the Rastafarians played any part in organizing or leading the riots. There was no suggestion in argument, nor any indication in evidence, that the Rastafarians, as a group or by their doctrines, were responsible for the outbreak of disorder or the ensuing riots. The Rastafarians, their faith and their aspirations deserve more understanding and more sympathy than they get from the British people. The true Rastafarian is deeply religious, essentially humble and sad. His philosophy is a striving towards a people's identity. His aspiration – the return to Africa from exile in 'Babylon' (a deliberate echo of the exile and lost tribes of Israel) – is embodied in a religious and peaceful discipline. He believes it is as legitimate to smoke cannabis as to drink alcohol – and less likely to lead to unruly behaviour; but, as Mr Jah Bones made clear in his evidence, the true Rastafarian accepts the law of the land. The dreadlocks, the headgear and the colours which he affects are a daily reminder to him of Africa and a witness to the world of his belief that his exiled people must return there. It is his great difficulty that young hooligans have aped the outward signs of his faith without accepting its discipline or adopting his religious approach to life.

3·107   It is a serious problem that some followers and imitators of

Rastafarianism are not as scrupulous to observe the law as is Mr Jah Bones. I have no doubt that cannabis smoking by some has done substantial harm to Rastafarian reputation in this country. The risk – to the Rastafarians themselves as well as to the rest of society – is that they will be overwhelmed by the wild and the lawless. In that event the good they represent will perish; the wrongs, which their imitators commit in their name, will be for what they are remembered, and will destroy them.

(3) Findings as to the nature of the disorders

3·108   My conclusions, therefore, on the nature of the disorders are these. They originated spontaneously. There was no premeditation or plan. They quickly became a riot, the common purpose of the crowds being to attack the police. Outsiders were attracted by the publicity into Brixton on Saturday; and some of them, white as well as black, participated in the Saturday riot. White people (as well as black people) helped to make and distribute petrol bombs on Saturday.

3·109   The violence erupted from the spontaneous reaction of the crowds to what they believed to be police harassment. When it did erupt, the publicity given to it attracted supporters from outside Brixton. And there can be no doubt that the rioters, both the young blacks whose spontaneous reaction against the police started it off and the supporters whom they attracted from Brixton and elsewhere, found a ferocious delight in arson, criminal damage to property, and in violent attacks upon the police, the fire brigade, and the ambulance service. Their ferocity, which made no distinction between the police and the rescue services, is, perhaps, the most frightening aspect of a terrifying weekend.

3·110   The foregoing analysis of the disorders and the analysis in Part II of the social conditions in which they occurred enable me to draw the following conclusions:

(1) The disorders were communal disturbances arising from a complex political, social and economic situation, which is not special to Brixton.

(2) There was a strong racial element in the disorders; but they were not a race riot.

(3) The disturbances on Friday and Saturday arose from police action common enough on the streets of Brixton, but the tension was such that each incident triggered off serious disorder.

(4) Once begun, the disorders on the Friday and the Saturday soon developed into a riot. The common purpose of the two riots was to attack the police. But the riots were neither premeditated nor planned. Each was the spontaneous reaction of angry young men, most of whom were black, against what they saw as a hostile police force.

(5) On Saturday, however, outsiders did participate in the rioting. They were attracted into the action by the publicity given to Friday's events. These people (some of whom were clearly identified as whites) played a significant part in intensifying the disorder by making and distributing petrol bombs, which were used for the first time on the Saturday.

(6) The Sunday riots were sporadic and spontaneous in character, stimulated almost certainly by the elation felt by many youngsters at their success, as they saw it, in defying the police with such dramatic results on the Saturday. No doubt some people were also attracted to participate in the disorders by the publicity which the media had given the events of Friday and Saturday.

(7) The riots were essentially an outburst of anger and resentment by young black people against the police.

Part IV
THE POLICE

A · Introduction

4·1   I have no doubt that a significant cause of the hostility of young blacks towards the police was loss of confidence by significant sections, though it should not be assumed by all, of the Lambeth public in the police. It is clear that the two Members of Parliament whose constituencies cover the area of the disorders were fully aware of the crisis of confidence and believed many of the complaints against police methods and action to be justified. The majority party of the Lambeth Borough Council were of the same opinion. And the evidence which I have heard and which has been confirmed by my visits to the area is to the effect that many of the young, particularly (but not exclusively) the young of the ethnic minority, had become indignant and resentful against the police, suspicious of everything they did. Whatever the reason for this loss of confidence, and whether the police were to blame for it or not, it produced the attitudes and beliefs which underlay the disturbances, providing the tinder ready to blaze into violence on the least provocation, fancied or real, offered by the police.

4·2   The loss of confidence and the attitudes and beliefs to which it gave rise represented a serious breakdown in relations between the police and the community they were serving. In this Part of the Report I analyse in detail the factors which brought about this breakdown. In summary, they were:

(i) the collapse of the police liaison committee in 1979;
(ii) the 'hard', vigorous policing directed particularly against street crime, using methods which caused offence and apprehension to many. The three methods to which objection was taken were: use of the SPG on the streets; use of the 'sus' law (being a suspected person loitering with intent to commit an arrestable offence); and the exercise of the statutory power to stop and search;

(iii) the police view that their operations could be prejudiced if made the subject of consultation. This view inevitably meant that 'hard' policing methods, in particular the use of the SPG, and operations such as 'Swamp '81', would have the worst interpretation put upon them;

(iv) a distrust in the procedure for investigating complaints against the police so great that many people would not even report their complaints;

(v) unlawful, and, in particular, racially prejudiced, conduct by some police officers when stopping, searching, and arresting young blacks suspected (or allegedly suspected) of street crime.

4·3   Incidents of misconduct (including harassment) were not as numerous as some would have me believe; but they did occur, particularly when an officer was young, inexperienced and frightened. Officers were, I am satisfied, sometimes guilty of harassment when purporting to exercise their powers on the street. The lack of consultation, to which I have already referred, and the distrust of the complaints procedure magnified the effect of such incidents, and also enabled a myth of police brutality and racism to develop. None of these incidents being the subject of consultation or investigation, it followed that the worst construction was invariably put upon the police action: the possibility that the victim's version might have been false or exaggerated had no chance of being tested.

4·4   In summary, by April 1981 there had arisen a serious gap between the police and important sections of the local community. In February 1979 mutual understanding had given way to mutual suspicion. Despite efforts by the police and some local leaders, the gap left by the collapse of the liaison committee was not effectively bridged: and it was deepened and widened by the publication in January 1981 of the Final Report of the Working Party into Community/Police Relations in Lambeth set up by the Lambeth Borough Council.[1] However well intentioned, this Report did harm to the cause of police/community relations in Brixton.

1. *Final Report of the Working Party into Community/Police Relations in Lambeth.* Published by the Public Relations Division, London Borough of Lambeth, Brixton Hill, London SW2, January 1981.

B · Police/community relations

(1) The organization

4·5   'L' District of the Metropolitan Police covers the area of the London Borough of Lambeth. It is divided into four Divisions based on Kennington, Clapham, Streatham and Brixton. Each Division is headed by a Chief Superintendent. The headquarters of the District is at Brixton. The District is the responsibility of a Commander, who is assisted by a District Chief Superintendent, and a Detective Chief Superintendent who is responsible for the CID officers in the District. At the time of the disturbances, the three senior officers in 'L' District were Commander Fairbairn, District Chief Superintendent Nicholson and Detective Chief Superintendent Plowman. Commander Fairbairn was in turn responsible to Deputy Assistant Commissioner Walker, in charge of No. 4 Area of the Metropolitan Police which includes 'L' District.

4·6   All officers in the Metropolitan Police are regarded as having responsibility for ensuring good relations with the community. But some officers have a particular responsibility in this respect. This specialist responsibility for community relations is divided between Community Liaison Officers (CLOs) in each District of the force and a central Community Relations Branch (A7) at New Scotland Yard. A7 Branch is headed by a Commander, at present Commander Ferguson. The CLOs are officers of either Chief Inspector or, in certain Districts, Superintendent rank.

4·7   The CLOs are each directly responsible to the operational Commander of their own District. At Brixton, Superintendent MacLennan is directly responsible to Commander Fairbairn for all community relations matters within 'L' District. His work involves coordinating and encouraging community relations activities, maintaining contact and liaison with all groups within the community, liaising with official bodies and representing the police on some of them (such as the Officers' Steering Group of the Inner City Partnership in Lambeth), and lecturing and talking both to police and to non-police gatherings about police/community relations. In a nutshell his role in this respect is to explain the police to the public and the public to the police. Like other CLOs he is also responsible

81

for the work of the Juvenile Bureau in the district, which handles cases involving those aged under seventeen who come to the notice of the police.

4·8   To help him discharge his responsibilities, Superintendent MacLennan has an Inspector as his deputy and a staff of two Sergeants and twelve Constables. Most of these officers work in the Juvenile Bureau, but two Constables, although attached to the Bureau, are known as community involvement officers and seek to involve themselves in, and thereby establish liaison with, youth clubs and other organizations in the area. The extent of police involvement in such organizations, not just through these two officers, is considerable, indeed it extends to several hundred organizations in the Lambeth area alone.

4·9   While he is directly responsible on a day-to-day basis to Commander Fairbairn, Superintendent MacLennan also has a general responsibility to the head of A7 Branch, Commander Ferguson. That Branch has a central responsibility for all community relations matters affecting the Metropolitan Police, including relations with ethnic minorities, matters concerning juveniles, the schools involvement programme and crime prevention. The Branch also gives policy guidance and support to the District CLOs as well as coordinating them in discharging their responsibilities. It is heavily involved in the community relations aspects of training for Metropolitan Police officers.

4·10   One of the major aspects of the force's community relations policy is establishing contact with children and teachers by visits to schools. In 'L' District, these visits are undertaken both by officers of the Juvenile Bureau and by home beat officers from the area. Home beat officers are not the responsibility of the CLO, but their role in the community relations field is vital. A home beat officer is an officer permanently posted to patrol on foot a specific area. He is, in short, the nearest the Metropolitan Police come to the traditional 'bobby on the beat'. In 'L' District as a whole there are forty-five home beat officers, thirteen of whom cover the Brixton area. The home beat officers deal with minor crimes on their beat, with complaints and with warrants of arrest, as well as visiting and keeping in touch with youth clubs, schools and other organizations in the area. The officers in Brixton are responsible to a Sergeant, who is also responsible for beat crimes, and through him to the Chief Inspector (Operations) at Brixton Police Station, although the Duty Inspector in charge of the relief at the Station also has some interest in them.

(2) The policing dilemma

4·11   Commander Fairbairn had only been in command of 'L' District for some five months prior to the disturbances. His predecessor, Commander Adams, had been there since December 1977. The essence of the policing problem which confronted both Commanders on their appointment to the District is as simple to state as it was, and remains, difficult to resolve: how to cope with a rising level of crime – and particularly of street robbery (in the colloquial phrase, 'mugging') – while retaining the confidence of all sections of the community, especially the ethnic minority groups. The crime problem included the presence, particularly in Railton Road, of illegal drinking and gaming establishments and of traffic in drugs: but street crime was the feature which most worried the two Commanders.

4·12   In statistical terms, the crime problem in 'L' District, and within it in Brixton, was presented to the two Commanders as follows. The number of serious offences recorded by the police in 'L' District in 1976 was 27,186; the figure for the Brixton Division was 9,423. By 1980 the figures were 30,805 and 10,626 respectively, an increase of 13 per cent in both cases (compared with a 15 per cent increase in the Metropolitan Police District [MPD] as a whole). During the five years 1976–1980, Brixton accounted for 35 per cent of all the crimes on 'L' District but for 49 per cent of robbery and other violent theft. The percentage increase in recorded offences of robbery and other violent theft from 1976 to 1980 throughout the Metropolitan Police District was 38 per cent. In 'L' District it was 66 per cent, and in Brixton 138 per cent. During the same period, 1976–1980, offences of robbery and other violent theft made up 2.2 per cent of all serious offences recorded in the Metropolitan Police District, 5.1 per cent of all serious offences recorded in 'L' District and 7.2 per cent of all serious offences recorded in the Brixton Division.

4·13   The conclusion the two Commanders drew from these figures was that 'L' District and Brixton in particular faced a particularly high level of street crime – indeed this was referred to in police evidence to the Inquiry as 'unique' – and one in which black people were disproportionately involved. Other submissions to the Inquiry – notably one by Concern – challenged this assessment, pointing out that crime statistics might be affected by factors such as policing policy, police strength and police recording practices, and emphasizing the importance of seeing the statistics in their full and correct social and demographic context. It was suggested that, viewed in this way, the police had 'wholly failed to substantiate that over 1976 to 1980 Brixton has presented a uniquely criminal situation that called for special policing'. Reference was also made to the study by the Home Office Research Unit, *Race, Crime and Arrests*,[1] which, it was submitted, supported the contention that the police had failed to establish the particular involvement of black people in violent crime, and in crimes of robbery and other violent theft in particular.

4·14   It is essential that senior police officers should be fully aware of both the strengths and the limitations of the statistical material at their disposal. It would be wholly reprehensible were police policy to be moulded on the basis of unsafe statistical generalizations, or were a false credibility to be given to racial stereotypes or myths by an over-simplistic assessment of statistical data. For those reasons, the analyses of crime available to senior police officers must be constantly checked both for their accuracy and their objectivity, as I believe the Metropolitan Police accept.

4·15   I do not believe that the analyses of crime available to successive Commanders of 'L' District were essentially unsound, or that they had a distorting influence on the perceptions of the Commanders as to the problems of policing the area. Policing decisions are founded not only on statistical analyses but on, among other things, close day-to-day knowledge of the crime in an area, based on reports from junior officers, on contact with offenders and victims, on perceptions as to community views of the important priorities, the whole pervaded by the exercise of professional judgement reflecting

1. *Race, Crime and Arrests*, Home Office Research Study No. 58, P. Stevens and C. E. Willis, HMSO, 1979.

years of police experience. There is no doubt that in the period under discussion serious crime in Brixton was increasing and that street crime formed a significant part of crime in the area. The submissions made to me on this point emphasize that statistics – or at least the analysis of statistics – is not necessarily an exact science and that crime statistics, like any other statistics, need handling with care. It may be that to describe the street crime situation in Brixton as 'unique' was to indulge in hyperbole. But the submissions do not explain away the practical impact nor the seriousness of the crime problem in 'L' District and in Brixton as it presented itself to Commander Adams and, subsequently, to Commander Fairbairn.

(3) The Brixton story

4·16   On his appointment to the District in December 1977, Commander Adams decided that he would have to adopt a two-fold response to the policing problem he confronted. First, he tried to establish what he himself called 'a positive system of street patrolling', using such manpower as he had available. Secondly, he wanted to establish 'a positive system of community relations'. He was particularly concerned about the relationship between young police officers, probation officers and social workers and the young people (especially black people) on the street.

4·17   Commander Adams made a number of imaginative innovations. With the help of Lambeth Borough Council he introduced an experimental community policing project on the Stockwell Park Estate in Brixton, which I have myself visited in the course of the Inquiry (the visit is noted in Appendix B). The project was successful in reducing crime levels on the Estate and in gaining the enthusiastic support of residents. He ran, for a while, a Juvenile Crime Prevention Scheme. He also tried to arrange for young police officers to be attached to youth clubs and the probation and social services, and to engage in group discussion meetings with black youths and specialist officers, including some members of the Special Patrol Group. It is unfortunate that, while successful liaison was established with the probation and social services, few of the proposed attachments to youth clubs occurred because of hostility and suspicion within the local community.

4·18   Yet by 1979 a breakdown of confidence and trust had de-

85

veloped between the police and important sections of the Brixton community. Many of the factors behind that breakdown were in existence before Commander Adams's arrival in Brixton; for example, a special meeting of the CCRL Executive with 'L' District officers was held on 10 August 1976 because of concern about the deteriorating state of relations between the police and the black community. Many factors were outside the Commander's control. Nevertheless, just as certain of his decisions were designed to improve relations between the police and the community, so others, contrary to his wishes, provided the occasion for a worsening of those relations.

4·19   The central concern of the Commander was the rising volume of crime in Lambeth and in Brixton in particular, and especially the number of street robberies. In order to counteract this increase, Commander Adams tried wherever possible to increase the number of foot patrols in the District and particularly in Brixton. He also argued for an increase in the permanent strength of officers. In 1980, manpower in Brixton was increased, although at the cost of other areas. But the general manpower situation facing the force was, until recently, unfavourable. Commander Adams therefore felt obliged to seek help from outside 'L' District.

(a) The Special Patrol Group

4·20   On four occasions between January 1978 and September 1980 Commander Adams mounted special operations against crime in 'L' District with the help of the Metropolitan Police's mobile reserve, the Special Patrol Group (SPG). From 13 January to 19 February 1978 officers of the Group patrolled Clapham to deal with street crime, in order to release local officers to deal with a spate of burglaries in the area. From 3 November to 2 December 1978 SPG officers were employed with CID and Traffic Patrol officers to tackle street crime in a number of parts of 'L' District including Brixton, although only 'L' District officers patrolled the Railton Road area. In 1979, from 5 November to 15 December, one unit of the SPG was used to support other officers in a crime prevention patrolling operation in 'L' District. Brixton was not, however, one of the areas affected by this operation. Finally, from 21 July to 2 September 1980, SPG and 'L' District officers conducted a further operation designed to combat street crime, although again only 'L' District officers patrolled the Railton Road area.

4·21   The object at least of the second and fourth of these operations was to deter street criminals by saturating an area with police officers, who then conducted frequent stops of people on suspicion and in many cases searched them too. The operations were generally successful in reducing the level of crime and particularly street crime in the parts of 'L' District they affected during the period over which they ran. But once the operations were over, crime reverted to its previous high, and increasing level. It is possible that the only, or principal, effect of these operations was to displace street crime into areas other than those in which the operations were conducted.

4·22   The effect of the operations on relations between the police and certain parts of the community in Brixton is, however, beyond doubt. They provoked the hostility of young black people, who felt they were being hunted irrespective of their innocence or guilt. And their hostility infected older members of the community, who, hearing the stories of many innocent young people who had been stopped and searched, began themselves to lose confidence in, and respect for, the police. However well intentioned, these operations precipitated a crisis of confidence between the police and certain community leaders. In particular they led to the breakdown of the formal arrangements for liaison between the ethnic minority communities, the local authority and the police.

(b) The collapse of formal community/police liaison
       arrangements

4·23   Before Commander Adams arrived in Brixton, his predecessor and the Principal Community Relations Officer of the Council for Community Relations in Lambeth (CCRL), Mr George Greaves, had discussed the establishment of a formal liaison committee between the two organizations. In February 1978, shortly after his arrival, Commander Adams told Mr Greaves of his own support for the proposal. On 10 May 1978, Mr Greaves sent draft terms of reference for the Committee to the Commander, who on 3 July indicated that he was content with them.

4·24   The first meeting of the Committee took place on 30 October 1978, with Mr Anthony Rampton, one of the CCRL officers, in the chair. Commander Adams addressed the meeting on the current crime problem and explained his conception of the role of the Committee. He made it clear that he was responsible for maintaining the peace in the area and that he would use whatever resources were available to him to do so. Among other matters, the meeting also discussed attacks on Asians in Streatham, policy on the sale of newspapers outside Brixton Underground Station and access to juveniles in custody.

4·25   Three days after this inaugural meeting, the special operation of November–December 1978 (paragraph 4·20, supra) involving SPG, CID and Traffic Patrol officers, directed against street crime and burglary, began in Brixton and other parts of 'L' District. Commander Adams did not inform community leaders in advance of the operation because he feared that, if he did so, news of it might become public and its effectiveness would be diminished. The omission greatly angered some of the community leaders. They objected also to what they saw as the aggressive style of the SPG operation. The failure of the police to inform the Liaison Committee of the proposed SPG operation encouraged CCRL members in the view that the police did not see liaison as a two-way process. There was a vigorous correspondence between the Commander, Mr Greaves and Mr John Tilley MP, who had attended the first meeting of the Liaison Committee. A number of people from the community made their views plain to Commander Adams at a meeting at Brixton Police Station on 27 November 1978.

4·26   Curiously perhaps, the matter was not discussed at the second meeting of the CCRL/Police Liaison Committee held on 8 January 1979, although a number of other matters usefully were. The next meeting of the Committee was arranged for 5 March, but it never took place. On 12 February 1979, three members of the staff of the CCRL were arrested and questioned at Brixton Police Station by police officers investigating an assault on two plain-clothes officers and a black barman by a number of black people in a Clapham public house. It would not be appropriate for me to comment on the incident since I understand that civil proceedings connected with it are pending. The incident became known locally as the 'Sheepskin Saga' – largely because it seemed that the only link between those who were wanted and those who were arrested was that they wore sheepskin coats. The following day, the Executive Committee of the CCRL held an emergency meeting. The members present saw the affair as the last straw in the continuing deterioration in relations between the police and the black community. They decided to withdraw from the Liaison Committee with the police and to rescind their permanent invitation to the police Community Liaison Officer to attend meetings of the Executive. They said that they would not return to the Liaison Committee unless the police made positive proposals to improve their relations with the community. The other community groups involved in the Liaison Committee subsequently also withdrew. The CCRL also called upon Lambeth Borough Council to set up an inquiry into policing in the area: it had previously asked the then Home Secretary to set up an inquiry but without success.

4.27 Commander Adams made various efforts to try to get the Liaison Committee re-started. He wrote to the Principal Community Relations Officer, Mr Greaves, on 20 February 1979, emphasizing that he wished the Committee to continue. He sought the help of the two MPs whose constituencies covered the Brixton area, Mr John Fraser and Mr John Tilley, and on 21 March 1979 they, Mr Knight the Leader of the Lambeth Borough Council, the two other MPs with Lambeth constituencies, Mr Greaves and Mr Courtney Laws of the Brixton Neighbourhood Community Association met him at his request. Although there is evidence that not all community leaders agreed with the decision to withdraw from the Liaison Committee, efforts to re-start it proved unsuccessful.

4.28 The demise of the Liaison Committee did not mean the end of all contact between community leaders and the police. There continued to be informal communications between the Principal Community Relations Officer and senior 'L' District officers. And, following discussions between Commander Adams and Mr Laws, some of the community leaders who disagreed with the decision to break off contact with the police continued to meet Commander Adams and other senior officers at irregular intervals: they included Mr Rene Webb of the Melting Pot Foundation. The first meeting of this new informal liaison group was held on 1 May 1979: further meetings were held, among others, on 3 April, 2 July and 8 September 1980.

(c) The Working Party into Community/Police Relations in
Lambeth

4·29   The break-up of the CCRL/Police Liaison Committee
marked a significant worsening in relations between the police in
Lambeth and important sections of the local community. It was also
important because of the request by the CCRL for the Borough
Council to establish an inquiry into police/community relations in
Lambeth. At its meeting on 13 March 1979 the Council did in fact
set up such an inquiry with the following terms of reference:

To inquire into the nature of policing in Lambeth in recent years and its
effect on the local community and to make recommendations.

Mr David Turner-Samuels QC was subsequently appointed Chairman of the Working Party conducting the Inquiry: its members included two Councillors from the majority party on the Borough
Council, one from the minority party, the Chairman of the CCRL,
the Borough Dean of Lambeth and a person nominated by Lambeth
Trades Council.

4·30   The Working Party began taking evidence in October 1979.
According to its report, it received a total of 275 submissions either
verbally or in writing from organizations and individuals in Lambeth by the end of March 1980. The police, however, refused
invitations to give evidence to the Working Party. They took the
view that since the Home Secretary, the Police Authority for the
Metropolis, had not accepted requests for an inquiry it would be
improper for them to become involved. They also doubted whether
the Inquiry was likely to be seen to be impartial, in particular since
some of its members were connected directly or indirectly with local
organizations which had been critical of the police in the past.

4·31   While the Working Party was sitting, both in the late Autumn
of 1979 and the Summer of 1980, Special Patrol Group officers were
again employed in Lambeth in special crime prevention operations
with 'L' District officers, though on neither occasion in the Railton
Road area. On the second occasion, on 10 July 1980, some eleven
days before the operation was due to begin, Commander Adams
announced his intention to carry out the operation by writing to a
number of community leaders and by informing the press. He also

held a meeting with many local leaders to outline his intentions (at which the SPG's supervising officers were present) and subsequently also met three of the local MPs. Nevertheless this further use of the Group in Lambeth was again criticized by some, although not all, community leaders. The Leader of Lambeth Borough Council, Councillor Knight, in a letter of 15 July to Commander Adams, described the decision as 'a serious error of judgement'. In a letter of 17 July 1980 to Commander Adams, Mr Greaves reiterated the CCRL's opposition to the deployment of the Group; three local MPs also criticized the move in a letter to the Commander of the same date.

4·32   The Working Party into Community/Police Relations in Lambeth published its Final Report in January 1981.[1] In the preface to its report, the Working Party noted that it had not been in a position to act as a judicial type of inquiry and that it made no findings of fact in relation to the truth or otherwise of the incidents submitted to it in evidence and mentioned in its Report. Nevertheless the tone of the Report was highly critical of the police. It described the police in Lambeth as an army of occupation and referred to the operations involving the SPG as 'attacks by the SPG on the people of Lambeth'. Quoting extracts from the submissions it had received, the Working Party described the police as intimidating and harassing working-class people in Lambeth and black people in particular. It criticized police use of powers to stop and search and of the suspected person provision (Section 4 of the Vagrancy Act 1824) as misuses of the law. A chapter headed 'Specific Areas of Attack' spoke critically of police raids on youth clubs, of police attacks on black homes and of police behaviour towards black parents. Alleged abuses of the Judges' Rules and of proper procedures on the taking of photographs and fingerprints and in the interrogation of juveniles were referred to: 'The submissions made to us [about police behaviour to juveniles inside police stations],' said the Working Party, 'present a picture of violence, intimidation, and induced confessions.' The Juvenile Bureau, police Community Liaison Officers and beat police officers were described as essentially, although not exclusively, public relations

1. Op. cit.

exercises by the police: 'Our evidence on beat police,' reported the Working Party, 'suggests that they are a liberal façade for the increasingly centrally controlled militarization of the police.' Police recruitment and training, the attitudes of police officers to black people, to the National Front, and to 'Gay People' (i.e. homosexuals), the impact of technological change on policing, and the police complaints procedure were among other aspects of policing which were criticized.

4·33 'The evidence we have presented,' concluded the Working Party, 'shows that the condition of community/police relations in Lambeth is extremely grave. This situation is created by the nature of the police force and basic policing methods.' The Working Party appeared to see the fundamental solution to this situation lying in a change in the arrangements for ensuring the accountability of the police to the community, although it refrained from making proposals 'since these issues are political and not administrative'. However, it made a number of recommendations which it suggested would bring about a 'limited improvement' in community/police relations. These included several designed to strengthen the safeguards for arrested and detained persons, the repeal of Section 4 of the Vagrancy Act 1824, and no future deployment of the SPG or any similar body in Lambeth. The Working Party's Report was welcomed by the Lambeth Borough Council. In a resolution adopted on 12 February 1981, it endorsed the Working Party's recommendations and called for the Metropolitan Police to be placed under the control of the GLC. I have no doubt that the style, language and contents of this Report succeeded only in worsening community relations with the police. But I am also satisfied that it reflected attitudes, beliefs and feelings widely prevalent in Lambeth since 1979.

(d) Moves to re-establish the Liaison Committee

4·34 On 20 November 1980, shortly after he took command of 'L' District, Commander Fairbairn wrote to Mr Knight, the Leader of Lambeth Borough Council, expressing his desire to increase contact between his senior officers and elected representatives of the Council and suggesting that informal meetings be held between them. After some further correspondence Councillor Knight replied on 7

January 1981 reiterating his own opposition to the use of the 'sus' law and deployment of the SPG in the Borough, but suggesting a positive effort to re-establish the former Liaison Committee. On 19 January Commander Fairbairn wrote to Mr Greaves proposing a meeting of representatives of the CCRL Executive and the police as a first step in re-convening the Liaison Committee.

4·35   He also, on 29 January, saw Mr Knight, along with the Chief Executive of the Borough Council and its Principal Race Relations Adviser, at Lambeth Town Hall. Mr Knight agreed to informal contact between Councillors and Council officials and senior police officers where necessary and desirable. The meeting also discussed the possible re-establishment of the Liaison Committee. Councillor Knight suggested that as a gesture of goodwill the Commander should announce his intention not to use the 'sus' provision or to deploy the SPG in Lambeth. The Commander replied that he could not promise not to make use of these tools in discharging his responsibility to police Lambeth. But he emphasized his desire to establish liaison with community leaders. Mr Knight did not rule out the possible re-establishment of the Liaison Committee, provided that the CCRL and other organizations originally involved in it agreed.

4·36   The moves to re-establish the Liaison Committee took another step forward on 1 April. The Executive Committee of the CCRL had responded promptly to Commander Fairbairn's letter of 19 January by nominating three of its members and Mr Greaves to hold exploratory talks with the Commander. On 1 April, after a long discussion, the Committee decided to set up a small sub-committee to recommend to it a number of positive proposals for discussion with the police. The police, for their part, were invited to prepare a similar list of items for discussion. This decision was reported to Commander Fairbairn by Mr Greaves in a letter dated 16 April, four days after the disturbances which are the subject of this Inquiry. It is significant, however, that in a press release on those disturbances delivered to Commander Fairbairn at the same time as the letter from Mr Greaves, the CCRL said 'Our experience of liaison with the police has been that it is totally ineffective in establishing constructive dialogue.'

The Police

(e) Operation 'Swamp '81'

4·37 When Commander Fairbairn arrived in 'L' District, he was confronted by the problem of a high level of street crime which had confronted his predecessor. That problem was the particular concern of Detective Chief Superintendent (DCS) Plowman, who on 12 January 1981 took over responsibility for crime operations in 'L' District. Detective Chief Superintendent Plowman, of course, studied the crime situation on his arrival, and when by mid-March he had seen no improvement in the situation he proposed to Commander Fairbairn that a special operation should be conducted. The operation would take the form of officers in plain clothes patrolling in pairs in areas of Lambeth where burglary and street robbery were particularly high. Commander Fairbairn approved Mr Plowman's proposal. Unlike the previous saturation exercises of this sort which had attracted criticism, the operation would be conducted by 'L' District officers only. The Commander knew of the previous criticisms of the use of the SPG and, anxious to avoid worsening relations with the CCRL, he decided not to seek the assistance of the SPG in conducting it. He did not, however, make known to community leaders his intention to mount the operation, and although the Community Liaison Officer on 'L' District, Superintendent MacLennan, was consulted about it, neither Deputy Assistant Commissioner Walker nor the home beat officers in the District were officially informed of the imminent operation. In the days before the operation was due to begin, neither the Commander nor Mr MacLennan sensed from their informal contacts with community leaders any particular tension in the community which caused them to question the wisdom of proceeding with the operation.

4·38 The operation, which became known, within the police, as 'Swamp '81' – an unfortunate name – was arranged to begin on Monday 6 April and end on Saturday 11 April. The Friday before it began, Friday 3 April, a number of premises in the 'Front Line' area of Railton Road were searched on warrant by uniformed officers and officers from the Brixton Crime Squad and the Robbery Squad, and some twenty-two people were arrested for various offences including drug offences. The suggestion was made to me that these raids contributed to a heightening of tension in the Railton Road area immediately prior to Operation 'Swamp', although the extent to which this was in fact so is unclear.

4·39   Operation 'Swamp' began, as scheduled, on Monday 6 April. Ten squads of between five and eleven officers, each squad supervised by a Sergeant, patrolled areas of Lambeth designated by Detective Chief Superintendent Plowman between the hours of 2 p.m. and 11 p.m. The ten squads were supervised by two Inspectors reporting to Mr Plowman. In all, 112 officers – drawn from the 'L' District Robbery Squad, the Divisional Crime Squads and uniformed officers – were involved. The operation envisaged the extensive use of the power of a Metropolitan Police Constable to stop and search people on the basis of a reasonable suspicion that they are in possession of unlawfully obtained property, contained in Section 66 of the Metropolitan Police Act 1839. The written instructions for the operation described its nature as follows:

> The purpose of this Operation is to flood identified areas on 'L' District to detect and arrest burglars and robbers. The essence of the exercise is therefore to ensure that all officers remain on the streets and success will depend on a concentrated effort of 'stops', based on powers of surveillance and suspicion proceeded by persistent and astute questioning.

Detective Chief Superintendent Plowman amplified these instructions when he briefed all the officers involved at 1 p.m. on Monday, 6 April. During this briefing, he emphasized that provided that at all times the officers acted in good faith, believing that their suspicions and reasons for stopping people were justified, and they were polite, civil but firm in their questioning, they would do well and achieve results.

4·40   Of the ten squads involved in the operation, four – consisting mainly of officers based in Brixton – were deployed in the Brixton area. One of these, Squad 7, patrolled the Railton Road/Mayall Road area. In the course of the operation, the ten squads between them made some 943 'stops', as a result of which 118 people were arrested. Slightly more than half of the people stopped were black. More than two-thirds were aged under twenty-one. Seventy-five charges resulted from these 'stops': these covered a variety of alleged offences, but included only one for robbery, one for attempted burglary and twenty charges of theft or attempted theft. A further eighteen alleged offences were referred to the Juvenile

Bureau. The remaining people arrested were released without charge or pending further investigation of their alleged offence. Although few of the charges brought related to burglary or robbery, it was said in evidence that during the period of the operation the number of reported offences of this category in the District was reduced by almost 50 per cent.

4·41   The community leaders had not been told of Operation 'Swamp' in advance. However, the existence of some special police effort on the streets rapidly became apparent to them and to the rest of the community. A number of those who gave evidence to me said that in the week of the Operation, tension in the streets of Brixton increased considerably. An indication of that tension occurred on Thursday, 9 April. At about 3 p.m. on that day, some twenty black youths began playing football across Atlantic Road outside the office of the private hire firm, S & M Car Hire. Traffic was stopped, and when the police intervened the youths refused to stop and one challenged an officer to a fight. After the intervention of the Duty Inspector from Brixton Police Station, Inspector Scotchford, the youths reluctantly ended their game. The Inspector, however, felt the tension in the air and the antagonism of the youths towards him.

4·42   The incident also caused concern to the Home Beat Officer whose beat covered Railton Road, PC 274 'L' John Brown. PC Brown responded to a call by a young officer for assistance in handling the youths: when he arrived, he did not recognize any of the youths playing football or standing around the area as local. He felt that the youths were seeking a confrontation with the police. Also anxious was Mr Courtney Laws, Director of the Brixton Neighbourhood Community Association. Mr Laws expressed his anxiety to PC Brown and told him that he had been trying to contact Superintendent MacLennan to discuss what could be done to reduce the tension which he felt now existed in the area. On his return to Brixton Police Station, PC Brown left a message for Mr MacLennan asking him to telephone Mr Laws. Superintendent MacLennan saw this message on the afternoon of the following day, some four hours before the disorders, which are the subject of this Inquiry, began. He tried to telephone Mr Laws, but without success.

(4) Comment and findings on police/community relations in Lambeth

4·43 Notwithstanding the good intentions and the efforts of Commander Adams and local leaders, the history of relations between the police and the people of Brixton during recent years has been a tale of failure. The Police Liaison Committee, after making a shaky start with Commander Adams's bleak and, as it appeared to its members, discouraging assertion that *he* was responsible for the public peace and would use the resources *he* believed necessary, soon passed into the shadow of the unannounced SPG operation (paragraph 4·25, supra), and ultimately suffered shipwreck on the rock of the 'Sheepskin Saga' arrests (paragraph 4·26, supra). The police and others tried to salvage something from the wreck; but their tiny retrievals (paragraphs 4·27–28, supra) were blown away in the storm of distrust which reached gale force with the publication in 1981 of the Lambeth Working Party's Report (paragraphs 4·32–33, supra). Commander Fairbairn after his appointment in 1980 did his best: but he failed to appreciate the risks of Operation 'Swamp '81'. Although I have no doubt that other factors played a part in heightening the tension in the streets of Brixton in the weeks prior to the disorders (some of them, perhaps, factors extrinsic to Brixton – I have in mind, in particular, the concern felt throughout the black community about the tragic deaths of thirteen people in a fire at a private house in Deptford on 18 January and the criticism expressed by some members of the community of the subsequent police investigation), I am equally certain that 'Swamp '81' was a factor which contributed to the great increase in tension observed by PC Brown, Mr Courtney Laws and others in the days immediately preceding the disorders.

4·44 Responsibility for the breakdown of relations between the police and the community in Brixton cannot, however, be laid wholly at the door of the police. It was not the police who abandoned the Liaison Committee, but the local leaders. The decision of the CCRL to withdraw from the Committee in February 1979 was no doubt made in good faith, but in my view it was wrong. In effect the public body committed to furthering better relations between all sections of the community in Lambeth was thereby refusing to deal officially with an organization (the police), which it itself saw as jeopardizing those very relations. There were, of course, genuine differences of view between the police and the CCRL on important matters of policing and approach. But the effect of the withdrawal was to deepen mutual suspicion between the police and some, though by no means all, of the community leaders.

4·45 The Report of the Lambeth Working Party which eventually followed increased this suspicion and in particular the police's sense that they were the constant subject of ill-informed and unbalanced criticism. The police felt that they were on the horns of a dilemma. As they rightly, and with very good reason, appreciated, it was necessary to do something to combat street crime: they would certainly be criticized if they did not, and no one had in their view come up with an alternative to 'saturation' policing operations. On the other hand, if they attempted to tackle street crime by a 'saturation' stop and search operation, they would be criticized for doing so. There was an underlying feeling that no matter how hard they tried to meet the apparently conflicting expectations of the community and no matter what measures were adopted, their efforts would continue to be the target for unreasonable criticism.

4·46 Neither the police nor the local leaders can therefore escape responsibility for the failure in police/community relations between 1978–1981. Both must accept a share of the blame. Neither police nor the local leaders foresaw the intensity of the coming catastrophe: but both, I believe, knew that as a result of their failure, the public peace – i.e. 'the normal state of society' (paragraph 4·57, infra), which it is the duty of everyone, but especially the police, to preserve – was seriously endangered. I pass now to the criticisms made of the police in the course of the Inquiry.

C · The main criticisms of the police

(1) 'Racial prejudice'

4·47 Some of those who have been represented at the Inquiry, and a considerable number of the witnesses whose evidence I have received, have no doubt that the riots were provoked – inevitably provoked, some say – by harassment of black people by a racially prejudiced police force not accountable to the community it is supposed to serve. This criticism is directed by some at the Metropolitan Police Force as a whole. The integrity and impartiality of its senior direction is as severely challenged as is the conduct of police officers on the streets.

4·48   Others do not go so far as to suggest that the entire Metropolitan Police is a racist police force. They reserve the criticism of racial prejudice and discrimination for the way in which individual police officers carry out their duty. They allege that officers pick on black people, especially young black people, disproportionately when exercising, for example, their powers to stop and search, and that they do not behave to them with the respect which is their due. Some suggest that this behaviour is the result of a tendency on the part of the police to stereotype all of the black community, or at least important sections of it, such as the Rastafarians, as criminals.

(2) 'Harassment'

4·49   Racial prejudice is not, however, the only charge levelled against police behaviour. Other critics allege that the police behave arrogantly and abrasively and that they frequently exceed or abuse their powers. These criticisms have been made to the Inquiry by representatives of both the white and the black community in Brixton, and they apply to police behaviour not only when stopping people in the streets but also during the arrest, questioning and detention in the police station of alleged offenders. They were applied with particular force by some of those who gave evidence to the behaviour of young police officers in Brixton: some people suggested that there was a dramatic gulf between the good intentions of senior officers and the actual behaviour of police constables. This criticism of harassment was well summarized in the words of Mr Rene Webb, the Director of the Melting Pot Foundation, quoted by learned Counsel representing the Foundation in his final address to the Inquiry: 'We do not object to what they do so much as to the way they do it.'

(3) 'Unimaginative and inflexible policing'

4·50   Many of those who voiced the immediately foregoing criticism of the police also voiced another: that the police were unimaginative and inflexible in their relationship with the community as a whole and with community leaders in particular, and in the methods of policing they adopted. The criticism was directed at all ranks of the force. It was said that they are insensitive to local opinion, unimaginative and uncomprehending in their dealings with the ethnic minorities, and have their priorities wrong. The critics suggest that a more responsive, and responsible, attitude might develop if the Metropolitan Police were made locally accountable. Lip service is paid, they say, by senior officers to the need for consultation and good relations with the community: an imposing façade has been constructed; but there is no legal requirement to consult, and the doctrine of the operational independence of the police is used to cut off any meaningful discussion of policing policies. Similarly there is no forum in which complaints about policing policy – as opposed to complaints about individual police officers – can be discussed.

4·51   One aspect of this criticism is the lack of local accountability: the other is criticism of the methods used by the police in coping with crime in Brixton. The reality of police practice, it is argued, is that, to the exclusion of other objectives, criminals must be sought out, pursued and arrested irrespective of the effect of the methods employed upon innocent people. The critics take particular exception to the exercise by the police of the 'sus' provision (Section 4 of the Vagrancy Act 1824) prior to its repeal; to the exercise of the power to stop and search; to the employment of the Special Patrol Group; and to saturation policing operations like 'Swamp '81'. This line of criticism has several variants, one of which is the blunt assertion that, even if some senior police officers have got their priorities right, the rank and file have not – with the notable exception of the home beat officer, who, however (it is suggested), is not thought of as an 'operational' policeman by his colleagues. In support of this latter point the critics draw attention to the failure to inform, let alone consult, home beat officers prior to Operation 'Swamp' and to the failure of senior officers to call in the home beat officers during the disorders of Saturday and Sunday. Another variant is that the Metropolitan Police have not yet fully solved the problem of maintaining the rule of law in a multi-racial society. Those who express this view do not quarrel with the principle that there is one law laid down by Parliament which must apply to all citizens: but they do ask whether the police have yet learned to enforce the law in areas with high ethnic minority populations with the same degree of discretion with which they are wont to enforce it in other parts of the country.

(4) 'Over-reaction to the disorders'

4·52   The disorders themselves have given rise to many criticisms reflecting different points of view as to the role of the police officer in a riot situation. The critics, to whose view I have already referred, allege brutality and aggressive behaviour, the use of unlawful weapons, the improper use of dogs, shields and truncheons, the exercise of unnecessary force and the adoption of undesirable tactics in the effort to suppress the disorders. They also allege an obstinate refusal by the senior command to withdraw when it should have been realized that it was only the presence on the streets of a militant police force which kept the rioters rioting and prevented them from dispersing. And they suggest that the heavy presence of police in Brixton on Sunday was a contributory factor in the disorders on that day.

(5) 'Delay and lack of vigour' (in handling the disorders)

4·53   But others, who, though not so vocal, probably represent the majority of the community, take a different line. They support police operations designed to reduce street crime and to enforce the law, are inclined to criticize the police for lack of success, and doubt whether the police reaction to the outbreak of disorder was sufficiently vigorous or swift. They ask whether the police were adequately equipped, trained or reinforced to quell the riot or protect themselves. They wonder whether the strategy and tactics employed by the police in handling the disorders were the right ones. Their case rests on the high volume of street crime in Brixton, on the devastating nature of the disorders, on the high figure of police casualties, and on the fact that for some two-and-a-half to three hours on Saturday night the police lacked the strength to quell the riots or disperse the rioters.

(6) 'Failure to act against looting'

4·54   Finally all the critics, whatever their point of view on other aspects of the policing of the riots, agree in deploring the failure, or inability, of the police to prevent the widespread looting and damage to property in the shopping centre, for which the riots offered a golden opportunity to the criminal fraternity and to excited children tempted by the good things of our material society made easy for the picking.

D · Two principles of policing

4·55   Before I deal with these criticisms, it will, I think, be helpful to refer to two well-known principles of policing a free society which are relevant to my Inquiry:

(1) 'Consent and balance', words which I take, with respect and gratitude, from the written evidence of the Chief Constable of Avon and Somerset;

and

(2) 'Independence and accountability'.

(1) Consent and balance

4·56   The function of our police has been authoritatively defined as:

The prevention of crime . . . the protection of life and property, the preservation of public tranquillity.[1]

This three-fold function requires 'consent and balance', words which I take to mean that, if the police are to secure the assent of the

---

1. Extract from Sir Richard Mayne's instructions to the 'New Police of the Metropolis' in 1829.

community which they need to support their operations, they must strike an acceptable balance between the three elements of their function.

4·57   What is the balance which they would seek to achieve? An authoritative answer has again been given: the primary duty of the police is to maintain 'the Queen's peace', which has been described as the 'normal state of society',[1] for in a civilized society, normality is a state of public tranquillity. Crime and public disorder are aberrations from 'normality' which it is the duty of the police to endeavour first to prevent and then, if need be, to correct. It follows that the police officer's first duty is to cooperate with others in maintaining 'the normal state of society'. Since it is inevitable that there will be aberrations from normality, his second duty arises, which is, without endangering normality, to enforce the law. His priorities are clear: the maintenance of public tranquillity comes first. If law enforcement puts at risk public tranquillity, he will have to make a difficult decision. Inevitably there will be situations in which the public interest requires him to test the wisdom of law enforcement by its likely effect upon public order. Law enforcement, involving as it must the possibility that force may have to be used, can cause acute friction and division in a community – particularly if the community is tense and the cause of the law-breaker not without support. 'Fiat justitia, ruat caelum'[2] may be apt for a Judge: but it can lead a policeman into tactics disruptive of the very fabric of society.

4·58   The conflict which can arise between the duty of the police to maintain order and their duty to enforce the law, and the priority which must be given to the former, have long been recognized by the police themselves, though they are factors to which commentators on policing have in the past often paid too little attention. The successful solution of the conflict lies first in the priority to be given in the last resort to the maintenance of public order, and secondly in the constant and common-sense exercise of police discretion. Indeed the exercise of discretion lies at the heart of the policing function. It is undeniable that there is only one law for all: and it is

---

1. *The Home Office*, Sir Frank Newsam, Allen and Unwin, 1955 (2nd edition).
2. 'Let justice be done, though the heavens collapse.'

right that this should be so. But it is equally well recognized that successful policing depends on the exercise of discretion in how the law is enforced. The good reputation of the police as a force depends upon the skill and judgement which policemen display in the particular circumstances of the cases and incidents which they are required to handle. Discretion is the art of suiting action to particular circumstances. It is the policeman's daily task.

(2) Independence and accountability

4·59   The independence of the police is the other principle of policing a free society to which I wish to refer. Neither politicians nor pressure-groups nor anyone else may tell the police what decisions to take or what methods to employ, whether to enforce the law or not in a particular case, or how to investigate a particular offence. The exercise of police judgement has to be as independent as the exercise of professional judgement by a doctor or a lawyer. If it is not, the way is open to manipulation and abuse of the law, whether for political or for private ends.

4·60   There are, nevertheless, limitations on the power of the police. First and foremost, the law. The police officer must act within the law: abuse of power by a police officer, if it be allowed to occur with impunity, is a staging-post to the police state. But there is also the constitutional control of accountability (see Part V, paragraphs 5·55–71, infra). The police must exercise independent judgement: but they are also the servants of the community. They enforce the law on behalf of the community: indeed they cannot effectively enforce it without the support of the community. The community pays them and provides them with their resources. So there has to be some way in which to secure that the independent judgement of the police can not only operate within the law but with the support of the community. At present, outside London, that mechanism is provided by the local police authority. A Chief Constable is independent, but accountable to his local police authority. The Metropolitan Police are differently placed. The Commissioner is accountable not to a local police authority but to the Home Secretary and, through him, to Parliament. Both these arrangements have been subject to criticism in the course of the Inquiry. I examine those criticisms later (Part V, paragraphs 5·55–71, infra). Suffice it to say for the present that the second basic principle of policing a free society which is of essential relevance to my Report is the independence of the police, coupled with the need to ensure that the police operate not only within the law but with the support of the community as a whole. Accountability and effective consultative machinery are needed to ensure this support.

E · Findings on the main criticisms of the police

4·61   Approaching the police problem with the two principles to which I have referred very much in mind, I now state my findings on the main criticisms of the police which have been developed by represented parties in the course of the Inquiry.

(1) 'Racial prejudice'

4·62   The direction and policies of the Metropolitan Police are not racist. I totally and unequivocally reject the attack made upon the integrity and impartiality of the senior direction of the force. The criticisms lie elsewhere – in errors of judgement, in a lack of imagination and flexibility, but not in deliberate bias or prejudice. The allegation that the police are the oppressive arm of a racist state not only displays a complete ignorance of the constitutional arrangements for controlling the police: it is an injustice to the senior officers of the force.

4·63   Such plausibility as this attack has achieved is due, sadly, to the ill-considered, immature and racially prejudiced actions of some officers in their dealings on the streets with young black people. Racial prejudice does manifest itself occasionally in the behaviour of a few officers on the streets. It may be only too easy for some officers, faced with what they must see as the inexorably rising tide of street crime, to lapse into an unthinking assumption that all young black people are potential criminals. I am satisfied, however, that such a bias is not to be found amongst senior police officers. They recognize that those black people in Brixton who are engaged in crime

are, like white criminals, a very small proportion of the total
population.

4·64   Nor is racially prejudiced behaviour by officers below the
level of the senior direction of the force common: but it does occur,
and every instance of it has an immense impact on community
attitudes and beliefs. The damage done by even the occasional
display of racial prejudice is incalculable. It goes far towards the
creation of the image of a hostile police force, which was the myth
which led the young people into these disorders. It is therefore
essential that every possible step be taken to prevent and to root out
racially prejudiced attitudes in the police service. This can be done
through careful checks in the recruitment of officers, through
training, through supervision and disciplinary arrangements. I set
out in Part V (paragraphs 5·6–40, infra) my recommendations on
these matters. The police cannot rest on the argument that since
they are a cross-section of society some officers are bound to be
racially prejudiced. Senior Metropolitan Police officers accept this.
They recognize that in this respect, as in others, the standards we
apply to the police must be higher than the norms of behaviour
prevalent in society as a whole.

(2) 'Harassment'

4·65   I have no doubt that some of the allegations of harassment
made against individual police officers in the course of the Inquiry
are true. While I am in no position to make findings on individual
allegations, the weight of criticism and complaint against the police
is so considerable that it alone must give grave cause for concern.

4·66   At the same time I have little doubt that behind some of the
criticism lies the power of gossip and rumour. There must be a
temptation for every young criminal – black or white – stopped in
the street or arrested in Brixton to allege misconduct by a police
officer: indeed, the position may almost have been reached where
not to do so is to endanger one's credibility in the eyes of one's
friends. Moreover, the circumstances in which arrests are made in
Brixton – where a hostile crowd normally gathers rapidly at the
scene on each occasion – are calculated to produce conflict, ending
in accusation and counter-accusation.

4·67   Having entered these cautionary notes, however, I do not doubt that harassment does occur. Stop and search operations in particular require courteous and carefully controlled behaviour by the police to those stopped, which I am certain was sometimes lacking. And in Brixton even one isolated instance of misconduct can foster a whole legion of rumours which rapidly become beliefs firmly held within the community. Whether justified or not, many in Brixton believe that the police routinely abuse their powers and mistreat alleged offenders. The belief here is as important as the fact. One of the most serious developments in recent years has been the way in which the older generation of black people in Brixton has come to share the belief of the younger generation that the police routinely harass and ill-treat black youngsters.

4·68   The police rightly and understandably respond to allegations of misconduct by saying that they must be tested through the complaints procedure. They point to the relatively small number of complaints against the police which are substantiated as evidence of the insubstantial nature of many of the complaints levelled against them. But a great deal of evidence submitted to me suggests that many people, particularly among the ethnic minorities, do not have any faith in the impartiality or efficiency of the existing system for considering complaints against the police. They regard the fact that the police investigate complaints against police officers as proof that the system is not impartial and are not persuaded that the independent scrutiny provided through the Director of Public Prosecutions and the Police Complaints Board is a sufficient safeguard. I do not doubt that a significant number of people have such little faith in the system that they do not bother to make formal complaints against the police even when they would be fully justified in doing so. I conclude that any system for considering complaints against the police, which is subject to the range and weight of criticism I have heard of the present system in this Inquiry, must be unsatisfactory and ineffective. Unless and until there is a system for judging complaints against the police, which commands the support of the public, there will be no way in which the atmosphere of distrust and suspicion between the police and the community in places like Brixton can be dispelled. I discuss ways in which the present system might be amended in Part VII (paragraphs 7·11–29, infra). The recommendations I make in Part V (paragraphs 5·16–40, infra) on training and supervision are also relevant.

(3) 'Unimaginative and inflexible policing'

4·69 'Unimaginative and inflexible policing' is too general an accusation to be a fair criticism. Its importance to my Inquiry is, however, crucial: for it represents what many, especially amongst the ethnic minority, believe to be true of the policy and methods of policing in Lambeth.

4·70 First, what is untrue in the accusation? The Metropolitan Police at District command level and above do not lack awareness of the need for good community relations. The senior command is not inflexible in its approach to policing. Officers at that level are well aware of the historic principle enunciated by Sir Charles Rowan that

the power of the police to fulfil their functions and duties is dependent upon public approval of their existence, actions, and behaviour, and their ability to secure and maintain public respect.[1]

Having heard the evidence of the two District Commanders, the Area Commander, Assistant Commissioner Gibson, and Deputy Assistant Commissioner Dear, I am satisfied that the basic policy of the Metropolitan Police is to police with the consent and approval of the people and to find and maintain the correct balance between the three police functions – the prevention of crime, the preservation of life and property, and the preservation of public tranquillity. But I am equally satisfied that, as my findings on community relations in sections A and B above make clear, the police in Lambeth have not succeeded in achieving the degree of public approval and respect necessary for the effective fulfilment of their functions and duties. In my judgement, police attitudes and methods have not yet sufficiently responded to the problem of policing our multi-racial society. A gap still remains in this area between theory and practice; between the recognition of principle and its detailed application in an ethnically diverse community. This is not to be attributed to lack of sincerity. The police, by and large, really do try. But there

1. Quoted in 'The Metropolitan Police Community Relations Branch', paper by Superintendent L. T. Roach, *Police Studies*, September 1978, pp. 17–23.

remains in the policing system a certain lack of flexibility in their approach; and, so long as that remains, it is a serious flaw. I would add that, though we rightly expect high standards of the police, we should not be surprised that the adjustment necessary to meet the problem of policing a multi-racial community is not yet as satisfactory as it should be. As Part II of the Report shows, British society as a whole is no better: we have not yet come to terms with ethnic diversity.

4·71   This lack of flexibility emerges as a feature of the history already told in the earlier sections of this Part of the Report. I, therefore, content myself at this stage with taking from my summary of the factors which brought about the breakdown in community relations two illustrations: the unwillingness to consult on police operations, and 'hard policing'. I would add, however, that other factors helped to build up the image of an unimaginative and inflexible police presence in Lambeth: notably the conduct of some officers in their dealings with black people, and the formal and complicated system for handling complaints against the police.

(a) Failure to consult

4·72   I have already dealt in detail with the collapse of structural and regular liaison between police and leaders of the local community. It is significant that one of the factors of this collapse was the refusal in 1978 of the District Commander to take the Liaison Committee into his confidence when planning a special operation (which included the use of the SPG) against street crime and burglary. Similarly at a much later date Commander Fairbairn, notwithstanding his determination to re-establish an effective process of regular consultation with local leaders, did not believe it wise or necessary to consult local opinion before launching 'Swamp '81'.

4·73   Neither Commander Adams nor Commander Fairbairn believed it wise, or appreciated the need, to consult locally before deciding whether or not to mount an operation against street crime. They saw such consultation as a danger to the success of the operation, as well as an intrusion upon their independence of judgement as police officers. This was, I am satisfied, an error of judgement. The proposition that consultation upon operations is inappropriate is too wide, as Assistant Commissioner Gibson recognized when giving evidence in Phase 2 of the Inquiry. The proposition that it interferes with, or may undermine, independence of judgement is a 'non-sequitur': for consultation informs judgement; it does not pre-empt it.

4·74   Some operations to prevent or defeat crime must plainly remain secret: if the criminals know what is coming, they will go to ground. But some operations need the support and approval of the local community, if they are to succeed in the long term (whatever their immediate impact). Street crime operations belong to the latter class: for they are dependent upon a stop and search procedure which is bound to inconvenience, and may well embarrass and anger, innocent people who are stopped. And, if they are undertaken in an area such as Brixton where their impact will be most directly felt by young black men – who constitute the most despairing and, therefore, the most sensitive (but not necessarily the most criminally infected) section of the community – the need for local understanding of what the police have in mind to do, and why, is clear.

(b) 'Hard policing'

4·75   My second illustration is the policy of 'hard policing' (see paragraph 4·2, supra) against street crime, of which 'Swamp '81', a saturation operation, was a typical example. Hard policing is often necessary. The police have an abiding duty to act firmly against crime. 'Mugging' is an especially offensive sort of crime: if it be given the name which in very many cases it deserves, i.e. robbery, its gravity is apparent. A direct attack on it requires the use on the streets of stop and search powers and of the occasional 'saturation' operation; and it was legitimate for the police to use Section 4 of the Vagrancy Act so long as it remained in the law. But, when a community becomes resentful and restless and there is widespread loss of confidence in the police, the particular circumstances may require a review of police methods. It is a situation calling for the exercise of a professional judgement which takes into account all the circumstances.

4·76   The view which I have reached is that Operation 'Swamp' was a serious mistake, given the tension which existed between the police and the local community in the early months of this year. I do not believe that, consistently with the principles of policing acknowledged as sound by the Metropolitan Police, it could have been authorized in April had there been consultation with local leaders as to the wisdom of mounting it.

4·77　It was submitted, however, that if street crime was to be tackled, there was no alternative way of doing the job. Even if this be correct, it was still necessary to assess the risk to public order. The seriousness of the risk arose from the presence in Brixton of hostile and resentful young black people whose anger against the police had affected also the attitudes and beliefs of the older, more responsible, members of their community. The question for the police was, therefore: was it wise in the circumstances to mount the operation? Had policing attitudes and methods been adjusted to deal fully with the problems of policing a multi-racial society, there would have been a review in depth of the public order implications of the operation, which would have included local consultation. And, had this taken place, I believe, as I have already indicated, that a street 'saturation' operation would not have been launched when it was, i.e. in April of this year.

4·78　I would add two further comments. First, the evidence (paragraph 4·21, supra) is not clear that a street saturation operation does diminish street crime: it may well only drive it elsewhere. And, after the operation is ended, street crime returns. If, therefore, such an operation is, in the short term, the only direct action possible against street crime, its efficacy is doubtful. But in the long term the development of a style of policing which is designed to secure public approval and respect is likely to be more effective. It is, therefore, remarkable that the opinion of the home beat officers, the importance of whose role is well understood by the senior command, was not sought on the wisdom of the operation.

4·79　For these reasons I conclude that attitudes and methods in the senior command of 'L' District had not become sufficiently adjusted to the problems of policing a multi-racial community. In the result, this failure became a factor not only in the loss of local confidence in the police but also in the causation of the April disorders.

4·80　It may well be that this failing reflected an even deeper misconception in the Metropolitan Police as a whole of the true place of community relations in the policing of a multi-racial society. Community relations are central, not peripheral, to the police function. I question whether this truth was as fully understood by all concerned before the riots as it is now. However, having heard Assistant Commissioner Gibson and Deputy Assistant Commissioner Dear give evidence in Phase 2 of the Inquiry, I am satisfied that senior police officers do now fully appreciate the importance of what has come to be called community policing. In the words of Mr Hazan QC for the Commissioner, there is already a new beginning. We are acquiring the experience which enables not only the police but the makers of policy in our society to apply Sir Charles Rowan's words (supra) to the task of policing in our ethnically diverse society. Much, however, remains to be done. I set out in Part V of the Report some suggestions and recommendations as to how progress may be made.

(4) 'Over-reaction to the disorders'

4·81   In general, I reject the criticism that the police over-reacted in the handling of the disorders. It is not possible in an Inquiry such as this to investigate specific instances of wrong-doing and lawlessness on the part of individual police officers. Nor is it appropriate: the proper forum for the adjudication of such complaints is to be found in the courts or in disciplinary proceedings. Nevertheless, I have little doubt from the weight of evidence that there were certain instances in which police officers over-reacted during the disorders, behaved aggressively and used excessive force. I am equally clear, however, that in general the police behaved, under great provocation, well and with restraint. I am confident that the Commissioner will investigate with vigour all the allegations of misconduct arising from the disorders, and will refer the results of his inquiries to the Director of Public Prosecutions or the Police Complaints Board for their independent scrutiny as appropriate.

4·82   Particularly worrying among the allegations of misconduct by police officers during the riots were those which concerned the use of unlawful weapons by police officers. Some of the allegations merely concern police officers throwing back at the rioters bricks and other missiles which were being thrown at them. That this occurred is clearly established. I do not condone it: it must be discouraged. But in the circumstances of the disorders it was understandable, even though, save in self-defence, it would not be excusable.

4·83   Other allegations of the use of unlawful weapons, however, were more serious. They were made in particular by three journalists, Mr John Clare, Miss Caroline Tisdall and Mr David Hoffman. These allegations must be most carefully examined by the Commissioner and, if verified, stringent action must, in my view, be taken against those concerned. Since the unfortunate death of Mr Blair Peach in Southall in April 1979, there has been some controversy about the extent to which police officers on public order duties may have had access to unauthorized weapons. It is essential that police officers engaged in these duties must be known only to possess authorized items of equipment. That puts a responsibility on Chief Officers of Police and on Police Authorities to ensure that the equipment available to the police is adequate for them to be able to fulfil their task. But it must also be clear that any officer found to have used unlawful weapons in discharging his duty will be subject to the most rigorous disciplinary procedure.

4·84   Other criticism of the police reaction to the disorders involved the alleged improper use of dogs, shields and truncheons. On two occasions – at Leeson Road on Friday, 10 April, and in Atlantic Road on Saturday, 11 April – dogs were deployed in an undesirable way in the handling of a crowd. All officers who gave evidence to the Inquiry recognized that dogs are not appropriate instruments for dispersing crowds in sensitive situations. Chief Superintendent Marsh clearly recognized as much when on Friday evening at Leeson Road he ordered the removal of police dog vans from the scene of the disorder. It appears dogs were present on these two occasions because their handlers responded to calls for urgent assistance without necessarily knowing the circumstances which had led to the calls being made, or appreciating their sensitivity. Arrangements must be introduced to prevent the deployment of dogs in handling major crowd disorders in the future.

4·85   It was suggested in the Inquiry that officers had used their protective shields improperly, in particular by beating on them with their truncheons and shouting in a manner reminiscent of ancient warriors going into battle. I find that this did happen. It was unfortunate. But it is to be remembered that the police were under heavy attack: they needed to preserve their spirits in the face of a ferociously hostile crowd. Such action, though understandable, was unworthy of a disciplined force. It was calculated to arouse fear and apprehension in those citizens, some of them no doubt perfectly peaceful, who heard it. Such behaviour, despite extenuating circumstances, must be stopped.

4·86   Some criticisms of the handling of the riots went deeper than these allegations of misconduct, however, and touched on police strategy and tactics. First, it was alleged with regard to Saturday that Commander Fairbairn should have responded to the suggestion of the mediators that the police withdraw from the scene. This criticism rests on the belief that since the fury of the crowd was directed at the police, that fury would cease if its object was removed. I reject it. The arson and looting in Railton Road were already under way by the time of the attempted mediation. It is only necessary to imagine the criticism which would have fallen on the head of Commander Fairbairn if he had withdrawn and, as I believe, the looting and disorder had continued, in order to realize how misdirected this argument is.

4·87   The other main criticism of the handling of the disorders by the police is the suggestion that the strategy agreed between Deputy Assistant Commissioner Walker and Commander Fairbairn of an advance in strength from either end of Railton Road involved surrounding the crowd so that, being trapped, it turned at bay on the police. The crowd attacked the police, so this argument goes, in a desperate attempt to escape from a trap which the police had sprung.

4·88   The fallacy of this argument is revealed by a glance at the map at Appendix E. While escape to the east of Mayall and Railton Roads is limited because of the railway line, there is an ample number of roads which provide means of escape to the west. Indeed, these were the roads which were used by looters and rioters, in the early stages of Saturday's disorder, to circumvent the police lines and, in their final phase, to escape the police advance. The crowd may have fought the police for a number of reasons: but being trapped was not one of them.

4·89   Before I pass from the criticisms of over-reaction by the police to the disorders, there is one other I should mention: that too many police officers were deployed in Brixton on Sunday morning and that this was a factor in the mounting tension which eventually sparked off the disorders of that day. (I have already dealt with the similar argument advanced about the police presence on Saturday morning in Part III, paragraph 3·26, supra). I reject this criticism. The police could hardly fail to respond to the disorders of the previous day, which had been on a scale beyond that of anything previously seen in Britain this century. They were naturally apprehensive of a recurrence of the disorders – rightly, as was proved – and anxious to have sufficient officers on hand to deal promptly with it. As it was, until the disorders did break out they kept many of their units in reserve, away from Brixton. I turn now to my findings on the criticism that far from over-reacting to the disorders the police were insufficiently prepared and ill-equipped to cope with them.

(5) 'Delay and lack of vigour' (in handling the disorders)

4·90   There is little doubt that the disorders revealed weaknesses in the capacity of the police to respond sufficiently firmly to violence in the streets. On Saturday – the height of the disorders – the rioters had the run of Railton and Mayall Roads and looting continued unchecked in the shopping centre of Brixton for some three hours before the police had assembled sufficient forces to regain the initiative and quell the disorders. It is no criticism of those officers who, under the most fierce attack, held the police lines at the Triangle and, later, near Effra Parade, to say that they were forced by the sheer weight of the attack to adopt a defensive posture, to contain the crowds before they were sufficiently reinforced to disperse them. The build-up of officers was slow; it did not really achieve a sustained momentum until after 8 p.m. on Saturday, some two-and-a-half hours after the serious disorder had first erupted.

4·91   Other deficiencies in police equipment and preparedness rapidly became apparent. The protective shields and helmets, when they became available, proved inadequate; the helmets provided insufficient protection to the head; the foam padding at the rear of the shields – themselves heavy and cumbersome – caught fire when petrol spilled over them. Officers untrained in the use of shields or in the command of men carrying them found themselves thrust into

115

the front line. Officers' uniforms were also ignited by the flames from petrol bombs. Police vehicles were totally unprotected from missile-throwing mobs. There were difficulties in radio communication between officers deployed at the scene and police control, and between different units of officers on the ground: most notably, it appears doubtful whether, at the time of the advance by Commander Fairbairn and Commander Adams from opposite ends of Railton Road, either of the two Commanders or Deputy Assistant Commissioner Walker were fully aware of the desperate situation of Chief Superintendent Robinson near Effra Parade. Indeed, Commander Adams did not even know that Mr Robinson was in Railton Road near Effra Parade. None of the Commanders seems sufficiently to have appreciated the extent to which in moving forward they were inevitably going to put Mr Robinson's serials under even greater pressure than they already were. There also appear, from the evidence of Mr Butler, a Deputy Assistant Chief Officer of the London Fire Brigade, to have been problems in the early stages of Saturday in establishing effective liaison between the police and the other emergency services.

4.92   I have no doubt that senior Metropolitan Police officers have learned a great deal about the successful handling of disorder from the experience of Brixton. Evidence given by Assistant Commissioner Gibson in Phase 2 of the Inquiry indicates that new arrangements have been introduced to ensure that an adequate reserve of officers, properly trained and equipped, is available for rapid deployment in the event of disorder. The communication arrangements of the Metropolitan Police were already the subject before the disorders of a major programme of improvement. It is one of those unfortunate mischances of timing, for which no one is to blame, that the disorders occurred a month before the Brixton Division was due to receive improved personal radio equipment which might have obviated at least some of the communication problems. It has been suggested by some that after the experience of the disorders in Bristol on 2 April 1980 and the conclusions of the subsequent review, which you, Sir, initiated, of police arrangements for handling serious disorder,[1] the Metropolitan Police should have been

1. House of Commons Official Report, 6 August 1980, Vol 990. Written Answers, col. 113.

better prepared for the disorders in Brixton than they were. I make no finding on this. I simply point out that the scale of disorder was far in excess of anything until then experienced by the police in Britain and, in particular, that the Metropolitan Police faced in the petrol bomb a sinister and dangerous weapon, which had not previously been used on any substantial scale, if at all, in the United Kingdom outside Northern Ireland.

4·93   There is one further criticism of the police handling of the disorders which I specifically reject. That is the criticism that the strategy adopted by the police on Saturday first to contain the disorder and then to quell it by an advance from both ends of Railton Road was misguided. Given the geography of the area, the resources available to them and the behaviour of the crowds, this was the only sensible approach open to Deputy Assistant Commissioner Walker and Commander Fairbairn. Nor do I think they can reasonably be criticized on the grounds that when eventually Commander Fairbairn and Commander Adams were able to advance, the crowd was trapped between their advancing cordons and those of Chief Superintendent Robinson near Effra Parade. There were means of escape open to the crowds, down Barnwell and Spenser Roads, for example, which eventually the crowds used. Any just criticisms of the police command on Saturday lie not in failures of strategic conception but in their preparedness and ability to execute that conception.

4·94   I find then the fifth main criticism of the police justified to the extent that the disorders revealed weaknesses in the police's capacity to respond firmly and quickly to large-scale street violence. I know that, with the added experience of the later disorders of this year, you, Sir, have already taken steps, together with Chief Officers of Police, to overcome these difficulties and to ensure that in the event of any repetition of disorder, the rule of law will prevail. I offer, in Part V (paragraphs 5·72–74, infra), some suggestions and observations on the police handling of disorder which I hope will assist in this process. However, for the reasons given in Part VII (paragraphs 7·31–40, infra) I do not think it necessary to strengthen the law, though its simplification and codification would in the long term be beneficial.

(6) 'Failure to act against looting'

4·95   Finally, there is the criticism that the police failed to stop the looting which ran unchecked in the centre of Brixton on Saturday evening. It is clear from the evidence that white people were as much involved in this as black people and, according to some evidence, they appear to have been the more systematic and organized in their approach. Some of the looters were young, but others were not. Many were people who had come from outside Brixton tempted by the prospect of easy pickings made possible while the police were preoccupied with the serious disorders in Railton Road.

4·96   Those who looted and damaged property in Brixton deserve the severest condemnation and punishment. They were, I am glad to say, roundly condemned by all who gave evidence to the Inquiry. Some indeed went so far as to suggest that they were so culpable that the police should have turned their attention from the disorders in Railton and Mayall Roads in order to deal with the looting. I cannot agree. The police could not have turned their back on the mayhem in Railton and Mayall Roads, even if the crowd there had been prepared to let them. I am satisfied that any delay by the police in stopping the looting arose not from any reluctance to do so but from the fact that because of the limited resources they had available in the early part of the evening, they could not cope with both the disorder and the looting. The police commanders felt they had to give priority to the former. I am satisfied that they were right to do so. Any fault lay in an inability to muster adequate numbers of officers, properly trained and equipped, sufficiently quickly, rather than in a failure either of police will or of operational judgement.

General comment on the criticisms

4·97   Nothing that I have heard or seen can excuse the unlawful behaviour of the rioters. But the police must carry some responsibility for the outbreak of disorder. First, they were partly to blame for the breakdown in community relations. Secondly, there were instances of harassment and racial prejudice among junior officers on the streets of Brixton which gave credibility and substance to the arguments of the police's critics. Thirdly, there was the failure to adjust policies and methods to meet the needs of policing a multi-racial society. The failures of the police, however, were only part of the story and arose in difficult circumstances. The community and community leaders in particular must take their share of the blame for the atmosphere of distrust and mutual suspicion between the police and the community which developed in Lambeth during the 1970s and reached its apogee in the weeks prior to the disorders. I hold it as a hopeful sign that in the closing stages of the Inquiry there was evidence of an apparent willingness on both sides to acknowledge past errors and to try to make a new start. And I repeat – the failures of the police and of the community leaders neither justify nor excuse the disorders or the terrifying lawlessness of the crowds.

4·98   The police response to the disorders, once they broke out, cannot however be criticized as 'over-reaction', 'unreasonable aggression', 'oppressive' or 'brutal' (to quote the descriptions I have heard offered by some in the Inquiry). The conclusion which I have reached is that, save in one or two respects where the true criticism is that they failed to act in sufficient time or with sufficient force, the police at command level and on the streets acted wisely, coolly and with commendable restraint (though there were some individual exceptions) in a testing, dangerous and alarming situation. It is a tribute to their restraint that no one was killed in the suppression of the disorders. Broadly, the police strategy and tactics in handling the disorders are to be commended, not criticized. Those who were privileged, as I was, to hear the evidence of a succession of Metropolitan Police Officers (both senior and junior) and of representatives of the London Fire Brigade, the London Ambulance Service and the British Transport Police during the Inquiry will have had many opportunities to marvel at and be thankful for the courage and dedication which was displayed by members of the police and emergency services in Brixton over that terrible weekend. They stood between our society and a total collapse of law and order in the streets of an important part of the capital. For that, they deserve, and must receive, the praise and thanks of all sections of our community.

4·99   Before we pass judgement on the quality of our policing, let us remember their many excellences even while we note and seek to remedy such defects as there may be.

Part V

POLICING – PROPOSALS
AND RECOMMENDATIONS

A · Introduction

5·1   In this Part I discuss proposals and recommendations for improving the quality of policing; they are derived from my study of the evidence and argument adduced in the course of the Inquiry. I am conscious that I have surveyed only part, albeit a central part, of policing our complex modern society, namely policing those areas in which ethnic diversity has become a significant feature of the life of the local community. It is necessary, therefore, to ensure that such proposals as arise from my Inquiry be tested by reference to general criteria applicable to the needs of society as a whole.

5·2   It is for this reason that in Part IV I ventured to formulate two policing principles of general application: 'consent and balance'; 'independence and accountability' (see paragraphs 4·55–60, supra). The proposals and recommendations which I put forward in this Part are an attempt to apply those general principles to one specific aspect of policing, namely the maintenance of public order in a multi-racial society, without undermining the two other requirements we make of the police, namely effective law enforcement and the protection of life and property. I remind myself, however, that of the three requirements public order is, in the last resort, the most important.

5·3   It is not surprising that the police forces of the United Kingdom today face a range of pressures wider and deeper than any which have previously confronted them. The pressures reflect changes in society, in social values and attitudes, and in policing itself. Society has become more fragmented and diverse in composition, and yet also more uniform in many of its perceptions and attitudes. This uniformity is largely due to the influence of the media. Social attitudes are more permissive; authority is no longer accepted without question. The police have been deeply affected by

120

the change. They are now professionals with a highly specialized set of skills and behavioural codes of their own. They run the risk of becoming, by reason of their professionalism, a 'corps d'élite' set apart from the rest of the community. Technological advances have offered new ways of preventing and fighting crime, of protecting life and property, and of quelling disorder without the necessity of maintaining close personal relations with the community. Indeed, not the least of the problems the police now face is how to take advantage of their technological aids without destroying the human factor, so essential if policing is to command public support.

5·4   The police are generally well aware of the conflicting pressures they face, perhaps more so than the rest of us. Crime must be dealt with firmly, yet the human face of the police must be retained. Traffic must be kept moving, but not so as to stop me doing what I want with my car. The police must ensure that free speech is preserved, except for some. Although research – by universities, by the Home Office, by the newly established Police Foundation – is gradually exposing the dilemmas which are often inherent, because of social attitudes, in police work, the degree of public knowledge about the problems which face police officers is generally limited to the image seen on the television screen, and much discussion of policing issues remains at the level of the catch-phrase or slogan.

5·5   The analysis in Part IV points to the view, which I have come to hold, that, notwithstanding an increasing awareness by police at all levels of the conflicting pressures imposed upon them by today's society, there is scope for a more coherent and better-directed response by them to the challenge of policing modern, multi-racial society. The point is not made as a criticism of the Metropolitan Police. It is a constructive comment, going to the heart of policing throughout the country. Indeed most of my proposals are of general application. They are not, save where the context clearly indicates otherwise, confined to London. They are designed as an agenda for a national discussion.

B · Recruitment

5·6   There is widespread agreement that the composition of our police forces must reflect the make-up of the society they serve. In one important respect at least, it does not do so: in the police, as in other important areas of society, the ethnic minorities are very significantly under-represented. The number of black officers serving in the Metropolitan Police on 6 October 1981 was 132, 0.5 per cent of the total strength of the force: on the same date, there were only 326 black officers in the police of England and Wales (0.3 per cent of the total strength). It is clear from the evidence I have heard that senior police officers are united with the leaders of ethnic minority groups in decrying the fact. Much has been done, for example through specially directed advertising campaigns, to try to attract black recruits. But these efforts have met with little success. The real problem is not that too many members of the ethnic minorities fail to meet the standards for appointment, but that too few apply. Independent research undertaken for the Home Office in 1979 underlined the fact that the reluctance of young West Indians to join the police is deeply rooted in the attitude of many members of that community to the police. The reasons most commonly given for lack of interest in a police career were a basic lack of interest in the job, a fear of being alienated from family and friends, and a fear of being ostracized because of colour prejudice within the service. Most disturbingly, however, the research revealed a strong undercurrent of hostility towards the police, which probably accounts, more than any other fact, for the failure of suitable people of West Indian origin to come forward as candidates for appointment. I have also heard evidence that, when black officers do join the police, they are treated with open hostility and contempt by at least some members of their own community.

5·7   A number of proposals were made in the course of the Inquiry designed to overcome the recruiting problem and to provide a higher proportion of black officers. It was suggested, for example, by, among others, the Chief Constable of Devon and Cornwall, that an annual quota of places in the police should be reserved for coloured minorities. This would, of course, involve a form of reverse discrimination in favour of ethnic minority members and I doubt whether such reverse discrimination would be acceptable. But there are several objections to the proposal on other, more practical grounds. A quota system would be ineffective as a means of making it more easy for members of the ethnic minorities to get into the police, unless it was accompanied by a lowering of entrance standards. Black officers recruited under a quota system in this way might feel that they had entered the police as second-class recruits. It would certainly be undesirable to divide police officers into two categories: those who had met the normal standards for appointment as a constable and those who had not. I understand that experience in American police forces, some of which introduced quota systems in the 1960s and early '70s, has not been universally satisfactory. For these reasons, I reject the quota system as a means of recruiting more black people to the police.

5·8   Nor do I accept an alternative suggestion made in evidence for a lowering of the standards for recruitment to police forces. I appreciate that such a lowering would apply to all recruits, black and white, and that its object would be, by reducing the threshold for entry, to secure a sufficient intake of black recruits to ensure that at least a good number completed the probationary period satisfactorily. The present minimum academic requirement for entry into the police is the possession of four 'O' levels including maths and English, or alternatively the obtaining of a minimum mark of 80 out of a total 200 in a standard entrance test. It is in my view possible to argue with at least as much force as to the contrary that the raising, not a lowering, of entrance standards is what we need. I therefore reject this proposal.

5·9   Nevertheless, vigorous action is required if the police are to become more representative of all the community they serve. A possible way forward (a suggestion which was made in evidence to the Inquiry) may lie in the provision of special additional training for would-be black entrants to the police. Many black applicants fail at present because they do not meet the physical or educational standards required. If the goal of securing more black police officers is accepted as essential, as in my view it must be, there is clearly a case for providing tuition for black applicants in order to assist them to meet at least the academic standard required for entry. It might be possible, for example, to recruit would-be black police officers to suitable civilian jobs in the police force (some 10 per cent of the civilian staff of the Metropolitan Police are, I understand, black), where such tuition could be provided, or to provide the tuition free on an evening class basis, or to adapt some of the Manpower Services Commission's schemes for the young unemployed to achieve this special end. It will no doubt be argued by some that to give such tuition would be to give black applicants an advantage over white. I doubt whether this would in fact be so, but it is justifiable and, moreover (as I think), lawful under Sections 37 and 38 of the Race Relations Act 1976.

5·10   Additional tuition arrangements of this sort would not be the whole answer. They would only be effective if coupled with a more purposeful drive to get black applicants to come forward in greater numbers. This drive – which must be given very high priority – must be conducted not simply through advertising but, I suggest, by means of personal contact through schools, youth clubs, unemployment offices and wherever else young black people are to be found. American police forces (such as the New York City Police) may have useful experience to offer here. At a time when there is no difficulty in attracting well-qualified white recruits, it may appear an unnecessary use of resources to engage in such a drive. But securing a police force fairly representative of the community as a whole requires that the effort be made.

5·11   There are, of course, other ways of recruiting black police officers. I have in mind the cadet scheme – under which young people of 16 are given, in the Metropolitan Police and certain other forces, a sound academic training coupled with an introduction to police work – and the Special Constabulary. If more black cadets can be recruited, they could in time provide an increased black presence in the regular police force. Black representation in the Special Constabulary is, I understand, already considerably better than black representation in the regular police force. Some community leaders in Handsworth, Birmingham, suggested to me on my visit there that if more of the older generation of black people could be recruited into the Special Constabulary, they might assist in bringing the black community into a deeper appreciation of the problems of the police, and of the need to support them by encouraging their young people to join the police. It may be that it would be easier to take up this suggestion with some minority communities than with others. Nevertheless I understand that the Police Advisory Board has the matter of the Special Constabulary under consideration, following the reports of two recent Working Parties of the Board on the subject of the 'Specials', and I hope that this suggestion is one which will be actively considered. There may also be other ways of involving members of ethnic minority groups in assisting the police. Again, American experience might have some useful leads to offer: I understand, for example, that in some areas with high ethnic minority populations, black youths have been enrolled by police forces in an auxiliary status in various aspects of police work. While American experience may not necessarily suit British conditions, projects of this nature would certainly seem to warrant further exploration.

5·12 Involving more black people in the police will take time. If it is to be achieved, it will require a gradual change in the attitude of many black people to the police. Leaders of the black community must, therefore, be fully involved and give their active support to the process. But it cannot be assumed that simply having more black police officers will solve all the problems in the relationship between some black people and the police: it will not. Nevertheless, in the long term, the process is of great importance. A police force which fails to reflect the ethnic diversity of our society will never succeed in securing the full support of all its sections.

5·13 I therefore *recommend* that the Home Office, with Chief Officers of Police, and in consultation with Police Authorities and representatives of the ethnic minority communities, conduct an urgent study of ways of improving ethnic minority recruitment into the regular police and of involving ethnic minorities more in police-related activities such as the Special Constabulary. The object of policy must be that the composition of the police fully reflects that of the society the police serve. Nothing less will suffice.

5·14 One other important aspect of police recruitment raised in evidence to the Inquiry is the need to ensure that racially prejudiced people are not selected as police officers. I am satisfied that police forces are aware of this. At present, they try to achieve it by a combination of checks, including inquiries as to character, interviews, and monitoring the behaviour and performance of recruits at training school and during their probationary period. A good deal of the evidence submitted to me questioned the effectiveness of these checks, and some recent research[1] which has been drawn to my attention – although not without its critics[2] – appears to support this evidence. It is clear from what was said in Phase 2 of the Inquiry by Deputy Assistant Commissioner Dear that the Metropolitan Police are fully alive to the problem and are exploring, with American help, whether attitude screening can be put on a more systematic, scientific basis.

5·15   It is unlikely, however, that racial prejudice can be wholly eliminated from the police so long as it is endemic in society as a whole. The destruction of racial prejudice requires a determined and concerted effort throughout society, including an unwavering lead from those in positions of authority in public life and in our major institutions. The police, of course, must make a parallel effort. We cannot rest on the cynical proposition, which I have heard, that, since the police will necessarily reflect social attitudes, racially prejudiced people are bound to be found in their ranks. I therefore *recommend* that the work currently being undertaken in the Metropolitan Police designed to identify scientific ways in which evidence of racial prejudice can be identified should be vigorously pursued with the support of the Home Office, and that the results should in due course be incorporated into the procedures for selecting recruits to all police forces.

C · Training the police

5·16   The training of police officers must prepare them for policing a multi-racial society. Much of the evidence submitted to me has suggested that the present training arrangements are inadequate. It was argued that the total time and resources devoted to training are insufficient, and in particular that inadequate emphasis is put in training on the problems of policing a multi-racial society. More attention should therefore be devoted, it was suggested, to the

1. *Conservatism, Dogmatism and Authoritarianism in British Police Officers.* Andrew M. Colman and L. Paul Gorman, Department of Psychology, University of Leicester.
2. Chief Inspector A. J. P. Butler's letter in *The Times*, 5 October 1981.

training of police officers in, for example, an understanding of the cultural background of ethnic minority groups and in the stopping and questioning of people in the street. And I have noted in Part IV (paragraph 4·91, supra) the evidence of inadequate training of both junior and senior police officers in the handling of disorder. Two particularly powerful submissions on the need to strengthen police training arrangements came in evidence from the Police Superinten-dent's Association of England and Wales and the Police Federation of England and Wales.

5·17 I am satisfied that improvements in police training are in hand. In particular, it was clear from the evidence of Deputy Assistant Commissioner Dear – which was welcomed by all parties represented in the Inquiry – that the Commissioner is well aware of the critical importance of training. (It is right, in passing, to pay tribute to the foresight of the Commissioner in establishing in November 1978 a comprehensive review of recruitment and train-ing in the Metropolitan Police, the results of which are now gradually being implemented.) The discussion and recommenda-tions which follow should, therefore, be studied against the back-ground of the fact that many improvements in training are well in hand. But the importance of adequate training is such that I make no apology for putting forward recommendations, some of which are already being implemented or considered: for the quality of training will benefit from the extensive public discussion which it is to be hoped will follow publication of this Report.

(1) Initial recruit training

5·18 I am satisfied that the length of the present period of initial training for recruits is insufficient. It cannot be right – and it is no criticism of them if I say so – that young men and women of nineteen or twenty are enabled to exercise the powers and responsibilities of the office of constable after a period of initial training which lasts only fifteen weeks in the Metropolitan Police[1] and only ten weeks in the training centres which serve the provincial forces. I appreciate that the initial course is not the total of the training given a recruit:

1. A proposal to extend this period by one week to 16 weeks is, I understand, currently under consideration.

that in the provinces further training may be undertaken within forces and that there is a two-week continuation course at the end of the probationary period; and that in the Metropolitan Police there are also continuation training arrangements and that, after initial training, four weeks are now spent on the 'street duties course' in which small groups of probationary constables are trained in basic police skills, a specially selected Sergeant and an experienced Constable being in charge of each group. Nevertheless, the recruit to a British police force receives a good deal less training in total than his counterpart in a number of other countries. I do not see how the increasing complexities of a police officer's task can be adequately covered – even at the basic level – in the present initial training period. I am fortified in this opinion by the fact that it appears to be the view not only of the great bulk of those non-police organizations and individuals who commented on training in submitting evidence to me, but of at least two of the three police representative organizations.

5·19 I therefore *recommend* that the minimum length of the initial training period for the police recruits be increased to six months. I am aware that this recommendation will undoubtedly have considerable resource implications, and I have the importance of resource factors in mind in making this and indeed all other recommendations in my report. In my view, however, resource considerations – important though they are – must not be allowed to stand in the way of the implementation of this recommendation. Indeed, if resources permitted, a case could be made for recommending a twelve-month initial training period. I do not, however, propose this: for, once a recruit has had a thorough grounding in his initial training, the sooner he begins to acquire experience, the better. The future effectiveness of the police requires, nevertheless, a significant increase in the initial training period.

5·20 Turning to the curriculum of an extended initial training course, there are bound to be many subjects which could usefully be treated in greater depth than they are at present. I draw attention to two which are particularly relevant to my terms of reference: the maintenance of public order, and an understanding of the cultural backgrounds and the attitudes to be found in our ethnically diverse society.

5·21 The prevention of disorder and the successful handling of it once it occurs must have very high priority in the recruit training curriculum. In respect of the handling of disorder, there must be training in the use of shields, in how to defend oneself against petrol bomb attack, and other practical matters arising out of a conflict situation. But this is not enough. There must be greater emphasis on the prevention of disorder, on training officers to handle and defuse potential situations of conflict with the public in the street. Stopping, searching and questioning members of the public, the handling of arrests, the execution of search warrants – all these ought to be matters in which police officers receive in the course of initial training the most thorough instruction. I know from the evidence in Phase 2, and from my visit to the Police College, Hendon, that much is already being done; and that the quality of the teaching is kept to a high standard. There is, however, a case for according the training of officers in the sensitive handling of situations of conflict even higher priority than it is given at present. The proposals for introducing human awareness training at present being considered in the Metropolitan Police should considerably improve this aspect of training.

5·22 The second subject is of critical importance – and is already known to be. I need not, therefore, go into any further elaboration of the subject.

5·23 More generally, the underlying theme throughout a recruit's initial training must, I suggest, be the police officer's role as a member of the community he polices and his need to maintain law and order through gaining the approval, confidence and respect of the community he serves. The recruit must learn that obtaining community support is not mere community relations window-dressing to be handled by a few specialists, but an essential element of the operational efficiency of the police in fighting crime and keeping the peace.

(2) The probationary period

5·24 The term 'probationary period' covers the first two years (or so) of police service, i.e. both the initial training course and the period after initial training when he or she is doing police work under supervision. I shall refer to this second period as 'probation'. It is an essential and integral part of the recruit training process. A system of continual assessment of an officer's performance and progress at present operates throughout the first two years of service. I do not recommend any change in the overall length of the probationary period: under my proposals, the first six months of the two-year period would be spent at the training school ('initial training') and the remaining eighteen months on probation, i.e. supervised police duties (subject to any necessary continuation courses). The object of the period spent on probation after leaving the training school must be to reinforce the academically based training at the school with individual experience 'on the job' in the street. This experience should include in particular practical training and supervision in the handling of people in situations of potential conflict such as stops in the street. I therefore welcome the introduction in the Metropolitan Police Probationer Training Programme of the 'street duty course', in which groups of probationer constables are given supervised training in the use of basic policing skills under the guidance of a specially selected Sergeant and senior Police Constable. I hope that the effectiveness of these courses will be carefully monitored and that the advantage of regional forces adopting a similar training concept will be actively considered.

5·25 One of the reasons for the introduction of the street duties course, however, was, I believe, the ending, because of manpower constraints, of the tutor or parent constable scheme, in which a probationer officer was sent out on the street in the company of an older, more experienced officer, who introduced the probationer to the skills of his profession. With the recent improvement in the police manpower position, I would hope to see schemes on the tutor or parent constable model encouraged wherever manpower permits. Any such scheme should be in addition to the street duties course. But if a choice had to be made, I would think that the street duties course is likely to be less effective in the long term than a sustained period of supervision and training on a one-to-one basis.

5·26 I also *recommend* that an officer's period on probation should include, if possible, a period in a city area where ethnic minorities form a substantial proportion of the population. I deal later in the

Report (paragraphs 5·34–35, infra) with the argument strongly put to me in evidence that it is inappropriate for young police officers to work in such areas. I simply observe, at this stage, that in the context of training it is in my view important that young police officers should have an opportunity to meet members of the minority communities and to understand at first hand the particular features of policing areas in which ethnic minority groups form a significant part of the population. Such periods of service should be designed not only to give direct experience in, for example, patrolling such areas, but, through contact with youth clubs, churches and other community organizations, an opportunity to appreciate the cultural background and other special features and needs of the ethnic minorities. Probationer constables should not, however, save in an emergency, go out alone on foot patrol in an inner city or any other racially sensitive area. One ill-judged incident involving an inexperienced constable can wipe out all the advantages one hopes to gain from introducing probationary constables more fully into the community they are to police.

(3) In-service training

5·27 The process of training a police officer does not, of course, end with the successful completion of his (or her) probationary period. The breadth of in-service training provided for the police – which includes broad courses provided at the Police Staff College at Bramshill, the management training courses for senior officers at the Police College, Hendon, and short specialist courses at regional force training centres – is impressive. It would be inappropriate for me to attempt here a comprehensive analysis of this considerable range of training. There are, however, two aspects of in-service training, of central relevance to my terms of reference, which I wish to mention: training in community relations; and training in the handling of disorder.

Training in community relations

5·28 Initial training courses already include an element – which, in my view, should be strengthened in an expanded course – of training in community relations, i.e. the need to establish and maintain good relations between the police and members of the public irrespective of racial, religious or social differences. Further training in community relations, of both a general and a specialist character, is provided for many officers, including those of more senior rank, but the exact extent and duration of the provision varies from force to force. Training courses designed to develop the understanding that good community relations are not merely necessary but essential to good policing should, I *recommend*, be compulsory from time to time in a police officer's career up to and including the rank of Superintendent. The theme of these courses should be the role of the police as part of the community, the operational importance of good community relations, the techniques of consultation, and the moral as well as legal accountability of the police to the public. I would hope to see community representatives, particularly from the ethnic minorities, playing a part in the design and execution of these training programmes.

Training in the handling of public disorder

5·29   Training in the handling of public disorder should also be provided, I *recommend*, for officers of all ranks up to and including Commander or its equivalent (Assistant Chief Constable) in the provinces. The disorders in Brixton and elsewhere have thrown doubt upon the adequacy of training currently provided on the policing of disorder. The precise nature of the training to be given in this subject is bound to vary somewhat according to the rank of the officer concerned: practical training in the use of shields and in meeting attack by petrol bombs, for example, is likely to be particularly important to the more junior ranks; training in the command of men and in the strategy and tactics for handling disorder is more appropriate for senior ranks. Further, the techniques for handling disorder are bound to develop and change. It is therefore essential that training programmes in this, as in other areas, should be constantly reviewed, and that refresher courses should be provided in order to bring officers up to date with the latest developments and techniques.

5·30   The effectiveness of existing arrangements under which one force may provide aid to another in the handling of disorder depends, however, not merely on officers being adequately trained but on them also undergoing a common pattern of training, so that officers from different forces can combine effectively when necessary in restoring order. Common standards are also desirable in my view in the equally vital area of community relations training. At present the provision of in-service training of any nature is the responsibility of individual Chief Officers of Police: the Home Office has no coordinating role. But the need to reassure the public that adequate training is being provided and the desirability on practical grounds of a common approach to training in important areas such as public order, both suggest the need for coordination in policy making and in direction. I therefore *recommend* that the Home Office, together with Chief Officers of Police, should seek to establish common programmes and minimum standards for in-service training in both community relations and the handling of disorder. Observance of these minimum standards by forces should be monitored through HM Inspectorate of Constabulary.

(4) Conclusion

5·31 I have touched in this brief discussion of police training only on those aspects of a large subject which seem to me directly relevant to my terms of reference. The training provided for police officers must, I suggest, be subject to constant review. The evidence I have received leads me to submit that there must be a greater emphasis on and provision for training throughout a police officer's career; and that the training provided must be effectively coordinated so as to achieve common minimum standards in all police forces, even though training needs will, I appreciate, vary according to the policing problems which characterize different areas.

5·32 Within the expanded training programme which I recommend, the period of practical 'on-the-job' training as a supervised probationary constable is the critical phase, though it needs, if it is to be effective, the grounding of an initial institutional training course, in which the central importance of community relations is explored in depth. The training programme must be considered as a whole and should be designed to bring the police and the public into closer contact. Above all, the central theme in all training must be the need for the police to secure the consent and support of the public if they are successfully to perform their duties of keeping the peace and preventing and detecting crime.

D · Supervision and monitoring

5·33 I have discussed ways in which the quality and representativeness of recruits to the police might be improved and in which those recruited might then be better trained to discharge their difficult role in contemporary society. But the need for careful monitoring, if mistakes, let alone misconduct, are to be avoided, does not end once a constable passes his probationary period. There continues to be a need for the effective supervision of individual officers, as well as a need for the regular monitoring of trends, and patterns in, for example, the nature of the complaints made against police officers, so that policing policy may be adjusted in order to maintain its effectiveness.

5·34 These needs were emphasized by the criticism made by a number of parties represented in the Inquiry of the deployment of young police officers in sensitive areas such as Brixton. It was claimed that because young officers lack years, they also lack maturity of judgement and therefore pose a real risk to good relations between the police and the local community. The relatively high number of young police officers deployed in 'L' District and elsewhere is not, however, a result of some misguided piece of personnel planning. It reflects the loss of experienced officers prior to the recent surge in recruitment following the Edmund Davies Report,[1] as well as, on occasion, more purely local factors (in the case of 'L' District, the significant increase in the strength of officers in the Brixton Division as a result of the decision made in 1980 – paragraph 4·19, supra). According to the Report of HM Chief Inspector of Constabulary for 1980,[2] some 36 per cent of police constables in England and Wales are between the ages of eighteen-and-a-half years and twenty-five. Young officers are therefore an unavoidable feature of contemporary policing. Moreover, they are likely to form a higher proportion of officers actually engaged in

1. *Report on Police Pay*, HMSO, Cmnd 7283.
2. HMSO, HC 409.

street patrol duty. As the Police Federation noted in its evidence to me, it would be wrong either to put all the blame for difficulties on these officers or to assume that everything was better in some apparently halcyon, but probably mythical, days of the past when older and more mature officers performed the duties now undertaken by the younger officers. (We all begin our lives by thinking how old policemen are; and it comes as a shock when our advancing years reveal how young they are.)

5.35   Young police officers are not only unavoidable: they are valuable. I have no doubt that they have a role to play in the policing of inner city areas which the older officer cannot understudy. No generation gap separates them from young people on the streets: they share with them recent school experience, the same interests and the same personal problems. The need is not to remove young officers from sensitive areas – age in itself is certainly no guarantee of wisdom – but to ensure that they receive proper guidance and supervision in discharging their difficult, delicate and indispensable function.

(1) Supervision

5.36   As far as supervision is concerned, the role of Inspectors and Sergeants is crucial. I am not wholly persuaded that its importance is sufficiently recognized either in the manning of forces or in the degree of management training given to officers in these ranks. It will be no good increasing through extended training the awareness of constables of the 'consent' principle and the need, for example, to avoid racially prejudiced behaviour if supervisory officers lack the skill to impart knowledge of these requirements or the alertness to spot error or misconduct. I therefore *recommend* that greater attention be given to management training in the supervisory responsibilities of officers of Inspector and Sergeant rank. At the same time these ranks must receive from their senior officers the support and recognition which is their due, since it is to their quickness of perception and firmness in action that we look for the elimination of abrasive, biased, and racially prejudiced conduct by policemen on the streets.

5.37   Close supervision is particularly important in stop and search type operations. Much criticism was directed in the Inquiry to the manner in which these are carried out: some people complained about the operations themselves, but many more, while accepting the need for such operations on occasion, spoke of the deep anger and resentment caused by discourteous and abrasive police behaviour. In the words of the submission of the Brixton Domino and Social Club: 'When police are conducting stop and search exercises, black persons object not to being stopped or searched, but to the way in which it is done. The police method is without respect, deliberately provocative and insulting and designed to strip the individual of whatever dignity he may possess.' On the other hand, it is clear from the evidence of, for example, Inspector Scotchford that efforts are made by supervisory officers to impress on young constables the need to treat people in the street with respect: 'I try,' he said, 'to get them to speak to people in a way they would wish to be spoken to.' Nevertheless, the balance of evidence suggests that far greater attention is necessary, not only in training but in the exercise of supervision by senior officers, to the manner in which stops, searches, questioning and arrest in the street are conducted. As far as training is concerned, the recommendations I have made earlier and the new street duty courses should help. But heightened supervision of officers on the street is equally important. I am acutely aware of the pressure on officers generated by the hostile circumstances in which essential police activities are often conducted in places like Brixton. This strengthens the need to ensure that stop and search operations and similar activities are conducted carefully and courteously, as well as firmly.

(2) Monitoring

5·38   The continuous monitoring of performance as a check against which policing policy and approach can be judged is equally essential. The existing system of checks and balances in the Metropolitan Police was described in oral evidence by Assistant Commissioner Gibson. I am satisfied that, properly operated, these checks should be sufficient. I draw attention, however, to two points which might benefit from further emphasis. First, the pattern of complaints both against individual officers and within police areas must be kept under continuous review in order to enable senior officers to detect points of potential friction and difficulty. I am aware that such monitoring is conducted in the Metropolitan Police at present; I simply underline its importance. Secondly, as I have already noted in Part IV (paragraph 4·14, supra), the statistics on which senior officers base their policy decisions must be reviewed constantly in order to avoid any danger of misinterpretation or stereotyping, and to check that there is no evidence that police officers are behaving in a biased or racially prejudiced manner. Again I am satisfied that this point is already appreciated by senior officers in the Metropolitan Police, but it is one which bears repeating.

5·39   One particular proposal for monitoring the conduct of officers was put to me in evidence by the Commission for Racial Equality (CRE) in Phase 2 of the Inquiry. This was that an addition should be made to the General Orders of the Metropolitan Police on the following lines:

> An officer not below the rank of Chief Superintendent and not based at the material station shall:
> (a) monitor the stop and arrest statistics of every station, and
> (b) where the statistics so require, investigate, and
> (c) where the result of the investigation warrants it, lay a disciplinary charge of discrimination
> wherever the statistics or other information show:
> (i) that one or more officers have stopped or arrested a substantially higher proportion of persons belonging to ethnic or national minorities than the proportion of such minorities in the local population, or
> (ii) that the proportion of members of ethnic or national minorities stopped or arrested for a particular class of offence substantially exceeds the proportion of such persons in the local population.

I appreciate the intention behind this proposal. It is, as I have noted, essential that procedures should exist to enable senior officers to monitor and supervise the pattern of individual and collective police behaviour in order to ensure that bias is eliminated. I do not, however, endorse the CRE's proposal, involving as it would an unacceptable presumption that disciplinary proceedings should be implemented whenever, regardless of the circumstances, an officer had stopped or arrested a substantially higher proportion of people belonging to ethnic or national minorities than the proportion of such people in the local population as a whole. The proposal is too rigid to warrant adoption.

5·40   In the analysis so far, I have concentrated particularly on the behaviour of police officers in the street and in other places, since there is no doubt in my mind that this was the aspect of alleged police misconduct principally responsible for the worsening of relations between the police and young members of the black community in Brixton. Nevertheless, the allegations of misconduct I have heard do not stop there: they extend to behaviour in police stations, particularly in the questioning and detention of suspects. The question of safeguards for those arrested has recently been exhaustively considered, together with other matters, by the Royal Commission on Criminal Procedure, chaired by Sir Cyril Philips,[1] and it would be presumptuous of me to attempt in this Report to go over that ground again. One proposal, not so far as I am aware considered by the Royal Commission, has, however, been made to me in evidence: that is for the introduction of an element of independent inspection and supervision in the treatment of suspects in police stations. I believe it to be sound, and in Part VII (paragraphs 7·7–10, infra) I consider it in more detail.

E · Discipline

5·41   Racially prejudiced or discriminatory behaviour is not at present a specific offence under the Police Discipline Code, although it is almost certainly covered by the Code's general offence of discreditable conduct.[2] It was suggested in evidence from, among others, the Commission for Racial Equality that it should be made a specific disciplinary offence, and when the suggestion was put to Assistant Commissioner Gibson in evidence he did not oppose it. A number of specific offences – such as corrupt or improper practice, improper dress or untidiness, drunkenness, and entering licensed premises – are included in the Code at present and the addition of racially discriminatory behaviour would help to emphasize the objection to conduct of this nature in a multi-racial society. While the precise formulation of the offence will no doubt require detailed

1. *Report of the Royal Commission on Criminal Procedure*, HMSO, Cmnd 8092.
2. See Schedule 2 of the Police (Discipline) Regulations 1977, SI 1977 No. 580.

consideration, I *recommend* that racially prejudiced or discriminatory behaviour should be included as a specific offence in the Discipline Code.

5·42   I am satisfied that when racially prejudiced behaviour is found it is stamped on by severe disciplinary action. It must continue to be so. While I do not go so far as to propose a fixed penalty for the offence, I do *recommend* that it should be understood throughout the police that the normal penalty for racially prejudiced behaviour is dismissal.

F · Complaints against the police

5·43   The evidence, which was given in the two Phases of my Inquiry and reinforced by my visits to the West Midlands and to Liverpool, has convinced me that there is a widespread and dangerous lack of public confidence in the existing system for handling complaints against the police. By and large, people do not trust the police to investigate the police. This may not be fair to the police: but unless there is a strengthening of the independent 'non-police' element in the system, public confidence will continue to be lacking. The problem is complex. I discuss it at length and put forward for consideration some proposals in Part VII (paragraphs 7·11–29, infra) of the Report.

G · Methods of policing

5·44   In the preceding paragraphs of this Part of my Report, I have been looking at ways in which – through recruitment, training, supervision and control – the conduct of individual police officers might be made more responsive to the needs of policing our contemporary, multi-racial society. The evidence I have received, however, is not limited to criticisms of alleged police misconduct; it extends to the policies and methods of policing itself. The criticisms I have heard are generally directed to the manifestations of so-called 'hard' policing seen in Brixton and certain other inner city areas: notably, the use of powers to stop and search, saturation police operations like 'Swamp '81', and the existence, or at least the deployment in sensitive areas, of units like the Special Patrol Group. The critics of the police generally draw a contrast between this style of policing and so-called 'community policing', a style best epitomized, perhaps, in the image of the Home Beat Officer or the friendly bobby-on-the-beat.

5·45   Senior police officers appear to respond to this criticism in two ways. First, they say that the demand for community policing ignores the harsh realities of crime in the inner city: they point out that styles of policing will vary and that what is good for a country market town is not necessarily appropriate to a deprived inner city area. Secondly, they emphasize that many, if not most, police forces are already doing much – as it is clear from the evidence they are – to meet the demand for community policing through, for example, re-introducing foot patrols and seeking improved contact generally with the community. As the debate on these matters developed in Phase 2 of the Inquiry, there seemed every danger of an unreal gulf developing between the proponents of one view of policing and the other.

5·46   Policing is, however, too complex a job to be viewed in terms of a simplistic dichotomy between 'hard' and 'soft' policing styles. Community policing – which I understand to mean policing with the active consent and support of the community – is too important a concept to be treated as a slogan. There are bound to be variations in the way the police seek to tackle different types of crime in different areas. There will in my view continue to be circumstances in which it is appropriate – even essential – for police commanders to utilize stop and search operations or to deploy special units such as the SPG, whatever the area concerned, just as there will be occasions where such methods should be avoided. It would be foolish to imagine that it is possible to discern a single blue-print guaranteed to produce successful policing in every area.

5·47   The value of the current debate about policing lies in the fact that it has revealed, or, more accurately, re-stated – for they have always been part of the British policing tradition – three fundamental points:

(i) the importance of policing by consent;

(ii) the need for this approach to policing in all aspects of police work. It is not something which can be put into a separate box labelled 'community relations';

(iii) that keeping law and order is the concern of the whole community, something in which all sections of the community have a responsibility as well as an interest.

I very much hope that the public debate about policing methods stimulated by Phase 2 of the Inquiry will continue after the publication of my Report. Central to the theme of that debate must be the question how these three fundamental points can best be reflected in the policing of today's society. I would hope in the coming months to see this question actively discussed among the Home Office, Chief Officers of Police, Police Authorities and representatives of local communities, especially leaders of the ethnic minority groups.

(1) The Home Beat Officer

5·48   An important issue in this context raised in the Inquiry is the role of the Home Beat Officer. There were clear indications in the evidence I received that the Home Beat Officer is regarded by other policemen as outside the mainstream of operational policing. His place in the operational structure of the police is, therefore, uncertain. These indications are to be found in the evidence of Inspector Scotchford and Police Constable Brown, in the failure to inform Home Beat Officers in advance of Operation 'Swamp', and in the failure of the police command in Brixton on Saturday, 11 April to call the Home Beat Officers to assist in quelling the disorders. The latter error was not, as some have suggested to me, crucial: for I am not convinced that Home Beat Officers could – to borrow a phrase from Mr Hazan – have stemmed the tide of disorder any more successfully than Canute dealt with the tide of the North Sea. But, with their knowledge of local people and local feeling, they could have provided a useful point of contact with the community and of information and advice to senior officers. The view apparently taken of Home Beat Officers by at least some of their police colleagues, which may be summarized in the nickname 'hobby bobbies', must be vigorously rejected. The example which I was myself fortunate to see of Police Constable Brown, the Home Beat Officer of Railton Road, controlling on the evening of 15 July 1981 a highly volatile crowd, enraged by some recent police raids, is itself sufficient to lay the myth of the Home Beat Officer as something other than a serious policeman.

5·49   There is, I suggest, a need for review of the role of the Home Beat Officer (or his equivalent in forces outside the Metropolitan Police), with particular regard to improving his supervision and ensuring his involvement in the mainstream of operational policing. Equally, however, there is a need to provide opportunities for other operational officers to develop their relationship with the community in non-conflict situations. The converse of the Home Beat Officer's lack of involvement in operational matters is the relative lack of opportunity for operational officers to be involved with the community. Of course many are much involved in their spare time – in youth clubs, sports activities, etc. – but this involvement is peripheral to their main police work. There is a danger, as Mr Gibson suggested, that Home Beat Officers become social workers rather than police officers: but there is equally a danger that the operational officer loses sight of his role as a servant of the community who needs to take the community with him in preserving law and order. Both these dangers must be avoided.

(2) Patrolling

5·50   A related issue to be considered is the relative balance of foot and mobile patrols. There is undoubtedly a widespread public feeling that the introduction of technological aids to policing – including the Panda car – while it has certainly enabled the police to respond more quickly to emergency calls, has had the effect of distancing the police from the public. There are no longer the opportunities, which in the early days a system of policing based exclusively on the beat patrolled by policemen on foot provided, for frequent and informal contact between the police and the public. The police must use today's technology, including the motor vehicle, to respond quickly to emergencies. At the same time, I welcome the recognition Chief Officers, including the Commissioner, have already given to satisfying the public demand for the re-introduction of officers on foot patrol. Some recent American research which has been brought to my attention[1] suggests that, while foot patrol does not have a significant effect on the volume of crime, it does reduce people's fear of crime. According to the research, people in areas policed on foot tend to perceive their neighbourhoods generally as more safe. The experience of Brixton confirms that the manner in which people perceive the policing of their area is as important as the reality of that policing. Moreover, it has been suggested in the Inquiry that a more visible permanent presence of police officers in the street would be a more appropriate means of deterring crime than occasional saturation policing operations. This hypothesis is clearly one worth testing by practical police initiative, carefully monitored through appropriate research.

(3) The status of the beat officer

5·51   There is, of course, a dilemma here. Everybody wants more foot patrols, but on the other hand, there are loud objections to anything which might be described as an oppressive police presence. The objection, I find, however, is not to the regular presence of officers policing on foot who are well known to the community but to a sudden influx of officers (particularly of officers unknown to a community) above normal levels. The solution lies, I suggest, in an approach to policing in areas such as Brixton which marries the work of Home Beat and operational police officers, achieving the effective coordination of their activities in a single policing style based on small beats regularly patrolled by officers normally operating on foot. If such an approach to policing is to be achieved successfully, the status of the beat officer will have to be enhanced. He must, in my view, be seen not as occupying the bottom of the police pecking-order (after the CID and specialist units have creamed off the best), but at its apex, in the forefront of the police team. Policing, like medicine, the law and the civil service, is a profession in which the general practitioner is as necessary as the specialist.

1. *The Newark Foot Patrol Experiment.* Published by the Police Foundation, 1909 K Street NW, Washington DC 20006, 1981.

(4) Personnel policies

5.52 A related factor of considerable importance is that police personnel policies must try to avoid a high rate of movement among officers posted to and from sensitive areas in particular. This applies at all levels: the rate of turn-over among senior police officers in 'L' District in the recent past is particularly noticeable and cannot have been of assistance in building up sustained relations with the community or enabling an informed judgement to be made of its needs. More continuity is essential, as is a careful attention to the mix of officers of different age groups in these areas. I have already rejected the notion that young police officers should be barred from serving in inner city districts like Brixton. But there is a need for senior officers to keep under regular review the proportion of young officers in these areas and to ensure that levels of supervision are adequate. I also *recommend* that procedures, which no doubt already exist, for briefing an officer transferred to an inner city area should be strengthened. A few days spent in getting to know the area and in hearing from leading members of the community about its character and needs might be invaluable in assisting an officer, once he is on his own, to respond sensitively yet firmly to the demands which will be put upon him.

(5) The Special Patrol Group

5.53 Where does this leave saturation policing, stop and search operations and units like the Special Patrol Group? They cannot in my view be wholly abandoned: there will continue to be circumstances in which their use is appropriate, even essential. The Special Patrol Group (SPG) was a particular target of criticism in this Inquiry (as at Red Lion Square). It was suggested that the Group should be disbanded, or that it should no longer be used in areas such as Brixton. I do not concur with either of these suggestions. It is in my view essential, given modern policing conditions, for the Metropolitan Police to have a small mobile reserve at its disposal and for this to be capable of deployment on general policing duties in any part of the Metropolitan Police District. Standards of supervision in the Group must, of course, be especially high, and a regular turn-over of officers is essential to prevent too inward-looking and self-conscious an ésprit de corps developing in the Group. I have no doubt that the effect of the changes in the structure and operations of the Group, announced by you, Sir, and the Commissioner on 10 March 1980,[1] are being carefully monitored in order to ensure that these objectives are being achieved. But it is a fair comment that the SPG has become a target of sustained criticism in some quarters not because of its failings, but because of its successes. I share the view that more could be done to make known to the public the purpose and achievements of the Group and I *recommend* that appropriate action be taken to achieve this.

(6) Conclusion

5.54   The important thing, I suggest, is not the imposition of a categorical ban on the use of the SPG or of special operations against crime in sensitive areas such as Brixton. It is that before these necessary tools of policing are used in such areas, there should be proper consultation with the local community. I appreciate of course that secrecy is essential to the success of certain operations and that consultation will not be possible or appropriate in those cases. Neither will consultation always produce an agreed result: in the end it will be necessary for the responsible police commander to take a decision. But the object must be to enable the community to understand fully why the police regard an operation as necessary, and there must be a willingness on the part of the police to listen to community views and to be prepared to modify their plans in the light of them. I set out in the next section of this Report my views on how such consultation might be achieved. For the present, I conclude this discussion of policing methods by *recommending* that, in consultation with their Police Authorities and with local community leaders, Chief Officers of Police should re-examine the methods of policing used, especially in inner city areas, with particular reference to:

(i) the pattern of patrolling, especially the mix of foot and mobile patrols;

(ii) the role of Home Beat Officers, with particular emphasis on

1. House of Commons Official Report, Vol. 980. Written Answers, cols. 395–6.

ways in which they can be integrated more effectively into the
mainstream of operational policing;

(iii) the provision of opportunities for operational officers to get to
know the community they are policing;

(iv) ways of ensuring greater continuity and a balanced spread of
officers of different ages in more sensitive inner city areas, and
of ensuring that officers transferred to work in such areas are
given an effective introduction to the problems and needs of
those areas.

I know that many of these matters are already under consideration by the Commissioner and other Chief Officers of Police. I
hope that the discussion of them in the preceding paragraphs will be
of value in this vital process.

H · Consultation and accountability

(1) General observations

5·55   I am satisfied that police forces generally recognize the importance of good relations with the community they police. Most if
not all forces express this recognition through the establishment of
specialized Community Relations or Community Involvement
Branches. The larger forces in particular usually also appoint
Community Liaison Officers at Divisional level with special responsibility for fostering good relations with the community. The
emphasis of most of these Branches is on securing good liaison with
the community and involving the police in the community. A
number of those who have given evidence to the Inquiry, however,
see these Branches as a mere public relations exercise. They instance
the reluctance, amounting in many cases to outright refusal, of
senior police officers to discuss operational questions with leaders of
the local community.

5·56   I need not rehearse my views on this topic, which are to be
found in Part IV, paragraphs 4·72–4·74. Community involvement
in the policy and operations of policing is perfectly feasible without
undermining the independence of the police or destroying the
secrecy of those operations against crime which have to be kept
secret. There will, of course, be some operational aspects of policing
– such as criminal investigations and security matters – which it

146

would be wrong to make the subject of consultation and discussion with representatives of the community. But the evidence I have received convinces me that the boundary between what may, and what must not, be disclosed has not been subjected to a close enough scrutiny. Until very recently, operational decisions were held by senior police officers to be inappropriate topics for community consultation. However, Assistant Commissioner Gibson has, as I have already mentioned, recognized the propriety of consultation and discussion, which would cover not only policy but the planning stage of some operational decisions. If a rift is not to develop between the police and the public as a whole (not just the members of the ethnic minority communities), it is in my view essential that a means be devised of enabling the community to be heard not only in the development of policing policy but in the planning of many, though not all, operations against crime.

5.57   Consultation and accountability are the mechanisms – in part administrative, and in part legal – upon which we rely to ensure that the police in their policies and operations keep in touch with, and are responsible to, the community they police. Under the existing law consultation is largely, but not entirely, an administrative matter: accountability has to be statutory. Accountability is, I have no doubt, the key to successful consultation and socially responsive policing. Exclusive reliance on 'voluntary' consultative machinery will not do, as the Brixton story illustrates. It must be backed by law.

5.58   Accountability is the constitutional mechanism which can provide the backing: for it renders the police answerable for what they do. Thereby it prevents them from slipping into an enclosed fortress of inward thinking and social isolation which would in the long term result in a siege mentality – the police in their fortress (happy as long as it is secure) and the rest of us outside, unhappy, uncertain and insecure (for we do not know what they will do, or how they will do it). English law does make the police accountable: but the law is imperfect in one respect, the importance of which has become apparent in the course of my Inquiry. There is no satisfactory or sufficient link between accountability and consultation. The link is tenuous to vanishing point in the Metropolitan Police District; more effective, but insufficiently developed, in the police areas outside London.

(2) Outside London

5·59   The legal position is to be found in Sections 1–5 and Section 12 of the Police Act 1964. A Police Authority is established by law for every police area. The Police Authority is a committee whose membership consists of local councillors and magistrates drawn from the police area for which it is responsible. It is the duty of the committee as Police Authority 'to secure the maintenance of an adequate and efficient police force for the area'. It has, subject to the approval of the Secretary of State, the power to appoint the Chief Constable and the duty to determine 'the number of persons in each rank' in the force for which it is responsible. It has the responsibility, subject to Regulations made by the Secretary of State, to provide and maintain the vehicles and equipment required in its area for police purposes. The Chief Constable is obliged to submit yearly 'a general report' in writing to the Police Authority and, by Section 12(2) of the Act,

shall, whenever so required by the Police Authority, submit . . . a report in writing on such matters as may be specified in the requirement.

5·60   The Chief Constable does, however, have a right to refer any such requirement to the Secretary of State if it appears to him that compliance would lead to a report which 'would contain information which in the public interest ought not to be disclosed, or is not needed for the discharge of the functions of the Police Authority': and, if he does so, the requirement is of no effect unless confirmed by the Secretary of State.

5·61   Subject, therefore, to the central supervision and direction of the Secretary of State, for which provision is made in Part II of the Act, police forces for areas outside the Metropolitan Police District are accountable to a committee drawn from the community they police. The committee has wide powers and can use them, in consultation with the Chief Constable, to ensure that liaison committees, or other means for local consultation, are set up within the area. The link between accountability and consultation can therefore easily be forged – even though there be no obligation upon the committee, as Police Authority, to establish consultative machinery.

5·62   The evidence which I have received is that, on the whole, the statutory machinery works well. But it is also clear that many Police Authorities are somewhat uncertain of themselves and do not always exercise the firmness which the statute envisages as necessary to the discharge of their awesome responsibility to secure the maintenance of an adequate and efficient police force for their respective areas. I would remind them that Section 4(1) of the Act makes it their *duty* to exercise for that purpose the powers conferred on them by the Act; and there can be no doubt that in our society a police force which does not consult locally will fail to be efficient. There is, of course, nothing in the statutory provisions to impair or undermine police independence. But they do emphasize that the relevant principle is not independence exclusive of responsibility but independence and accountability.

5·63　Three imperfections, it has been suggested to me, are to be found in this system of accountability. First, the presence of magistrates on police committees. Secondly, the limits on the power of the committees in relation to the appointment and promotion of senior officers. Thirdly, the absence of a duty, as distinct from a power, of the committee to require the establishment of consultative machinery at police divisional or sub-divisional level. I have not the evidence, nor in any event would I think it within my terms of reference, to comment on the first two matters. There is, however, some force in the third point.

5·64　On the basis of the evidence I have received, the urgent need is, however, not a change in the formal powers (or duties) of Police Authorities, but that Chief Officers of Police should take Authorities fully into their confidence, and should cooperate with Police Authorities in establishing consultative arrangements in their police areas. I note that, in delivering the annual James Smart Lecture in Edinburgh a year ago, you yourself observed, Sir, that 'it has become increasingly desirable that Police Authorities should see themselves not just as providers of resources but as a means whereby the Chief Constable can give account of his policing policy to the democratically elected representatives of the community and, in turn, they can express to him the views of the community on these policies'. It is necessary also that Chief Officers of Police should accept and, indeed, encourage Police Authorities in their adoption of this role. A police force, the Chief Officer of which does not discuss, or allow his senior officers to discuss, matters of policing policy openly and responsively with the community, is certain in the long run to find its efficiency undermined by loss of community support.

5·65   Police committees would, I believe, act more vigorously and with greater confidence if, instead of a power of uncertain extent (as under the existing law) there was imposed upon them (and upon Chief Officers of Police) a statutory duty to cooperate in the establishment and supervision of liaison committees, or other consultative machinery, at police divisional and sub-divisional levels. But, since the *power*, though not the duty, to take these steps does exist in the law, the urgent need is, as I have already emphasized, that cooperation should begin *now*.

5·66   While, therefore, I do recommend legislation to impose the duty discussed in the foregoing paragraphs, I *recommend* even more strongly that Police Authorities and Chief Officers of Police should act at once, if they have not already, under their existing statutory powers. But, I believe, the imposition by statute of a duty would ensure that the task was accomplished. I so *recommend*.

(3) London

5·67   In the Metropolitan Police District the statutory provision for accountability is different. Very briefly, the Secretary of State is the Police Authority and the Commissioner, who is appointed by the Sovereign, is the Chief Officer of Police.[1] In effect, therefore, the Metropolitan Police are nationally, but not locally, accountable. No committee drawn from the community they police has the right to receive a report, or to make a requirement. The opportunity to ignore local (but not national) opinion exists for the Metropolitan Police; and he would be a bold man (bolder than I) who would affirm that the existence of an opportunity does not breed the temptation to make use of it, especially when it is convenient or saves trouble.

5·68   It was, therefore, no surprise to hear from the Lambeth Borough Council and other represented parties the submission that it was no longer appropriate for you, Sir, to be the Police Authority for the Metropolis and that this responsibility should be passed to

1. Section 62 and Schedule 8 of the 1964 Act and Sections 1, 4 and 5 of the Metropolitan Police Act 1829 (as later amended).

the Greater London Council (GLC). The object of such a change would be to allow London rate-payers a say in policing similar to that at present enjoyed by rate-payers in other areas. I recognize the force of the demand for people in London to have a greater say in the manner in which their community is policed. I do not, however, recommend any change in the law substituting some other body for the Secretary of State as Police Authority. You, Sir, are of course accountable to Parliament. There are good reasons for the national accountability of the Metropolitan Police. I do not believe that Parliament would wish to see ultimate responsibility for the policing of the nation's capital transferred from a senior Minister responsible to it and put in the hands of a local body, however important.

5·69   There is nevertheless a need for the development of more effective channels of communication between the Metropolitan Police and the various communities it serves. The urgent need, in my view, is at the level of the London Borough. I am aware that in recent years the Commissioner has been seeking to develop, with your encouragement, liaison machinery at Borough level on a voluntary basis. The difficulty about voluntary arrangements – as the experience of Brixton amply demonstrates – is that they depend too much on the willingness of all parties to participate: if, for any reason, a local difficulty prompts one of the parties to withdraw, the arrangement collapses and discussion stops. I therefore *recommend* that a statutory framework be developed to require local consulta-tion between the Metropolitan Police and the community at Borough or Police District level. The members of local consultative or liaison committees might, I suggest, include appropriate police officers, elected Councillors and perhaps other community repre-sentatives: the precise composition of the committees, the arrange-ments for appointment of their members, their powers and respon-sibilities will, however, require further consideration and, no doubt, consultation with those concerned. It is, nevertheless, essen-tial that any such local machinery should not simply be a statutory talking-shop but should have real powers, which I envisage might include a role in the complaints procedure (Part VII, paragraphs 7·25–27, infra) and in the inspection of detention areas within police stations (see also Part VII, paragraphs 7·7–10, infra), and the right to make representations to a Metropolitan Police Advisory Board, if, as I suggest in the next paragraph, such a Board were to be established. Any aspect of police policy should be regarded as a matter appropriate for discussion through the machinery, including operational questions other than those which, in the view of the Commander of the District, must remain confidential.

5·70   There is, I suggest, a case also for the establishment of an Advisory Board or other consultative arrangement between the Home Office, the Commissioner and the London Boroughs at force level, i.e. covering the Metropolis as a whole. I think the possibility should be studied. But, whether or not such an arrangement is deemed advisable, the Borough is in my view the critical area where a statutory framework is necessary.

(4) Conclusion

5·71   I have emphasized the responsibility resting on Chief Officers of Police to take the community into their confidence in the development of policing policies, and on the Home Office and HM Inspectorate of Constabulary to encourage Chief Officers to put their problems and policies on the table for discussion with the community. I *recommend* the establishment of statutory liaison committees, or other appropriate consultative machinery. At the same time, I stress the responsibility resting on community leaders to respond constructively to the opportunities to influence policing which such machinery would provide. As Assistant Commissioner Gibson rightly pointed out in evidence, mutual trust and goodwill must be established. Community representatives must seek to appreciate the difficulties (and dilemmas) of the police, and to avoid extravagant language or ill-informed criticism. If, as I believe to be essential, a relationship of mutual trust and respect is to be fostered between local communities and the police, both sides will have to be prepared to give and take and to work positively to establish and maintain such a relationship.

I · Police handling of disorder

5·72 'However good relations between the police and a local community may be, disorder may still occur. The police must be equipped and trained to deal with this effectively and firmly wherever it may break out. In responding swiftly to disorder, the police deserve and must receive the full support of the community. The analysis of the disorder in Brixton in Parts III and IV of this Report, and experience of the handling of disorder elsewhere, underline in particular the need for:

 (i) means of ensuring that available police units are rapidly reinforced in the event of disorder by sufficient, properly trained and equipped officers. Effective reinforcement arrangements both within and between police forces are particularly important, because the traditional British approach to handling disorder requires, if it is to be effective, the presence of large numbers of officers;

 (ii) increased training of officers, at both junior and command levels, in the handling of disorder. I have recommended earlier the adoption of common minimum standards and programmes for such training (paragraph 5·30, supra);

(iii) more effective protective equipment for officers – including better helmets, flame-proof clothing and, perhaps, lighter shields;

(iv) vehicles for transporting police officers which have some form of protection against missiles;

 (v) improved arrangements for communication between officers involved in handling disorder and their operational commanders;

(vi) a review of police tactics for the handling of disorders.

5·73 The disorders in Brixton reveal a possible danger that the use of protective shields carried by officers can serve to attract missiles from a crowd and encourage officers to adopt a largely defensive posture, with the result that lines of police officers behind shields effectively become 'Aunt Sallies' for the crowd to aim at. There may be scope for the adoption by the police of a more positive, interventionist role in quelling disorder in order to speed dispersal and reduce casualties. There is also clearly a need for the development of techniques by the police to meet the threat of the petrol bomb, and for a re-affirmation of the importance of avoiding the use of police dogs in dispersing a disorderly crowd. And there may be benefit in studying ways in which community leaders and police officers can cooperate in tense situations to help defuse them. (This would be a suitable topic for study and action by statutory liaison committees, if they be established, as I recommend.)

5.74 I deal with these matters very shortly because I am aware that each of them is already under review. At your instruction, for example, a Working Party of senior police officers and Home Office officials has recently examined the protective equipment available to the police. Changes are no doubt needed if the police are to be able to cope successfully with disorder on the scale the country has recently experienced. At the same time, while the improvement now in hand in the ability of the police to deal with disorder must be completed, there should, I suggest, be no change in the basic approach of the British police to policing public disorder. It would be tragic if attempts, central to the thrust of my Report, to bring the police and the public closer together, were to be accompanied by changes in the manner of policing disorder which served only to distance the police further from the public. I am glad to note that most Chief Officers of Police agree that it is vital that the traditional appearance and role of the British police officer is preserved, as far as possible, in the public order role of the police as in other aspects of their duties. I recognize the importance, and necessity, of your decision that such equipment as water cannon, CS gas, and plastic bullets should be available in reserve to police forces: however, such equipment should not, I suggest, be used except in a grave emergency – that is, in circumstances in which there is a real apprehension of loss of life – and then only on the authority of the Chief Officer of Police himself. I so *recommend*.

J · Conclusion

5.75 The approach to policing I have sought to suggest in Parts IV and V of the Report is not necessary merely as a response to the presence of ethnic minority groups in our cities: it would, in my view, be necessary as a response to modern social developments even without the presence of such groups. The ethnic minority leaders from whom I have heard evidence in the Inquiry are not asking for special treatment or for a different standard or quality of policing from that which is provided for the rest of the community. As learned Counsel appearing for the Council for Community Relations in Lambeth put the matter in his closing address in Phase 2 of the Inquiry:

If there be any persons – and there may be – who believe that crimes should go unpunished because they are committed by persons of a particular shade of skin, the Council are not of their number. If there are any who believe that some of the violence to person and property which accompanied the Brixton disturbances were the legitimate self-expression of an oppressed minority, the Council do not share those beliefs.

That view was echoed by other parties represented in the Inquiry, including Mr Wilton Hill in his closing address on behalf of the Brixton Neighbourhood Community Association, the Brixton Domino and Social Club and the Melting Pot Foundation, three important black organizations in Brixton. 'Our position,' he said, 'is that we do not in any way condone breaches of the law. As a matter of fact, my clients tend to view black crime more severely than other members in the community, because we feel that black people, by committing crime, tend to let down the side.'

5.76 Nor would it be right to allow differing standards to apply in the application of the law. The law is the law. It extends to all and it must be applied firmly and fairly. But it must also be applied sensitively: and the existence of the discretion, which the law has always recognized as possessed by the police, enables them to police with sensitivity as well as firmly and fairly. To quote the Chief Constable of the Greater Manchester Police in his written evidence to me:

A commonly held view in the police service is that the police should merely enforce the law without concessions to any sections of the community. Fundamentally, this is not an unfair stance, but in reality it is much too simplistic. When any groups of people with different aspirations and cultural backgrounds adopt a style of living apparently at variance with the norm, it is clearly just not good enough for the police to aver that all must be treated alike. It is right that the integrity of the law should be preserved but the means to achieve this can be different. In short, therefore, it is patently obvious that when various social pressures and tensions exist within any particular community, it is imperative that police officers on duty in the area adopt a sensible and sensitive approach. This is not to say that they must negate their basic duty under the law or act otherwise than totally impartially, for it would surely be folly to expect the police to employ double standards of law enforcement to placate or stifle the protests of unreasonable activists or to show undue favour to racial minorities.

5·77   I have no doubt that many of the points I have made in this Part of my Report are already under discussion between Chief Officers of Police, Police Authorities and the Home Office. There are, of course, bound to be variations in approach between police forces. What I am anxious to see develop is a programme of action designed overall to re-affirm the position of the police as a respected part of the whole community, responsible to it, dependent on it and receiving its active support. The need for an imaginative, dynamic attempt to tackle the tremendously difficult issues currently facing the police, an attempt which requires the cooperation of Parliament, the Home Office, Chief Officers of Police, the police representative organizations, Police Authorities and local communities, is clear. I hope that the recommendations I have made will help to provide an agenda for a continuing dialogue between the police and the public about the nature of policing in today's society – a dialogue which, if it be based on mutual understanding and respect, will serve to strengthen, without de-humanizing, the forces of law and order.

Part VI
THE DISORDERS AND SOCIAL POLICY

A · General observations

6·1   The police do not create social deprivation, though unimaginative, inflexible policing can make the tensions which deprivation engenders greatly worse. Conversely, while good policing can help diminish tension and avoid disorder, it cannot remove the causes of social stress where these are to be found, as those in Brixton and elsewhere are, deeply embedded in fundamental economic and social conditions. Any attempt to resolve the circumstances from which the disorders of this year sprang cannot therefore be limited to recommendations about policing but must embrace the wider social context in which policing is carried out.

6·2   This inevitably raises questions which some may regard as going not only beyond the proper scope of an Inquiry under Section 32 of the Police Act 1964, but beyond the competence of a judge. It is not, however, possible to exclude the social problem from the Inquiry: the policing problem is only one aspect – although admittedly a vital one – of the social problem, and cannot be properly understood in isolation. You yourself, Sir, recognized this when responding to questions in the House of Commons following your statement on the establishment of the Inquiry.[1] An unavoidable limitation lies in the fact that, as a judge conducting a quasi-judicial Inquiry, it would be inappropriate for me to make specific suggestions or proposals in the field of Government financial or economic policy. I do, however, consider it part of my duty to comment on those aspects of policy which touch on the social problem which is inextricably bound up with the matters referred to me under Section 32. One consequence of the limitation is that I refrain from discussing that part of the written evidence, submitted to me by the Lambeth Borough Council and others, which was intensely critical

1. House of Commons Official Report, 13 April 1981, cols. 21–31.

of the restrictions imposed by the Government on local authority expenditure and of the effect of recent changes in the Rate Support Grant system. While I do not consider it proper to express a view on these matters, I do feel it necessary to mention them in view of the weight of attention they received in the written evidence.

6·3   In July of this year there was published the report by the House of Commons Home Affairs Committee on racial disadvantage to which I have already referred.[2] It is a masterly review and deserves not only the close consideration which I am sure it will receive, but also a positive response, from Government.

6·4   It may nevertheless be helpful to you, Sir, and your colleagues, as you consider the twin problems of the inner city and of racial disadvantage, if I identify and set out a number of themes and issues which the weight of evidence to the Inquiry suggests merit urgent attention. I also offer for your consideration my own thoughts and proposals as to priorities and needs. If they lack detail, it is because I am conscious that I am moving into a field which it is for others, not me, to cultivate.

B · The inner city

6·5   The failure of the many attempts over the last three decades to tackle the problem of inner city decline successfully is striking. The proportion of national resources devoted to resolving the problem is clearly an important consideration; but it is noticeable that large sums have been spent to little apparent effect. The underlying national economic decline is no doubt one important reason – not just as a factor limiting the total of resources which Governments have felt able to spend on the inner city, but in reducing the effectiveness of what has been spent.

6·6   There may, however, be other factors. One of these, I suggest, is the lack of an effective coordinated approach to tackling inner city problems. Looking at the examples of Brixton and Merseyside, conflicting policies and priorities – as between central

1. *Racial Disadvantage*, 5th Report from the Home Affairs Committee, House of Commons, HC 424–1, HMSO.

and local government or between the different layers of local government – appear to have been a frequent source of confusion and reduced drive. I am aware that there have been a number of attempts to overcome this problem: the Inner City Partnerships are the latest in a series of attempts to secure a better coordinated and directed approach. It is, however, apparent from Brixton that the Partnerships – valuable though they are – are not the complete answer, at least in anything but the very longest term; and they only cover, of course, a limited number of areas of deprivation. While I have neither the evidence nor the experience to recommend any reorganization of local government, I do note the apparent existence of a striking problem of coordination – not only in London, Merseyside and the other great conurbations, but also in an area like Bristol where a sizeable city is located in a largely rural county. In the result, there emerges a lack of coordinated policy for the control of services which must be central to any strategy designed to tackle the related, but not identical problems of inner city decline and minority disadvantage. I conclude that much could be done to achieve a better coordinated and directed attack on inner city problems, and I *recommend* action to achieve it. One of the objects of such an approach must be to ensure that the resources which the Government judges the nation is able to devote to the inner city are effectively spent.

6·7   The approach to inner city problems also appears to have been deficient in two other important respects. First, local communities should be more fully involved in the decisions which affect them. A 'top down' approach to regeneration does not seem to have worked. Local communities must be fully and effectively involved in planning, in the provision of local services, and in the management and financing of specific projects. I should like to see, for example, greater consultation than exists at present between local authorities and community groups about the allocation of resources to projects under the Urban Programme. I have been impressed by the quality of the evidence I have received from community groups in Brixton and elsewhere, and by the enthusiasm evident, for example, among tenants' groups and ethnic minority leaders during the visits I paid to housing estates in Brixton and to community groups in Handsworth. Inner city areas are not human deserts: they possess a wealth of voluntary effort and goodwill. It would be wise to put this human capital to good use.

6·8   A second deficiency appears to lie in the extent to which the private sector – banks, building societies and other business companies – is involved in the process of inner city regeneration. The private sector is not, in my view, an alternative to adequate public sector involvement: both are needed. I have, however, noted with interest the evidence contained in a paper submitted to me on behalf of the Railton Road Youth and Community Centre which describes the work of The Local Initiative Support Corporation (an offshoot of the Ford Foundation) in developing community programmes in decaying central city neighbourhoods in the United States of America. It may be that here, as in other respects, American experience has valuable insights to offer.

6·9   I have emphasized in Part V of the Report the importance of involving the community in aspects of policing; but there must also be effective police involvement in the community. Provision must be made for the police to be involved, like other important social agencies, in community re-development and planning. The social functions of the police – in handling the problems of the elderly, domestic disputes and juveniles, for example – are important to the social health of a community. The police derive from these functions a wealth of experience which can be of great value to those involved in planning and in determining social provision. It is vital that the law and order implications of environmental and social planning should be taken into account at the earliest stage. A good illustration of the need for this is provided by the Stockwell Park Estate, whose garages, pedestrian walkways and numerous small recesses, though a planner's dream, have provided opportunities and escape routes for thieves and vandals, and create major policing problems. The involvement of the Metropolitan Police in the Lambeth Inner City Partnership machinery is a welcome recognition of the important contribution the police can make in this sphere. There is also, I suggest, scope for much closer liaison between the police, the other local services – the probation service, social services and housing departments – and the voluntary sector such as the churches. In London both the Commissioner and Commander Adams – it is apparent from the evidence – long ago recognized the value of such links and have tried, in different ways and at different levels, to strengthen them. Law and order is a community problem and the police are not the only service which has a function in this area, although they carry, admittedly, the leading responsibility.

C · The ethnic minorities

6·10   The problems associated with inner city decline are not to be equated with those of ethnic minority groups: the former go much wider. Conversely, while many in the ethnic minority communities stand to benefit from a concerted strategy to regenerate the inner cities, such a strategy will not solve all of their problems. By no means all ethnic minority members live in inner city areas, and the particular problems they face must be recognized wherever they are. As the analysis in Part II of the Report and the recent Select Committee report on Racial Disadvantage show, the ethnic minorities tend both to suffer the same problems as the rest of society, but more severely, and to have certain special problems of their own. A more ready recognition of the ethnic minority need within the more general problem of deprivation is required, as is a clear and co-ordinated response to it from government at all levels.

6·11   I have identified in Part II some of the respects in which black people (mainly West Indian) in Brixton are particularly disadvantaged. Other minority groups – such as the Asian and Muslim communities – have somewhat different problems. The character of these problems has been extensively surveyed in the Select Committee report. I do not wish, nor am I equipped, to duplicate that report. There are, however, three areas of disadvantage which emerge from the evidence I have received as particularly important:

 (i) Housing;
 (ii) Education;
 and
 (iii) Employment.

Each of these are matters which deeply affect the lives of all people living in inner city areas but particularly those who come

161

from ethnic minority groups. In the next paragraphs, I discuss both some of the general aspects of these specific problems and their particular implications for the ethnic minorities.

(1) Housing

6·12   Many of our inner cities suffer from acute housing stress. Much has clearly been done, by central and local government and their agencies, to try to alleviate this stress. Severe problems continue, however, as the statistics on housing in Brixton (Part II, paragraphs 2·6–2·9, supra) indicate.

6·13   Resources are obviously a crucial part of the answer. But large scale clearance and re-development may be too costly to contemplate in present economic circumstances. Moreover there are many indications – of which the example of Stockwell Park Estate is one – that large scale re-development, although still perhaps appropriate in certain circumstances, is not necessarily always a successful solution. Over the last ten to fifteen years, there has been increasing recognition of the value of *rehabilitation*. It has proved preferable – and, perhaps, financially less exacting – to improve existing properties, so avoiding the total upheaval and destruction of existing communites. The streets off Railton Road[1] are a tribute to what this approach, and individual effort, can together achieve. Housing associations and private groups have an important part to play in this process. There is, I suggest, a strong case for a more purposeful attempt to draw in important housing agencies, such as building societies and housing associations, as part of a coordinated approach with the public sector to rehabilitating housing in inner city areas.

6·14   Housing provision – whether through public, mixed or private sector schemes – is a specific example of an area in which *community participation* is needed. I was impressed, for example by the neighbourhood management approach adopted at the Stockwell Park and Tulse Hill Estates. At these estates, management has been devolved by the Housing Departments involved to estate level; it appears more responsive to tenants; and an attempt is being made to draw tenants themselves into the management process and to get

1. See Part II, paragraph 2·5.

them to accept a share in the responsibility for the effective running of the estates. The police are involved together with other agencies in the development of a team response to problems – such as vandalism – on the estate. Local residents, and the local police, have much to contribute not only to management but to re-development. The experience of neighbourhood associations and police could, if drawn upon, avoid some of the planning mistakes which have resulted in housing estates becoming centres of juvenile crime – places where the elderly and the weak go in fear of assault, robbery and theft.

6·15 The matters I have mentioned affect all the community. There is, however, evidence, noted in Part II, that *ethnic minorities* face particular problems in housing. West Indians, for example, seem to rely particularly heavily on public sector housing provision, and to be over-represented, within that sector, in the poorer quality housing. Council housing allocation policies must be seen to be fair. Some Councils – among whom Lambeth Borough Council is certainly one – are well aware of the ethnic minority dimension of their housing policies. Others appear to be less aware. There is a strong case, as the Home Affairs Committee recently noted,[1] for local authorities reviewing their housing policies – particularly their criteria and procedures for the allocation and transfer of council houses – in order to ensure that they do not, wittingly or unwittingly, discriminate against minority groups.

(2) Education

6·16 I have already noted in Part II the evidence of under-achievement among West Indian schoolchildren – which has been examined in depth in the interim report of the Committee of Inquiry into the Education of Children from Ethnic Minority Groups (the Rampton Report)[2] – and of dissatisfaction among West Indian parents about the schooling their children are receiving. The report of the Home Affairs Committee suggests that while there is not the same evidence of under-achievement among Asian pupils – if anything they appear to do better than their white compatriots – the

1. Op. cit., paragraphs 87–88.
2. Cmnd 8273, HMSO, 1981.

dissatisfaction felt about schooling is not limited to West Indians but is also felt by many Asian people.

6·17   The main criticisms of educational provision, chiefly voiced by West Indian parents, during the Inquiry were:

   (i) a lack of discipline in schools. This partly reflects the different school experience of many West Indian parents, but also other cultural differences;

  (ii) the alleged failure of teachers to motivate West Indian pupils sufficiently. It was suggested that teachers tend to stereotype black pupils as ill-disciplined or unintelligent and accordingly set too low a performance standard for these pupils;

 (iii) lack of sufficient contact between parents and schools;

 (iv) lack of understanding by teachers of the cultural background of black pupils;

and

   (v) failure of the curriculum sufficiently to recognize the value of the distinctive cultural traditions of the various ethnic minorities.

6·18   It is obvious from the evidence I have received, and from my own visit to Tulse Hill School, that much dedicated work is being done – in HM Inspectorate, in local education authorities and in individual schools – to try to adapt our education system to meet the special needs of the ethnic minorities. The Inner London Education Authority, for example, has undertaken much pioneering work in this respect. It is equally clear, however, from the Rampton and the Select Committee reports, that we are still some way from having resolved all the problems. The reconstituted Rampton Committee, now under the chairmanship of Lord Swann, is looking at these problems in the remainder of its remit. In the paragraphs which follow, I set out certain points which I hope will prove of help to the Swann Committee and to the Department of Education and Science (DES) as it considers the Rampton and Select Committee reports.

(a) Under-fives

6·19   The provision of facilities for under-fives is a matter which concerns, at central government level, the DHSS as well as the DES. The need for adequate pre-school provision is particularly marked among ethnic minority children. The need arises among West Indian children partly as a result of the problem of family breakdown to which I have referred in Part II, and partly because of the importance of early tuition in language. Among Asian children, this second reason is the primary source of the need. A greater provision of play groups, nurseries and organized child-minding facilities which can serve all the community is particularly important in places like Brixton if children are to be given the right support at the formative early age. The report of the Rampton Committee contains several important proposals in this respect. I endorse the recommendation of the Select Committee that 'central Government and local authorities take a joint initiative as a matter of the highest priority to ensure that both local authority and voluntary provision for care of the under-fives comes closer to meeting the demand for it in the ethnic minority community in particular'.[1]

(b) Teacher training

6·20   There is a clear need for improved training of teachers in the particular needs, the cultural background, and the expectations of minority group children and parents. Again the Rampton Committee and the Home Affairs Committee reports contain valuable recommendations in this respect, which I do not need to repeat. Teachers must, however, be warned against the danger of a 'reverse racialism' in attributing all the ills of black people to exploitation by white people. A balanced approach, in this, as in much else, is needed.

(c) Language

6·21   While it is right that the curriculum should fully recognize the value of different cultural traditions, I echo the Home Affairs Committee's view that the primary object of schooling must be to prepare all our children, whatever their colour, for life in Britain. It is essential, therefore, that children should leave school able to speak, read and write effectively in the language of British society, i.e. English. This is of the first importance if young black people are

1. Op. cit., paragraph 90.

to have a chance to make their way, and to contribute to the extent they have it in them to do, to British society.

(d) Home/school liaison

6·22   It is apparent from the evidence that the extent of contact between parents and schools varies considerably, but that black parents in particular are often, for whatever reason, apparently hesitant to take a full and active part in the schools. Unless they do so, however, teachers will remain unaware of the way they view the needs of their children and the effectiveness of the school system. I hope that black parents will in future take a more active interest in the education of their children and that teachers will for their part recognize the desirability of taking positive steps to encourage such an interest. Only if parents and schools can be brought closer together will parents appreciate what schools are trying to do for their children and teachers understand the parents' expectations.

6·23   This last point is clearly not solely of relevance to ethnic minority parents: it applies to all. Nevertheless, although I appreciate that some have already, and others are currently, examining the matters which I have mentioned in far greater depth, looking at the issues as a whole I think I can say that the time has come for a Government initiative in ethnic minority education, and particularly in the four respects I have mentioned. A lead is necessary. I endorse the Select Committee's view that a failure to act, now the facts are generally known, will cause widespread disappointment and ultimately unrest among the ethnic minority groups of our society.

6·24   There is another aspect of education relevant to my terms of reference which I wish to mention, that is the question of *police involvement in schools*. The extent of police involvement in schools – through participation in discussion groups, classes on the police, road safety activities, etc. – is already very extensive. I hope that teachers and parents will welcome and encourage this. Obviously there are limits to the proper activities of the police in schools – it would be wholly inappropriate, for example, for police officers routinely to enter school premises in order to question children about suspected offences. Police assistance in the education of children in the fundamentals of an ordered society can, however, be of great value. Indeed, as the pressures on our society grow in intensity, the need for programmes of instruction for all children in the way government works, in the law, and in the duties, as well as the rights, of citizenship, increases.

6·25   I make one final comment which arises from the discussion about employment which immediately follows. Children must be educated in the use of leisure. As time spent in working diminishes, the increased leisure must result not in boredom and idleness but in satisfying activity. Sport, the arts and recreational activity assume a great importance.

(3) Employment

6·26   Unemployment is a problem which faces both white and black people. There is evidence, however – to which I have referred in Part II and which is more fully discussed in the Home Affairs Committee report[1] – that its weight falls disproportionately heavily on black people. Unemployment among black people is no doubt mainly the result of factors which also affect the employment prospects of the white majority. But there are other factors peculiar to the black community, for as the Home Affairs Committee note in paragraph 168 of their report, 'Asians and West Indians continue to be at a substantial disadvantage in employment long after their arrival in Britain and their children may also suffer substantial disadvantage in this respect.' The Select Committee note various possible reasons for this, of which racial discrimination, past and present, is one of the more important.

6·27   There is then a need, in the sphere of employment as in other spheres, for a fuller recognition of the particular problems of the ethnic minorities, and for action to overcome them. Various proposals are made by the Select Committee for remedial action; others have been put to me in evidence from the Commission for Racial Equality (CRE). Not the least important of these in my view are the suggestions, by both the Committee and the CRE, for improving support, including private financial and advisory support, for ethnic minority businesses. The encouragement of black people to secure a real stake in their own community, through business and the professions, is in my view of great importance if future social

1. Op. cit., paragraph 164 ff.

stability is to be secured. It is, I think, unnecessary for me to discuss the measures suggested by the Select Committee and the CRE, for they are already under consideration: but I do urge the necessity for speedy action if we are to avoid the perpetuation in this country of an economically dispossessed black population. A weakness in British society is that there are too few people of West Indian origin in the business, entrepreneurial and professional class.

6·28 Whatever the special employment problems of black people, and of young black people in particular, unemployment remains nevertheless an evil that touches all the community. There can be no doubt that it was a major factor in the complex pattern of conditions which lies at the root of the disorders in Brixton and elsewhere. In a materialistic society, the relative (not by any means – given our social security system – absolute) deprivation it entails is keenly felt, and idleness gives time for resentment and envy to grow. When there is added the natural aggression of youth, and with the media ever-present to relay examples of violence, there arises a devastating and dangerous combination of factors tending to unrest and disorder. The solution, of course, depends on a successful outcome of current economic problems. In the meantime, Government – in the shape of the Department of Employment and the Manpower Services Commission (MSC) – is clearly already doing much to try to alleviate the worst effects of unemployment, particularly among the young. The effectiveness of those programmes, and the broad thrust of economic policy, lie outside the scope of my Inquiry. I therefore simply note the criticisms made to me of the MSC programmes that they do not prepare young people sufficiently well for skilled work, and that they do not cater adequately for ethnic minority needs. Both the nature of the training provision to be made for the young unemployed and the wider economic issues are already the subject of vigorous national debate: it is unnecessary for me to comment on them.

6·29 I do, however, offer one thought for consideration in that debate. The structural causes of unemployment – which include remarkable developments in technology, an effect of which is that leading developed countries are losing the attributes of a labour-intensive economy – are deeper and more complex than the mere existence of the current recession. If this analysis is right, we shall have to face its implications. In order to secure social stability, there will be a long term need to provide useful, gainful employment and suitable educational, recreational and leisure opportunities for young people, especially in the inner city. For instance, it has been suggested to me that young people could be encouraged to participate in projects to clean up and regenerate the inner city. There is attraction in projects which could use the idle labour available in the inner cities to tackle the physical decay which is there so evident. It should not, I suggest, be too difficult to devise satisfactory schemes for such sorts of activities in place of current unemployment and social security programmes.

D · The response to ethnic minority needs

6·30   In the preceding paragraphs, I have discussed three particular areas of deprivation which touch on all who live in our inner cities but have a particularly severe impact on ethnic minority groups. It is essential, as I have earlier suggested, that if alienation among the black community is not to develop, there should be a more ready recognition of the special problems and needs of the ethnic minorities than hitherto. One problem in responding to these needs, noted in the Home Affairs Committee's report, is the lack of precise statistical information about the extent of ethnic minority problems. This raises the question of the *monitoring* of these problems by both central and local government. The issue is one which arouses strong feelings, as the Home Affairs Committee has observed. I concur with the Committee, however, when it comments: '. . . it is self-defeating to admit on the one hand the existence of a national pattern of racial disadvantage and to try however haltingly to shape policies and practices to come to terms with that condition, and on the other hand, to deny oneself the necessary tools to measure its scale and its spread'.[1] I therefore endorse the Select Committee's proposals for improving the extent of the information available about ethnic minority needs, including its call for the inclusion of an ethnic question in the Census and for ethnic monitoring by local authorities of the services they provide.[2]

1. Op. cit., paragraph 9.
2. Op. cit., paragraph 85.

6·31   The Select Committee's report provides ample evidence of failures by both central and local government to give sufficient recognition to the ethnic minority aspects of deprivation. It also provides ample evidence that, although some effort is undoubtedly being made, there is a lack of a sufficiently well-coordinated and directed programme for combating the problem of racial disadvantage. Unless a clear lead is given by Government, in this area as in others, there can be no hope of an effective response. The evidence I have received suggests that the black community in Britain are still hoping for such a lead, although they are cynical about what they see as the previous lack of response from all governments of whatever persuasion. If their hopes are again dashed, there is a real danger that cynicism will turn into open hostility and rejection. This must not be allowed to happen.

6·32   This leads me to the question how far it is right to go in order to meet ethnic minority needs. It is clear from the evidence of ethnic minority deprivation I have received that, if the balance of racial disadvantage is to be redressed, as it must be, positive action is required. I mean by this more than the admirable approach adopted by at least some central and local government agencies at present, which is intended chiefly to persuade the ethnic minorities to take up their share of general social provisions. Important though this is, it is not, in my view, a sufficient answer. Given the special problems of the ethnic minorities, exposed in evidence, justice requires that special programmes should be adopted in areas of acute deprivation. In this respect, the ethnic minorities can be compared with any other group with special needs, such as the elderly, or one-parent families. I recognize the existence of a legitimate and understandable fear on the part of both public and private institutions that programmes which recognize and cater for the special needs of minority groups will stimulate a backlash from the majority. I suspect that this fear, rather than 'institutional racism', is the primary factor inhibiting the necessary development of such programmes. I believe that if the justification for any such special programmes were fully explained, the backlash threat might prove to be over-rated. Nevertheless, it must not be allowed to prevent necessary action. Certainly special programmes for ethnic minority groups should only be instituted where the need for them is clearly

made out. But need must be the criterion, and no other. The principle has already been recognized by Parliament (Sections 35, 37, 38 of the Race Relations Act 1976), and must be made effective.
6·33   As I have already indicated, I do not consider it appropriate to make recommendations about the scale of resources which should be devoted to either inner city or ethnic minority needs. It is for Government and Parliament in the final analysis to judge the relative priority they should be given. There is, however, one particular matter connected with resources on which I do consider it appropriate to comment – *Section 11 of the Local Government Act 1966*. Under this Section, local authorities can be reimbursed by the Home Office for 'special provision in the exercise of any of their functions in consequence of the presence within their areas of substantial numbers of immigrants from the Commonwealth whose language or customs differ from those of the community . . .' Grants, which cover 75 per cent of eligible expenditure, are made only if claimed by the local authority, and only in respect of the employment of staff. The importance of Section 11 lies in the fact that, as the Home Affairs Committee has put it, grants under the Section, currently totalling some £50 million per annum, are the 'only Government finance earmarked directly and exclusively for combating racial disadvantage . . .'[1]
6·34   The defects of Section 11 have been fully chronicled and discussed by the Select Committee: 'There is,' the Committee notes, 'no single aspect of Section 11 payments which has escaped criticism.' The defects include the limitation of the Section to Commonwealth immigrants and the exclusion of voluntary bodies and of non-salary costs from its scope. Other problems arise from the way in which the grants are administered. The Section is currently being considered by the Home Office. I endorse the Select Committee's view that reform of Section 11 must not be long delayed. It was drafted to meet a different and narrower purpose than what is presently required, namely an effective means of providing finance to meet all ethnic minority special needs. A broad approach to Section 11 is necessary; and, when an opportunity occurs, the Section itself should be amended so as to bear more directly on the pattern of today's needs.

1. Op. cit., paragraph 48 ff.

E · Discrimination

6·35   All the evidence I have received, both on the subject of racial disadvantage and more generally, suggests that racialism and discrimination against black people – often hidden, sometimes unconscious – remain a major source of social tension and conflict. I have discussed in Part V ways in which the danger of racially discriminatory behaviour by police officers might be avoided. You, yourself, Sir, are considering the relevant aspects of the law in your review of the Public Order Act 1936 and related legislation. Changes in legislation are not, however, I suggest, the principal requirement if discrimination is to be rooted out, as it must be. What is required is a clear determination to enforce the existing law, and a positive effort by all in responsible positions to give a lead on the matter. Eliminating discrimination will undoubtedly take time. It would be disastrous, however, if there were to be any wider doubt than at present exists among the ethnic minorities about the will of Government, employers, trade union leaders and others in positions of authority to see this through. There are already signs among some black youths, despairing of an end to white discrimination, of a disturbing trend towards a total rejection of white society and the development of black separatist philosophies. Pride in being black is one thing, but black racialism is no more acceptable than white. A vigorous rejection of discriminatory and racialist views is as important among black people as among white if social harmony is to be ensured.

F · Community Relations Councils, and the Commission for Racial Equality

(1) Community relations councils

6·36   Local Community Relations Councils (CRCs) are, or should be, at the centre of attempts to foster a harmonious, multi-racial society. The evidence I have received, however, suggests that CRCs are sometimes torn between their role in fostering community relations, which requires them to keep a dialogue going with authority, and the need, equally important in their view, not to lose credibility with the ethnic minority groups. There is a difficult balance to be achieved. While I appreciate the difficulty, there can be no excuse for the failure of some CRCs to recognize that their primary duty is to foster harmony, not to undermine it. The evidence I have received included the following criticisms of CRCs:

(i) some appear to have a tendency to act purely as a special interest lobby for minority groups;
(ii) some are too readily influenced by extreme political views;
(iii) many too often expect to be the sole channel of contact and communication between the ethnic minorities and official bodies.

It would be outside my terms of reference to inquire closely into these matters and I therefore make no finding or comment on them, save that the evidence suggests that it is time that the role of CRCs was reviewed.

(2) The Commission for Racial Equality

6·37 In view of the Home Affairs Committee's examination of the CRE, I simply mention here one suggestion affecting the Commission which was made in evidence given by Assistant Commissioner Gibson of the Metropolitan Police to the Inquiry. This was that the CRE should be prepared to intervene more positively as mediator in a local situation, like that which arose in Brixton, where a breakdown of relations between the police and the community has occurred. I appreciate that this may present difficulties for the Commission. But the suggestion that the CRE should adopt more of a trouble-shooting role in such circumstances seems to have merit, and I commend it for consideration by the Commission and the Select Committee.

G · The media

6·38 I have discussed so far the social context of the disorders, with particular reference to the inner city environment, unemployment and ethnic minority needs and problems. There is, however, one other factor which I identified in Part II as figuring in the causation of the disorders following upon Brixton – the 'copy-cat' element. This raises the question of the role of the media, particularly the broadcasting media, in circumstances of major social disorder such as those experienced in Brixton and elsewhere.

6·39   The question raises difficult issues. On the one hand, there is the need to preserve the independence of the media from political interference and to recognize their important role in informing the public of current events. On the other, the media are under a duty to achieve balance and must be prepared themselves to recognize the possible social effects of their reporting. Is there not a Gresham's law of the press to be feared and resisted – that the bad drives out the good? The media, particularly the broadcasting media, do in my view bear a responsibility for the escalation of the disorders (including the looting) in Brixton on Saturday 11 April and for their continuation the following day, and for the imitative element in the later disorders elsewhere. I do not propose legislation to curb the freedom of the media to report such events: that would introduce a potential evil far greater than the one which has to be remedied. The duty to publish (and 'be damned') is real, and never to be forgotten. But I do urge editors and producers to accept that there is also a responsibility to assess the likely impact on events of their own reporting of them, to ensure balance in the coverage of disorder, and at all times to bear in mind that rioters, and others, in their exhibition of violence respond alarmingly to what they see (wrongly, but understandably) as the encouraging presence of the TV camera and the reporter.

6·40   There is one other matter concerning the media which I would mention: that is, the criticism made frequently to me that the media do not report fairly the problems of areas such as Brixton. I have heard this criticism made by both residents and by others, including police officers. There is a feeling that the media always focus on problems and difficulties, and ignore the good. It is believed by many that the bad name which some areas have got is itself a factor in preventing their regeneration and improvement. The criticism of lack of fairness is also made about the reporting of matters involving members of the black community, and the police. I cannot say whether the criticism is well founded or not. But I hope that over the next few months, it will be considered by those concerned.

6·41   To conclude, the matters to which I have referred deserve, if they have not already received, the fullest consideration by the Press Council, the Board of Governors of the BBC, the Independent Broadcasting Authority and newspaper editors.

H · Conclusion

6·42   In this Part of my Report, I have sought to draw attention to some matters in respect of which urgent action is required if the social conditions which underlay the disorders in Brixton and elsewhere are to be corrected. I have emphasized in particular:

   (i) the need for a concerted, better co-ordinated attack on the problems of the inner city;

  (ii) recognition of and action to meet the special problems and needs of the ethnic minorities, based on an acceptance of them as full and equal members of a culturally diverse society;

 (iii) the need to involve not just black people, but all the community, both nationally and locally, in a better directed response to these problems. It is essential that people are encouraged to secure a stake in, feel a pride in, and have a sense of responsibility for their own area;

 (iv) the role of the police as essential participants in any effective response by the community;

  (v) the need for newspaper editors, television and radio producers, and journalists to give continuous attention to the social implications of their awesome power to influence the minds, the attitudes and the behaviour, not only of the reading, viewing and listening public, but also of those whose unlawful behaviour they report.

These themes must be kept constantly in view if the social context in which the police operate is not to continue to breed the conditions of future disorder.

Part VII
LAW REFORM

7·1   Some proposals for the reform of the law have been made to me in the written and oral evidence presented to the Inquiry. They include:

(a) stricter control of the 'stop and search' power of the police;

(b) repeal not merely of the 'sus' law (which in fact was repealed after the Phase 1 hearings), but of the offence (vehicle interference) which was enacted in partial substitution for it;

(c) provision for independent inspection and supervision of the detention and interrogation procedures operating inside police stations;

(d) radical reform of the system for handling complaints against the police;

(e) local accountability of the Metropolitan Police, and a strengthening of local consultation machinery, not only in London but throughout the country;

(f) a new Riot Act.

A · Stop and search

7·2   The power is, I am convinced, necessary to combat street crime. The formulation to be found in Section 66 of the Metropolitan Police Act 1839, i.e. that 'a constable may . . . stop, search, and detain . . . any person who may be reasonably suspected of having or conveying in any manner anything stolen or unlawfully obtained', is sound in that the power may be exercised only if there be reasonable grounds for suspicion. (It has been adopted in a number of local Acts applying to inner city areas outside London.)

7·3   The problem, of course, is how to enforce the safeguard of reasonable suspicion. If it be clear that the test of reasonableness is objective and that the exercise of the power is subject to review by the courts, no reform of principle is required. The state of the law is,

however, a mess, as the Royal Commission on Criminal Procedure[1]
has shown: see paragraph 3·12 of its Report. I respectfully agree
with the Commission's proposals for the rationalization of the law
and for certain additional safeguards: see paragraphs 3·20–3·28 of
the Philips Report.

B · The 'sus' law, and its repeal

7·4   The Criminal Attempts Act 1981 received the Royal Assent
on 27 July. Section 8 of the Act repeals so much of Section 4 of the
Vagrancy Act 1824 as applies to suspected persons and reputed
thieves loitering with intent to commit an arrestable offence. Section 9 creates a new summary offence, i.e. vehicle interference: it is
an offence 'to interfere' (word not defined) with a motor vehicle with
the intention of theft of the vehicle, or of theft of anything carried in
it, or of taking and driving it away without consent. A provision,
which, juristically, is an anomaly and may prove difficult for the
courts, is to be found in sub-section (2):

 . . . and, if it is shown that a person accused of an offence under this
section intended that one of those offences should be committed, it is
immaterial that it cannot be shown which it was.

Sub-section (4) confers on a constable the power to arrest without
warrant anyone who is, or whom he with reasonable cause suspects
to be, guilty of an offence under the Section. Loitering with intent to
snatch a bag or pick a pocket (the other mischief which the 'sus' law
was used to prevent) is no longer an offence unless the facts establish
an attempted theft.

7·5   It is too soon to undertake a review, or to recommend reform,
of the new offence. The new legislation must be seen in action first.
A risk does exist that the new offence may prove no better than that
which it replaces. But it does have the advantage over the Vagrancy
Act offence of being drafted in terms appropriate to the mischief it is
intended to prevent, namely car theft. This must be a step forward
from a law which was designed to protect Cobbett and his contem-

---

1. Cmnd 8092, HMSO (the Philips Report), 1981.

poraries as they moved in their rural rides around the countryside of England in the aftermath of the Napoleonic wars.

7·6   I *recommend*, therefore, no more at this stage than that a careful watch be kept on how the law develops.

C · Lay police station visitors

7·7   I know, Sir, that you have under review the whole problem of safeguards for suspected persons under interrogation or detention in police stations. I am also aware that reform (which I recommend) of the procedure for handling complaints against the police will itself constitute an additional safeguard. But more, I believe, requires to be done.

7·8   In its Report on deaths in police custody, the House of Commons Home Affairs Committee recommended:

that Chief Officers of Police should arrange for sufficient random checks to be carried out to ensure that the procedures are properly observed.[1]

I respectfully endorse the recommendations, but would add that, as a safeguard, it would be greatly strengthened if it were backed by a statutory system of independent inspection and supervision of interrogation procedures and detention in police stations.

7·9   It was suggested to me, as I understand it was also suggested to the Committee of Inquiry into the Interrogation Procedures in Northern Ireland,[2] that a system comparable to the Boards of Visitors of HM Prisons might be established. I am not persuaded by the arguments adduced by the Northern Ireland Committee that such a system would be unlikely to have any significant effect. On the contrary, I suggest that, if it were known that members of police committees (outside London) and of the statutory liaison (or consultative) committees, whose establishment I recommend both in London and outside, had the right to visit police stations at any time and the duty to report upon what they observed, the effect would be salutary.

7·10   I do not pretend to offer a blue-print for legislation. It should

1. Third Report of the Committee, Session 1979–80, HC 632, paragraph 13.
2. Cmnd 7497, HMSO, 1979.

not, however, be difficult to include amongst the provisions which I recommend for the strengthening of local accountability and consultation, provision for random checks by persons other than police officers on the interrogation and detention of suspects in the police station. I so *recommend*.

D · Reform of the police complaints procedure

7·11   No matter how effective recruitment methods, training, and supervision and monitoring procedures are, instances of alleged police misbehaviour will arise about which the public wish to complain. It is essential therefore that a procedure for considering complaints is established which carries the confidence of both the public and the police. I have heard much evidence during the Inquiry, including my visits to the West Midlands and Liverpool, to the effect that the existing complaints procedure does not command the confidence of the public.

(1) The existing procedure

7·12   The existing procedure is based on two statutes. Section 49 of the Police Act 1964 requires the police to record any complaint received against a police officer forthwith and to investigate it. The Chief Officer of Police may, and shall if so directed by the Secretary of State, request the Chief Officer of Police for any other police area to provide an officer to carry out the investigation, and that Chief Officer must comply with the request. Under the Police (Discipline) Regulations 1977, a complaint which suggests that the officer concerned may have offended against the Regulations must be investigated by an officer of the rank of Superintendent or above (in the Metropolitan Police, of the rank of Chief Inspector or above) and from a different Division of the force. When the investigating officer has completed his report, it is considered by the Deputy Chief Constable of the force. Unless he is satisfied that no criminal offence is involved, Section 49(3) requires him to send the report of the investigation to the Director of Public Prosecutions. The Director recommends whether or not the officer should be charged with a criminal offence. After the Director has made his decision, the

Deputy Chief Constable decides whether the circumstances are such as to justify bringing a disciplinary charge against the officer in accordance with the Police (Discipline) Regulations.

7·13   The Police Act 1976 requires the Deputy Chief Constable to send to the Police Complaints Board a copy of the investigating officer's report together with a memorandum stating whether he has decided to bring disciplinary proceedings against the officer concerned and, if he has not, his reasons for not doing so. If the Board disagree with a decision of the Deputy Chief Constable not to bring proceedings, they may recommend that disciplinary charges be brought. Where such charges are preferred and are denied by the officer, the Board can direct that they be heard by a tribunal of two members of the Board in addition to the Chief Officer, instead of by the Chief Officer sitting alone. In the last resort, the Board may direct that charges be brought, and in these circumstances, if they are denied by the officer, they must be heard by a tribunal. Finally, under Section 50 of the Police Act 1964, every Police Authority in carrying out its duty with regard to the maintenance of an adequate and efficient police force, and HM Inspectors of Constabulary in carrying out their duties with respect to the efficiency of any police force, are required to keep themselves informed as to the manner in which complaints are dealt with by the Chief Officer.

(2) The evidence received by the Inquiry

7·14   The passing of the Police Act 1976 – which was accompanied by considerable public debate – was intended to introduce a convincing independent element into the consideration of complaints against police officers of a disciplinary nature (the Director of Public Prosecutions [DPP] already providing an independent element in criminal cases). The clear indication from the evidence I have received, however, is that the Act has failed to stem criticism of the existing procedure. I have indeed received considerable evidence of a lack of confidence in the impartiality and fairness of the procedure, not only among members of the ethnic minority communities but generally. It has been suggested to me that because of this lack of confidence, there is a widespread reluctance to lodge complaints. People, it is said, do not believe that their complaint will be investigated or judged fairly, and they are worried that if they do complain they will subsequently be subjected to harassment and intimidation by the police. The chief criticisms centre on the fact that under the present system the police investigate themselves.

7·15   This is by no means the only source of complaint, however. Many criticize the formality of the system, particularly in relation to the consideration of relatively minor complaints. They see it as slow and cumbersome, and as operating in a way which is likely to widen the rift between the complainant and the police, rather than to reconcile them. A third main criticism is that the existing procedure focuses on complaints made against individual officers: it does not cater for the situation in which the complaint is directed against Force policy rather than individual misconduct. Alongside these main criticisms, I have heard a number of others of a lesser but still important nature, such as, for example, the allegedly unhelpful nature of letters sent to complainants informing them of the outcome of their complaint, and the working of the so-called 'double jeopardy' rule. One of the most important implications of this rule is that it generally prevents the Deputy Chief Constable or the Police Complaints Board from taking action for an offence against the Discipline Code if the evidence has been found by the DPP to be insufficient for a criminal charge.

(3) Findings on the evidence

7·16   Some people, including many police officers, respond to these criticisms with the suggestion that the present system is on the whole satisfactory: the defect lies in lack of knowledge among the public about the safeguards the existing procedure contains, which better publicity should remedy. There is undoubtedly some truth in the suggestion that the public is insufficiently aware of the checks and balances in the present system. But more publicity alone will not establish the necessary degree of public confidence in the complaints procedure. I find that the existing system is more concerned with the determination of disciplinary matters concerning individual police officers than with satisfying the complainant. It lacks a sufficiently convincing independent element, particularly in the consideration of the more serious complaints. In relation to less serious matters, it is over-formal and rigid. It is also expensive, wasteful of the time and resources of the police, the Director of Public Prosecutions and the Police Complaints Board. There is insufficient discussion of policy matters arising from complaints. In short, if a proper level of public confidence in the system is to be obtained, changes in the system, as well as more publicity about it, are necessary.

7·17   The objective of a complaints procedure which is fair both to the complainant and to the accused police officer is as easy to state as it is difficult to achieve. One constant problem – which no procedural change can overcome – is that many complaints resolve themselves into a conflict of evidence between the complainant and the accused police officer, with no third element present which could objectively resolve the conflict. This situation is, of course, common in a court of law; but whereas few feel aggrieved if a defendant is acquitted because of lack of evidence, someone complaining against the police is unlikely to accept a similar 'not guilty' verdict – particularly as it is very often conveyed in a letter describing the complaint as being dismissed because it has been found 'unsubstantiated'. A 'not proven' verdict has never satisfied anyone south of the Anglo/Scottish border. The point is important because it suggests that, whatever the system for considering complaints, none is going to satisfy all complainants or silence all critics. But this should not prevent attempts to find a system which is generally accepted as fair and impartial. The weight of evidence I have received suggests that the present system is not so accepted among significant sections of the population.

(4) Possible reforms

(a) Independent investigation of complaints

7·18   How might a satisfactory level of public confidence in the system be achieved? It is clear to me that many will continue to criticize it so long as the investigation of complaints remains in police hands. These people argue that the fact that the police investigate the police means that the investigation, if not obviously rigged in favour of the accused police officer, is likely to be generally favourable to him. Only the establishment of an independent service for the investigation of all complaints against the police will silence their criticisms.

7·19   The difficulties in the way of establishing an independent investigatory system are largely, though not exclusively, practical. They include such matters as how the investigation service would be staffed, who would appoint its members, what their powers would be, to whom they would be accountable and what their relationship would be with HM Inspectorate of Constabulary, the Director of Public Prosecutions and the Police Complaints Board. There is also the difficult question of the relationship of any independent investigation service with Chief Officers of Police, who would remain responsible for discipline within their forces. Resources are an additional important consideration. The total cost to the Police Service of the existing system of complaints investigation ˉwas estimated in 1980–81 at about £9 million a year. An independent service of investigation is unlikely to be less expensive than the present system and might well be more. Compensating savings on police expenditure would probably be hard to find. The annual cost of an independent team to investigate only the 150–300 most serious cases a year (as recommended in the Triennial Review Report of the Police Complaints Board[1]) has been estimated at about an additional £1 million.

7·20   There is a further most important factor, which is sometimes overlooked. In their Triennial Review Report, the Police Complaints Board expressed themselves satisfied that 'in the vast majority of cases which come before them, a thorough and fair investigation has been made by the police into the complainant's allegations . . .'[2] The Board is uniquely placed to judge the quality of police investigations and its findings on this matter must be given considerable weight. I conclude that the decision whether to establish a new procedure for the independent investigation of complaints must rest on a judgement whether the gain in public confidence which would ensue outweighs the resource and financial costs involved.

7·21   My own view is that if public confidence in the complaints

---

1. Police Complaints Board, *Triennial Review Report, 1980*, Cmnd 7966, HMSO.
2. Ibid., paragraph 62.

procedure is to be achieved any solution falling short of a system of independent investigation available for all complaints (other than the frivolous) which are not withdrawn, is unlikely to be successful. Any such system should include a 'conciliation process' (paragraphs 7·24–26, infra).

7·22 Should the balance of advantage be felt to fall otherwise, however, so that the conclusion reached is that practical considerations rule out more radical change, a package of more limited measures could help to improve public confidence and to remedy some of the defects in the existing system. Such a package might, I suggest, include the introduction of a 'non-police' supervisor as recommended by the Plowden Working Party (infra) but with a greater involvement in the investigation than envisaged in their report, and the establishment of a conciliation process for minor complaints.

(b) The lay supervisor

7·23 The Police Complaints Board in their Triennial Review Report (supra) recommended an independent service for the investigation of serious complaints, i.e. complaints of serious injury or, I would add, of corruption. The Working Party set up by you, Sir, under Lord Plowden to consider the Board's proposal rejected it.[1] I would respectfully agree with their rejection. If an independent service is to be set up, it should be along the lines of the radical proposal I have already considered, and which I favour: i.e. available for all complaints which are not withdrawn or resolved by the conciliation process (which I recommend, infra). The Working Party, however, did recommend an extension of existing arrangements under which investigating officers may be drawn from another police force by the appointment of a non-police supervisor to oversee the investigation of the most serious complaints. If the radical proposal is not thought practicable, I endorse this recommendation, subject to its strengthening in two important respects. First, Deputy Chief Constables should be placed under an obligation to appoint an officer from another force to investigate all complaints of a serious nature rather than having discretion in the

1. Cmnd 8193, HMSO, 1981, paragraph 18–20.

matter; this could be achieved by you, Sir, issuing an administrative direction under Section 49 (1) of the Police Act 1964. Secondly, the independent supervisor – who should, I suggest, be the Chairman of the Police Complaints Board or his nominated representative – should be involved in the investigation process. He should be treated as a member of the investigating team: that is, he should keep regularly in touch with the progress of the investigation and should be able to offer guidance and to influence its conduct. He must not be treated as an irrelevant fifth wheel on the investigation coach.

(c) Conciliation

7·24   An attempt should be made to explore ways of increasing the element of conciliation in the handling of minor complaints, that is, all those which do not raise any question of criminal proceedings and which do not, when viewed initially, seem likely to result in proceedings under the Police Discipline Code. Many people do not want to make a formal complaint with all that it entails, but they do want to register a grievance and to receive some sort of apology or explanation. An officer of Inspector rank could be nominated in every police station, with the duty of receiving all complaints and, before recording them, of seeking to conciliate the complainant. Something of this sort is already done on an informal basis, but what is required is a procedure by law under which, if both the police officer complained of and the complainant agree, the conciliation process is substituted for the statutory 'recording' of the complaint. The complaint would be considered by a senior police officer (possibly sitting with a lay person). It would be open to him (or the two of them) to seek conciliation by explanation or apology or in any other way, including the withdrawal of the complaint, which proved acceptable. The process would be conciliation, not arbitration. It would have to be clear that, if a solution by conciliation proved impossible, the complainant retained the right to require the complaint to be recorded and investigated, in which event no reference would be allowed by law to be made in subsequent proceedings to what was said and done in the unsuccessful conciliation attempt.

7·25   Police Authorities, local consultative or liaison committees (see paragraphs 5·55–71, supra) and Citizens Advice Bureaux I envisage as having a role to play. A complainant should be able to lodge his complaint at a police station or with any of these bodies, who would pass them on to the police. These bodies could also maintain a list of persons ready to assist in the conciliation process by sitting with the senior police officer.

7·26   An effective conciliation procedure might be one way of reducing the rigidity and formality of the existing complaints procedure. There are other steps which might also be taken. The requirement to refer all criminal cases to the DPP is, I think, excessive and burdensome. I concur with the recommendation in the Police Complaints Board's Triennial Review Report that minor criminal complaints should no longer be referred to the Director: such complaints would of course continue to be referred to the Board. This would require legislation. I would also urge more flexibility in the administrative guidance which helps to underpin the so-called 'double jeopardy' rule. I doubt whether it can ever have been intended that the effect of this rule should be to reduce the possibility of effective redress in cases where, notwithstanding the decision not to prosecute, disciplinary proceedings appear to be appropriate.

(d) Complaints other than those against individual officers

7·27   Complaints which involve policing policy or administration must be given an opportunity for an airing and appropriate consideration. In this respect, Police Authorities might be encouraged to be more active in discharging their responsibilities under Section 50 of the 1964 Act. The way in which Authorities currently discharge their responsibility under this Section appears to vary considerably. Police Authorities might, for example, require the Chief Officer of Police to produce an analysis for them on a regular basis of all complaints made and of the type of circumstances in which complaints have been generated. It ought to become obvious from such an analysis what areas of police activity are particularly productive of complaints. Alternatively, all complaints which raise policy matters, and are not directed against the behaviour of an individual police officer, might be considered by a committee of the Authority. In London, the local consultative or liaison committees, which I recommend, could be given a role in this field. Outside London,

HM Inspectors of Constabulary could specifically discuss complaints with Authorities during their annual inspection of forces.

(5) Conclusion

7·28   Each of the changes I have mentioned would, I suggest, be a useful modification of the existing complaints procedure: taken together, they would represent a significant strengthening of existing arrangements. Each requires, I acknowledge, further consideration and study before it can be implemented. This must not be allowed to inhibit necessary change. A complaints procedure which is generally acknowledged to be fair and impartial – to the public and to the accused police officer – is essential if the police are to enjoy the degree of public support they must have in order to discharge their onerous and necessary task. If public confidence in the complaints procedure is to be secured, the early introduction of an independent element in the investigation of complaints and the establishment of a conciliation process are vital. I so *recommend*.

Postscript

7·29   Since writing the foregoing paragraphs, I have had my attention drawn to interesting developments in this field in Canada and Australia. In Ontario the Government has this year introduced a Bill to establish 'a project to improve methods of processing complaints by members of the public against police officers' of the Toronto Metropolitan Force. It would establish an independent system, while making provision for the 'informal resolution' of complaints. In Australia the Government has introduced the Complaints (Australian Federal Police) Bill 1981, which makes provision for investigation in some cases by the Commonwealth Ombudsman and for the establishment of a disciplinary tribunal, whose President will be a Judge. The Toronto proposal appears to me to merit serious consideration as a possible model for reform of our procedure.

E · Consultation and accountability

7·30   My recommendations are to be found in paragraphs 5·55–71, supra.

F · A new Riot Act?

7·31   The Commissioner of the Metropolitan Police, through his Counsel, submitted, in effect, that a new Riot Act is now needed. He proposed a new statutory offence, punishable summarily: namely, failing to disperse after a public warning. He was supported by Counsel to the Inquiry in his closing address. It was suggested that the present law needs strengthening in two respects:

(1) the power of arrest in a situation of public disorder;
(2) the absence from the criminal law of any offence appropriate to riot conditions which poses no evidential or other obstacles in the way of swift justice.

Existing powers of arrest are said to be insufficient to support the 'snatch squad' technique of dispersing a disorderly crowd: and Section 5 of the Public Order Act 1936, which makes it a summary offence to behave in a threatening way conducive to breaches of the peace in a public place, is said not to be adequate to meet the problem of disorder, which often renders it impossible for the police, whose primary task is to quell the disorder, to prove that the accused was himself acting in a threatening way.

7·32   The Riot Act 1714 (in its draconian way) met, it is said, both needs. Passed for 'preventing tumultuous and riotous assemblies and for the more speedy and effectual punishing of the rioters', it achieved its two purposes by making it an offence punishable by death to fail to disperse after a public warning by a Magistrate. It authorized officers of the law to seize and apprehend those who, after the statutory time limit of one hour from the warning had expired, 'riotously and tumultuously' continued together.

7·33   The Act was repealed as obsolete in 1967.[1] Nobody suggests its draconian penalty should be revived. But the principle that it should be an offence to fail to go away from the disturbance, i.e. to 'disperse', after a public warning should, it is submitted, form the basis of a new offence punishable summarily.

7·34   I disagree: and for these reasons. First, the law does provide ample support for the power of arrest. Secondly, Section 5 of the Public Order Act 1936 appears to work well enough in practice, and

1. Criminal Law Act, 1967.

is correct in principle in that it requires the prosecution to prove positive acts of criminal behaviour by the accused. Thirdly, there are very real difficulties in incorporating a public warning given in the din of turmoil as a necessary ingredient of the offence. I now consider these three reasons.

(1) Power of arrest

7·35   There is at common law a power of arrest (significantly the only common law power of arrest to survive the march of legislation), which is exercisable where a breach of the peace has been committed, or is reasonably apprehended, and there are reasonable grounds for apprehending its continuance or immediate renewal.[1] There is also a power of arrest without warrant vested in a constable who reasonably suspects anyone of committing an offence under Section 5 of the Public Order Act 1936.[2] Further, the common law also recognizes a power, and in so doing imposes a duty, upon the police to take reasonable steps, short of arrest, e.g. by moving people on or dispersing a crowd, to prevent or quell disorder – though the extent of this power has given rise to a degree of uncertainty in the case law: see, for example, Humphries v. Connor (1864) 17 Ir. CLR 1, Beatty v. Gillbanks (1882) 15 Cox CC 138, Wise v. Dunning (1902) 1 KB 167, Duncan v. Jones (1936) 1 KB 218.

7·36   I am not persuaded by anything I have heard that these powers are insufficient. When they are considered together with the statutory powers of arrest (general, as in Section 2, Criminal Law Act 1967, and particular as in Section 1 [3], Prevention of Crime Act 1953 and in Section 137, Highways Act 1980), I find myself persuaded to the contrary, namely that the powers of the police on the street are sufficient for the purpose of dealing with disorder.

(2) The Public Order Act offence

7·37   Section 5 (with Section 5A added by Section 70, Race Relations Act 1976, which makes incitement to racial hatred an offence)

1. For a recent discussion of the power, see R v. Howell (1981) 3 All E R 383.
2. Section 7 (3) of the Act.

can, I appreciate, present evidential difficulties. But they are no greater than one has to accept in a criminal law, the 'golden thread' of which is the presumption of innocence. And the difficulties are slight when compared with those which will inevitably arise with the proposed new statutory offence.

(3) The practical difficulties of a new statutory offence

7·38   The essence of the offence, as I understand it, would be the failure to disperse after the expiry of a time limit from the giving of a public warning by a senior police officer present at the scene of the disturbance. It would, on the proposal put to me, be a defence for the accused to show that he had a reasonable excuse to be where he was.

7·39   I foresee these difficulties. First, it would be contrary to principle to find the offence established, unless it were proved that the accused heard, or ought reasonably to have heard, the warning. But, given the din of public disorder (and Brixton was very noisy), how can one be sure? And what if the accused arrived on the scene after the warning had been given but before the expiry of the time limit? Secondly, the mind boggles at the litigation which could develop over the defence of 'reasonable excuse'. With such problems we could well find ourselves in a forensic confusion as great as that which now prevails when a jury has the complex task of deciding whether the necessary elements of riot (or unlawful assembly) have been proved. Thirdly, is the warning to define the area from which dispersal is to be made? And, if it does, what happens when, as will happen, the crowd moves out of the area but without scattering? These difficulties could well frustrate the intention of the proposed legislation.

7·40   To conclude, therefore, I am not persuaded that the existing law (which, of course, includes not only the Public Order Act but the common law offences of riot, unlawful assembly, and affray as well as a range of statutory offences, e.g. offences against the person, assaulting a police officer in the execution of his duty and wilful obstruction of the highway) is inadequate either in the powers of arrest which it confers or in the number and nature of the offences available for prosecution. Though I favour a modern restatement of the law relating to public disorder, I see no urgent need for piecemeal reform: and in this Report, I am concerned only with what is urgent.

G · 'Selective' ban on processions – Section 3 of the Public Order Act, 1936

7·41   In addition to the foregoing proposals I have considered whether there is a need to strengthen the statutory powers to control marches, processions, and demonstrations which are likely to stir up racial hatred. The question does not directly arise in respect of the Brixton disorders, which arose not from any march or demonstration but from police action sparking off a crowd reaction. But I have received evidence, notably about the Southall disturbances, which suggests strongly that the existing law, which is said not to allow 'selective' banning of marches, and under which, for example, the National Front may choose racially sensitive areas in which to march and enjoy, as they march, the protection of the police, undermines the confidence of the ethnic minorities in the impartiality of the police. (See Part II, paragraph 2·26.)

7·42   The existing law is in Section 3 of the Public Order Act 1936. If a Chief Officer has reasonable ground for apprehending 'serious public disorder', he may impose such conditions as appear to him necessary for the preservation of public order: sub-section (1). In practice, the most common of the conditions imposed are as to timing and route. I do not think it would be lawful for him to impose conditions, the practical effect of which would be to ban the march or procession. For instance, he could not impose a 'condition' prohibiting the march from entering Brixton: the power is to impose conditions, not to prohibit processions.

7·43   If a Chief Officer considers that his power to impose conditions will not enable him to prevent 'serious public disorder', he is under a duty to apply to the district council concerned for an order prohibiting for a period not exceeding 3 months 'the holding of all public processions or of any class of public procession' in the district or any part of it; and the council may, with the consent of the Secretary of State, make an order: sub-section (2). Somewhat different provision is made for the London police, but the principle is the same. The ultimate power is, therefore, with the Secretary of State: but he can act only on application. An important feature of the power to prohibit is that it may apply to a class of procession, specified in the order. In other words, a ban limited to a class of procession is permitted by law.

7·44   In the Green Paper *Review of the Public Order Act 1936 and Related Legislation*[1] presented to Parliament by you, Sir, and the Secretary of State for Scotland in April 1980, the power to control processions conferred by Section 3 of the Act is reviewed and some tentative suggestions made for reform of the law. They include:

    (*a*) a national requirement of advance notice to the police of an intended procession (paragraph 72);
and
    (*b*) a less stringent public order test for imposing conditions or banning processions (paragraph 45).

7·45   First, in my Report on the Red Lion Square Disorders, I expressed the view that the need for advance notice to the police had not been established. I think subsequent events have shown that the need does exist – though the procession urgently called without notice in protest against some sudden, unforeseen, event must be protected (if not by law, at least by the exercise of the discretion not to prosecute).

7·46   Secondly, I think the test of *'serious'* public disorder is too stringent (if it has any meaning, which I doubt). I would merely delete 'serious' and leave the test as one of 'reasonable grounds for apprehending that the procession may occasion public disorder'.

7·47   But there remains the difficult question: ought the power to prohibit some, without having to prohibit all, processions be extended to include the power to prohibit *one* specified procession? I appreciate the political and constitutional sensitivity of the issues raised. It would be better, if it be possible, to avoid them by a bolder use of the power to prohibit a specified class of procession (which the Section already provides) than appears hitherto to have been the practice. As a matter of law, I would think it possible to specify a

1. Cmnd 7891.
2. Cmnd 5919, HMSO, 1975, paragraph 128.

class of procession which, because it was likely to stir up racial hatred, was a sufficient threat to public order to justify a class prohibition. But, as a matter of practice, I can foresee drafting difficulties in formulating the class.

7·48 If the conclusion is reached that it is not possible to ban 'racist' marches or processions in racially sensitive areas by the use of the existing law because of the practical difficulties of specifying a class, I see no reason why the Public Order Act should not be amended so as to empower the district council, with the consent of the Secretary of State and upon an application originating from the appropriate Chief Officer of Police, to prohibit one specified march. The safeguard would have to be that the Chief Officer, the council and the Secretary of State had reasonable grounds for believing that the march or procession was a threat to public order as being likely to stir up racial hatred. The safeguard should be so drafted as to make possible judicial review of the decision.

7·49 Accordingly I *recommend* that the Public Order Act be amended:

(1) to include a requirement of advance notice of a procession to the police;
(2) by deletion of 'serious' from the public order test.

I would recommend an amendment to enable one specified march to be banned, only if it were to be considered impracticable to make use of the existing power to ban a class of procession.

Part VIII
SUMMARY OF FINDINGS
AND RECOMMENDATIONS

Part I · Introduction

8·1   The problem of policing a deprived, multi-racial area like Brixton cannot be considered without reference to the social environment in which the policing occurs (paragraphs 1·2–1·7).

Part II · Social Conditions

8·2   In its appearance and amenities Brixton, in the central part of the London Borough of Lambeth, shares many of the features of other decaying inner city areas (paragraphs 2·1–2·5).

8·3   The Borough suffers from very serious housing problems (paragraphs 2·6–2·9), and a lack of sufficient leisure and recreational facilities (paragraphs 2·10–2·11).

8·4   The population of the area, which is declining, tends to be relatively young, working class and transient. There is a marked incidence of social problems. Some 36 per cent of the population of Brixton are black: the percentage is higher among young people (paragraphs 2·12–2·15).

8·5   The black community in Brixton faces similar problems to those facing the white community, but more severe. The family, education, unemployment and discrimination are particular areas of difficulty (paragraphs 2·16–2·22). As a result, young black people may feel a particular sense of frustration and deprivation. Spending much of their lives on the street, they are there bound to come into contact with criminals and with the police (paragraph 2·23).

8·6   While differences undoubtedly exist between Brixton and other areas which have experienced disorder this year, the similarities are more striking (paragraphs 2·24–2·30).

8·7   The social conditions in Brixton do not provide an excuse for disorder. But the disorders cannot be fully understood unless they are seen in the context of complex political, social and economic factors which together create a predisposition towards violent protest (paragraphs 2·31–2·38).

Part III · The Disorders

Friday, 10 April

8·8   The disorders followed an incident involving an injured youth. The police officers involved in this incident acted reasonably. The disorder was spontaneous. The decisions taken subsequently by the police were appropriate in the circumstances: but it was unwise to continue Operation 'Swamp '81' on Friday evening and Saturday (paragraphs 3·4–3·27).

Saturday, 11 April

8·9   Many young people, especially many young black people, were spoiling for a row as a result of their frustrations, fancied or real, and of their beliefs as to what had happened on Friday. An incident outside the S & M Car Hire Office, involving two plain-clothes police officers questioning a suspect and subsequently arresting another man, provided the spark. The actions of the two officers concerned were not unlawful: but they lacked discretion and judgement (paragraphs 3·28–3·80).

Sunday, 12 April

8·10   A day of aftermath. The disorders, though less intense than those of Saturday, were serious and more widespread (paragraphs 3·81–3·93).

The nature of the disorders

8·11   On each of the three days, the disorders constituted a riot. They were not premeditated. They began as a spontaneous reaction to what was seen as police harassment: but once they had begun, an element of leadership and direction did emerge; and strangers were observed participating in the disorders. White people, as well as black people, helped to make and distribute petrol bombs on Saturday.

8·12   The disorders were communal disturbances arising from a complex political, social and economic situation, which is not special to Brixton. There was a strong racial element in the disorders; but they were not a race riot. The riots were essentially an outburst of anger and resentment by young black people against the police (paragraph 3·96–3·110).

Part IV · The Police

Police/community relations

8·13   A major cause of the hostility of young blacks towards the police was loss of confidence by significant sections, though not all, of the Lambeth public in the police. The reasons for this loss of confidence included the collapse of the police liaison committee in 1979; 'hard' policing methods which caused offence and apprehension to many; lack of consultation about police operations; distrust of the procedure for investigating complaints against the police; and unlawful and, in particular, racially prejudiced conduct by some police officers (paragraphs 4·1–4·4).

8·14   The dilemma facing the police Commanders in Brixton is as simple to state as it was, and remains, difficult to resolve: how to cope with a rising level of crime – and particularly of street robbery ('mugging') – while retaining the confidence of all sections of the community, especially the ethnic minority groups. The crime problem may not have been 'unique'; but it was serious (paragraphs 4·11–4·15).

8·15   Commander Adams sought to deal with the problem in a number of ways, one of which was the deployment of officers of the Special Patrol Group (SPG) to assist local officers in special operations against crime. However well intended, the operations provoked the hostility of young black people and precipitated a crisis of confidence between the police and certain community leaders. In particular, when combined with other incidents, they led to 'the breakdown of the formal arrangements for liaison between the ethnic minority communities, the local authority and the police (paragraphs 4·16–4·28).

8·16   Following the breakdown of the liaison arrangements, the Lambeth Borough Council appointed a Working Party into Community/Police Relations in the Borough. The Final Report of the Working Party, published in January 1981, succeeded only in worsening community relations with the police, although it reflected attitudes, beliefs and feelings widely prevalent in Lambeth since 1979 (paragraphs 4·29–4·33).

8·17   Moves to re-establish the liaison committee followed the appointment of Commander Fairbairn to 'L' District. But the launching of Operation 'Swamp '81' in the week of 6–11 April 1981, contributed, along with other factors, to increased tension in the streets of Brixton (paragraphs 4·3–4·42).

8·18   Neither the police nor the local leaders can escape responsibility for the breakdown of relationships between the police and the community in Brixton. Both must accept a share of the blame (paragraphs 4·43–4·46).

The main criticisms of the police

8·19   Six main criticisms were made of the police in the course of the Inquiry:

(1) 'racial prejudice';
(2) 'harassment';
(3) 'unimaginative and inflexible policing';
(4) 'over-reaction to the disorders';
(5) 'delay and lack of vigour' (in handling the disorders);
(6) 'failure to act against looting'.

I consider these bearing in mind two principles of policing a free society:

(1) 'consent and balance';
and
(2) 'independence and accountability' (paragraphs 4·47–4·60).

8·20   I find that the direction and policies of the Metropolitan Police are not racist. But racial prejudice does manifest itself occasionally in the behaviour of a few officers on the streets (paragraphs 4·62–4·64).

8·21   Harassment does occur: and in Brixton even one isolated instance of misconduct can foster a whole legion of rumours which rapidly become beliefs firmly held within the community (paragraphs 4·65–4·68).

8·22   The Metropolitan Police at District command level and above do not lack awareness of the need for good community relations. But the police in Lambeth have not succeeded in achieving the degree of public approval and respect necessary for the effective fulfilment of their functions and duties. Attitudes and methods in the senior command of 'L' District had not become sufficiently adjusted to the problems of policing a multi-racial community (paragraphs 4·69–4·80).

8·23   Although there were sometimes instances of misconduct by police officers during the disorders, in general I reject the criticism that the police over-reacted in the handling of them. In particular, I reject the criticisms that the police should have withdrawn on the Saturday, and that the police strategy encircled the crowd so that, being trapped, it turned at bay on the police (paragraphs 4·81–4·89).

8·24   I find that the disorders did reveal weaknesses in the capacity of the police to respond sufficiently firmly to violence in the streets. The weaknesses lay not in failures of strategic conception but in the police's preparedness and ability to execute that conception (paragraphs 4·90–4·94).

8·25   I am satisfied that any delay by the police in stopping the looting on Saturday arose not from any reluctance to do so but from the fact that, because of the limited resources they had available in the early part of the evening, they could not cope with both the disorder and the looting. The police commanders felt that they had to give priority to the former. They were right to do so (paragraphs 4·95–4·96).

8·26   I conclude that, while nothing can excuse the unlawful behaviour of the rioters, both the police and the community leaders must carry some responsibility for the outbreak of disorder. Broadly, however, the police response to the disorders, once they broke out, is to be commended, not criticized (paragraphs 4·97–4·99).

Part V · Policing – Proposals and Recommendations

8·27   There is scope for a more coherent and better directed response by the police to the challenge of policing modern, multi-racial society (paragraphs 5·1–5·5).

Recruitment

8·28   I reject proposals that an annual quota of places in the police should be reserved for coloured minorities and that standards for recruitment might be lowered. Nevertheless vigorous efforts are required to recruit more black people into the police. A possible way forward may lie in the provision of special additional training for would-be black entrants to the police. This would only be effective if coupled with a more purposeful drive to get black applicants to come forward in greater numbers. Other ways of involving black people in the police – such as the cadet scheme and the special constabulary – must also be considered. I *recommend* that the Home Office, with Chief Officers of Police, and in consultation with Police Authorities and representatives of the ethnic minority communities, conduct an urgent study of ways of improving ethnic minority recruitment into the regular police and of involving the ethnic minorities more in police-related activities (paragraphs 5·6–5·13).

8·29   Efforts must be made to avoid racially prejudiced people entering the police service. I *recommend* that the work currently being undertaken in the Metropolitan Police designed to identify scientific ways in which evidence of racial prejudice can be identified should be vigorously pursued with the support of the Home Office, and that the results should in due course be incorporated into the procedures for selecting recruits to all police forces (paragraphs 5·14–5·15).

Training the police

8·30   Improvements in police training are in hand. But there is scope for further improvement. In particular the length of the present period of initial training for recruits is insufficient. I *recommend* that it be increased to a minimum of 6 months. More attention should be given, in an extended curriculum, to training in the prevention, as well as the handling, of disorder, and in an understanding of the cultural backgrounds and the attitudes to be found in our ethnically diverse society (paragraph 5·16–5·23).

8·31   The period spent by a recruit on probation after the initial training course is an essential and integral part of the recruit training process. It should include practical training and supervision in the handling of people in situations of potential conflict such as stops in the street, training provided either through a 'street duties course' or, preferably, through a tutor or parent constable scheme. An officer's period on probation should include a period in a city area where ethnic minorities form a substantial proportion of the population. Probationer constables should not, however, save in an emergency, go out alone on foot patrol in an inner city or any other racially sensitive area (paragraphs 5·24–5·26).

8·32   As for in-service training, courses designed to develop the understanding that good community relations are not merely necessary but essential to good policing should, I *recommend*, be compulsory from time to time in a police officer's career up to and including the rank of Superintendent. Training in the handling of public disorder should be provided for all ranks up to and including Commander (Assistant Chief Constable). The Home Office, together with Chief Officers of Police, should seek to establish common programmes and minimum standards for in-service training in both these areas (paragraphs 5·27–5·30).

8·33   Above all, the central theme in all training must be the need for the police to secure the consent and support of the public if they are successfully to perform their duties (paragraphs 5·31–5·32).

Supervision and monitoring

8·34   Young police officers are an unavoidable, indeed valuable, part of the modern police service. The need is not to remove them from sensitive areas but to ensure that they receive proper guidance and supervision (paragraphs 5·33–5·35).

8·35 As far as supervision is concerned, the role of Inspectors and Sergeants is crucial. I *recommend* that greater attention be given to management training in the supervisory responsibilities of officers of these ranks. Close supervision is particularly important in stop and search type operations (paragraphs 5·36–5·37).

8·36 The continuous monitoring of performance as a check against which policing policy and approach can be judged is equally essential. I reject, however, a proposal made by the Commission for Racial Equality (CRE) as to how this might be improved (paragraphs 5·38–5·40).

Discipline

8·37 I endorse a proposal by the CRE that racially prejudiced or discriminatory behaviour should be included as a specific offence in the Police Discipline Code. I also *recommend* that it should be understood throughout the police that the normal penalty for racially prejudiced behaviour is dismissal (paragraphs 5·41–5·42).

Methods of policing

8·38 I discuss some of the issues raised by the debate about community policing. I find that there will continue to be circumstances in which the use of 'hard' policing methods, including the deployment of the Special Patrol Group, is appropriate, even essential. Nevertheless, I conclude by *recommending* that, in consultation with their Police Authorities and with local community leaders, Chief Officers of Police should re-examine the methods of policing used, especially in inner city areas, with particular reference to:

(1) the pattern of patrolling, especially the mix of foot and mobile patrols;
(2) the role of the Home Beat Officers, with particular emphasis on ways in which they can be integrated more effectively into the mainstream of operational policing;

(3) the provision of opportunities for operational officers to get to know the community they are policing;

(4) ways of ensuring greater continuity and a balanced spread of officers of different ages in more sensitive inner city areas, and of ensuring that officers transferred to work in such areas are given an effective introduction to the problems and needs of those areas (paragraphs 5·44–5·54).

Consultation and accountability

8·39   Community involvement in the policy and operations of policing is perfectly feasible without undermining the independence of the police or destroying the secrecy of those operations against crime which have to be kept secret. There is a need to devise means of enabling such involvement. Outside London, Police Authorities can use their existing powers to set up local consultative or liaison committees. Chief Officers of Police should take Authorities fully into their confidence, and should cooperate with Police Authorities in establishing consultative arrangements in their police areas. I *recommend* that a statutory duty should be imposed on Police Authorities and on Chief Officers of Police to cooperate in the establishment of such consultative arrangements. I also *recommend* that meanwhile Police Authorities and Chief Officers of Police should act at once under their existing powers to set up such arrangements (paragraphs 5·55–5·66).

8·40   In London, I do not recommend any change in the law substituting some other body for the Secretary of State as Police Authority. I do, however, *recommend* that a statutory framework be developed to require local consultation between the Metropolitan Police and the community at Borough or Police District level. The possibility of an Advisory Board or other consultative arrangements between the Home Office, the Commissioner and the London Boroughs at force level should also be studied (paragraphs 5·67–5·71).

Police handling of disorder

8·41 I suggest that the experience of the disorders in Brixton and elsewhere reveals the need for a number of improvements in police arrangements for handling disorder. Many of these are already in hand. I recognize the importance, and necessity, of your decision that such equipment as water cannon, CS gas and plastic bullets should be available in reserve to police forces. I *recommend* that such equipment should not be used except in a grave emergency – that is, in circumstances in which there is a real apprehension of loss of life – and then only on the authority of the Chief Officer of Police himself (paragraphs 5·72–5·74).

Conclusion

8·42 I conclude that the approach to policing I have suggested is not necessary merely as a response to the presence of ethnic minorities in our cities: it would be necessary as a response to modern social developments even without the presence of such groups. Differing standards must not be allowed in the application of the law. But the law must be applied sensitively, as well as firmly (paragraphs 5·75–5·77).

Part VI · The Disorders and Social Policy

8·43 Any attempt to resolve the circumstances from which the disorders of this year sprang cannot be limited to recommendations about policing but must embrace the wider social context in which policing is carried out. As a Judge conducting a quasi-judicial inquiry, it would be inappropriate for me to make specific suggestions or proposals in the fields of Government financial or economic policy. I do, however, consider it part of my duty to comment on those aspects of policy which touch on the social problem which is inextricably bound up with the matters referred to me under Section 32 (paragraphs 6·1–6·4).

The inner city

8·44   The failure of the many attempts over the last three decades to tackle the problem of inner city decline successfully is striking. One of the reasons for this, I suggest, is the lack of an effective co-ordinated approach to tackling inner city problems. I conclude that much could be done to achieve a better coordinated and directed attack on inner city problems, and I *recommend* action to achieve it. I also *recommend* that local communities must be fully and effectively involved in planning, in the provision of local services, and in the management and financing of specific projects. The private sector and the police must also be more effectively involved in the attempt to tackle inner city problems (paragraphs 6·5–6·9).

The ethnic minorities

8·45   I draw attention to three particular areas of need:

(1) housing;
(2) education;
(3) employment (paragraphs 6·10–6·11).

8.46   In a discussion of housing policies, I refer to the increasing recognition of the value of rehabilitation and to the need to involve the community in housing management and development. I also endorse the finding of the Home Affairs Committee of the House of Commons in its Report on Racial Disadvantage that there is a strong case for local authorities reviewing their housing policies in order to ensure that they do not, wittingly or unwittingly, discriminate against minority groups (paragraphs 6·12–6·15).

8.47   I discuss the criticisms of educational provision made during the Inquiry and draw attention to four areas for potential improvement. These are the provision of facilities for under-fives; the training of teachers in the particular needs, the cultural background and the expectations of minority group children and parents; the teaching of English; and the involvement of parents, and of black parents in particular, in the work of the schools. I suggest that the time has come for a Government initiative in ethnic minority education, particularly in the four respects I have mentioned. I also refer to the importance of police involvement in schools, and to the

204

need to educate children in the use of leisure (paragraphs 6·16–6·25).

8·48   Unemployment is a problem which faces both white and black people, but there is evidence that its weight falls disproportionately heavily on black people. The encouragement of black people to secure a real stake in their own community, through business and the professions, is of great importance if future social stability is to be secured. There can be no doubt that unemployment was a major factor in the complex pattern of conditions which lies at the root of the disorders in Brixton and elsewhere. The solution, of course, depends on a successful outcome of current economic problems. But the structural causes of unemployment are deeper and more complex. In order to secure social stability, there will be a long-term need to provide useful, gainful employment and suitable educational, recreational and leisure opportunities for young people, especially in the inner city (paragraphs 6·26–6·29).

The response to ethnic minority needs

8·49   I suggest that if alienation among the black community is not to develop, there should be a more ready recognition of the special problems and needs of the ethnic minorities than hitherto. I endorse the proposals of the Home Affairs Committee for improving the extent of the information available about ethnic minority needs, including the Committee's call for the inclusion of an ethnic question in the Census and for ethnic monitoring by local authorities of the services they provide (paragraph 6·30).

8·50   I suggest that there is a lack of a sufficiently well-coordinated and directed programme for combating the problem of racial disadvantage. It is clear from the evidence of ethnic minority deprivation I have received that, if the balance of racial disadvantage is to be redressed, positive action is required (paragraphs 6·31–6·32).

8·51   I endorse the Home Affairs Committee's view that reform of Section 11 of the Local Government Act 1966 must not be long delayed (paragraphs 6·33–6·34).

Discrimination

8·52   I call for a clear determination to enforce the existing law on racial discrimination, and a positive effort by all in responsible positions to give a lead on the matter (paragraph 6·35).

Community Relations Councils, and the Commission for Racial Equality

8·53   I note the criticism of Community Relations Councils made in evidence to the Inquiry and suggest that the time is right for a review of the role of CRCs (paragraph 6·36).

8·54   I commend for consideration by the Commission for Racial Equality and by the Home Affairs Committee in its current inquiry into the CRE the suggestion made by Assistant Commissioner Gibson of the Metropolitan Police in evidence to the Inquiry that the CRE should be prepared to intervene more positively as mediator in local situations, like that which arose in Brixton, where a breakdown of relations between the police and the community has occurred (paragraph 6·37).

The media

8·55   I discuss questions about the role of the media raised by the disorders. I urge Editors and Producers to accept that they have a responsibility to assess the likely impact on events of their own reporting of them, to ensure balance in the covering of disorder, and at all times to bear in mind that rioters, and others, in their exhibition of violence respond alarmingly to what they see (wrongly, but understandably) as the encouraging presence of the TV camera and the reporter. I suggest that the matters to which I have referred deserve, if they have not already received, the fullest consideration by the Press Council, the Board of Governors of the BBC, the Independent Broadcasting Authority and newspaper editors (paragraphs 6·38–6·41).

Conclusion

8·56   I conclude that the themes I have mentioned in this Part of the Report must be kept constantly in view if the social context in which the police operate is not to continue to breed the conditions of future disorder (paragraph 6·42).

Part VII · Law Reform

8·57   In this Part of the Report, I discuss a number of proposals for the reform of the law made to me in the written and oral evidence presented to the Inquiry (paragraph 7·1).

Stop and search

8·58   I conclude that the power of stop and search is necessary to combat street crime. The state of the law is, however, a mess, as the Royal Commission on Criminal Procedure has shown. I respectfully agree with the Commission's proposals for the rationalization of the law and for certain additional safeguards (paragraphs 7·2–7·3).

The 'sus' law, and its repeal

8·59   I *recommend* that a careful watch be kept on how the Criminal Attempts Act 1981 develops (paragraphs 7·4–7·6).

Lay police station visitors

8·60   I *recommend* provision for random checks by persons other than police officers on the interrogation and detention of suspects in the police station (paragraphs 7·7–7·10).

Reform of the police complaints procedure

8·61   On the basis of the evidence I have received, I find that there is a lack of public confidence in the existing system for considering complaints against the police. I discuss a number of possible reforms of the system and conclude that if public confidence in the complaints procedure is to be secured, the early introduction of an independent element in the investigation of complaints and the establishment of a conciliation process are vital (paragraphs 7·11–7·29).

A new Riot Act?

8·62   I discuss the proposal that a new Riot Act is now needed. I conclude that the existing law is not inadequate and that there is therefore no need for the proposed reform (paragraphs 7·31–7·40).

'Selective' ban on processions – Section 3 of the Public Order Act, 1936

8·63   I *recommend* that the Public Order Act 1936 be amended:

(1) to include a requirement of advance notice of a procession to the police;
(2) by deletion of 'serious' from the public order test.

8·64   I suggest that it should be possible to ban 'racist' marches or processions in racially sensitive areas by the use of the existing power to prohibit a specified class of procession. But, if for practical reasons this proves difficult, I would also *recommend* an amendment to the Act to enable one specified march to be banned (paragraphs 7·41–7·49).

Part IX
CONCLUSION AND
ACKNOWLEDGEMENTS

A · Conclusion

9·1   The evidence which I have received, the effect of which I have outlined in Part II, leaves no doubt in my mind that racial disadvantage is a fact of current British life. It was, I am equally sure, a significant factor in the causation of the Brixton disorders. Urgent action is needed if it is not to become an endemic, ineradicable disease threatening the very survival of our society. It would be unfair to criticize Government for lack of effort. The real question is whether the effort, which is undoubted, has been properly directed. Funding (e.g. grants pursuant to Section 11, Local Government Act 1966, the Urban Programme and the Inner City Partnership schemes) has been made available on a substantial scale. The administrative effort of central and local government has been equally substantial: an illustration is to be found in Lambeth itself where the work done by the Borough Council and central government to relieve racial disadvantage deserves high praise. And, though the Race Relations Act 1976 and the CRE have their critics, they are clear evidence of the will and the commitment of Parliament and government to the cause of racial equality. 'Institutional racism' does not exist in Britain: but racial disadvantage and its nasty associate, racial discrimination, have not yet been eliminated. They poison minds and attitudes: they are, and so long as they remain will continue to be, a potent factor of unrest.

9·2   The role of the police has to be considered against this background. As I have said in Part VI, the police do not create social deprivation or racial disadvantage: they are not responsible for the disadvantages of the ethnic minorities. Yet their role is critical. If their policing is such that it can be seen to be the application to our new society of the traditional principles of British policing, the risk of unrest will diminish and the prospect of approval by all responsible elements in our ethnically diverse society will be the greater. If they neglect consultation and cooperation with the local community, unrest is certain and riot becomes probable.

9·3 A new approach is required. I am satisfied, as Mr Hazan QC submitted in his final speech on behalf of the Metropolitan Police, that it has already begun. But determination and persistence in the formulation and application of the necessary policies will be required. I would add that an equal persistence in striving to the same end is also required of all sections of the responsibly minded public.

9·4 On the social front, I find myself broadly in agreement with the House of Commons Select Committee. The attack on racial disadvantage must be more direct than it has been. It must be coordinated by central government, who with local authorities must ensure that the funds made available are directed to specific areas of racial disadvantage. I have in mind particularly education and employment. A policy of direct coordinated attack on racial disadvantage inevitably means that the ethnic minorities will enjoy for a time a positive discrimination in their favour. But it is a price worth paying if it accelerates the elimination of the unsettling factor of racial disadvantage from the social fabric of the United Kingdom. I believe this task to be even more urgent than the task of establishing on a permanent basis good relations between the ethnic minorities and the police. Good policing will be of no avail, unless we also tackle and eliminate basic flaws in our society. And, if we succeed in eliminating racial prejudice from our society, it will not be difficult to achieve good policing.

9·5 I end with the quotation from President Johnson's address to the nation, which appears at the very beginning of the US Report of the National Advisory Commission on Civil Disorders (1968):

. . . The only genuine, long-range solution for what has happened lies in an attack – mounted at every level – upon the conditions that breed despair and violence. All of us know what those conditions are: ignorance, discrimination, slums, poverty, disease, not enough jobs. We should attack these conditions – not because we are frightened by conflict, but because we are fired by conscience. We should attack them because there is simply no other way to achieve a decent and orderly society in America . . .

These words are as true of Britain today as they have been proved by subsequent events to be true of America.

B · Acknowledgement and thanks

9·6   Finally, I wish to acknowledge, and in doing so to express my gratitude and great appreciation for, all the help I have received in the conduct of the Inquiry and the preparation of the Report. My thanks include all those who submitted evidence to the Inquiry: I was greatly impressed by the quality of much of the evidence I received.

9·7   I have already expressed my appreciation of the assistance given me by those who were instructed on behalf of the represented parties. But I have not yet mentioned the impressive and immensely valuable role of Counsel to the Inquiry. Theirs was a very difficult task calling for adroit and skilful handling of witnesses, a mastery of the voluminous written evidence and the exercise of independent judgement both in advising me and in conducting, on my behalf, the proceedings of the Inquiry. I thank them most sincerely for their great help to me and for the successful discharge of their onerous duty.

9·8   I wish also to place on record my appreciation of the services of the Treasury Solicitor, and to pay a personal tribute to those in his office who handled the business of the Inquiry. The office has acquired an expertise in the work of public inquiries, which is an asset of great value to the nation. This expertise, to which must be added energy, skill and a calm determination to overcome all difficulties almost before they arise, was put unreservedly at my disposal. My thanks are great indeed.

9·9   I leave to the last the expression of my profound respect and gratitude for the services of Philip Mawer, Secretary to the Inquiry and Nicholas Montgomery Pott, the Assistant Secretary. I cannot adequately express my admiration, or the magnitude of the debt I personally owe them, for their great services. They faced many formidable challenges in the organization of the hearings and of the visits which together constituted the proceedings of the Inquiry: they overcame them, and the progress of the Inquiry is the best evidence of their skills and patience. In the preparation of the Report they have exhibited the ability to analyse and master complex and voluminous evidence and to present it lucidly for consideration, which is the mark of a fine civil servant. They were

211

admirably supported by Mr Ted McCormick and Miss Melissa Grant of the Home Office. I offer my most sincere thanks to the whole team.

SCARMAN

P. J. C. MAWER
(Secretary)
30 October 1981

Appendix A
BRIEF HISTORY OF THE INQUIRY

Appointment

1   On 13 April 1981 the Home Secretary (the Rt Hon. William Whitelaw CH, MC, MP) announced in a statement to the House of Commons that he was appointing Lord Scarman to conduct an inquiry under Section 32 of the Police Act 1964 with the following terms of reference:

> . . . to inquire urgently into the serious disorder in Brixton on 10–12 April 1981 and to report, with the power to make recommendations.

The Warrant of Appointment is set out at page 5 of this Report.

Collection of evidence

2   Advertisements were placed in national, local and West Indian newspapers in the week beginning 4 May 1981 announcing that Lord Scarman intended to conduct his Inquiry in two Phases: an examination of the events of 10–12 April and their immediate causes (Phase 1); and an assessment of the underlying reasons for the disturbances, focusing in particular on the policing of multi-racial communities (Phase 2). The advertisements also invited the submission of written evidence to the Inquiry through the Treasury Solicitor in respect of both Phases 1 and 2, and requested those parties wishing to be represented at the Inquiry to apply in writing to the Secretary of the Inquiry.

3   Leaflets giving similar information were distributed to households in the Brixton area and supplies of leaflets were made available to various local community organizations. In addition evidence was specifically invited from a number of Government Departments and organizations and individuals who, it was believed, had a contribution to make to the Inquiry. These included police forces, local authorities and community relations councils in a number of areas outside London with a high ethnic minority population. Details of

the witnesses heard in Phases 1 and 2 and of the written evidence received in Phase 2 are set out in Appendix C.

4   Copies of statements by witnesses called to give oral evidence in Phases 1 and 2 of the Inquiry were circulated to the parties represented, together with a police report on the disturbances and transcriptions of police radio messages. Some sixty-eight written submissions of evidence in respect of Phase 2 were circulated to the parties represented and made available to the press in advance of the Phase 2 hearings. Transmitted television news film of the disturbances was shown to the represented parties at Lambeth Town Hall on 18 June 1981 and recorded police radio messages were played to the represented parties on 2 July 1981. At the conclusion of the Inquiry, one copy of the written submissions made public in Phase 2 of the Inquiry and of the transcripts of the public hearings was deposited in the Public Records Office and another in the Library of the University of London.

Visits

5   As part of the process of informing himself on the issues in the Inquiry, Lord Scarman undertook the following visits:

15 July – Melting Pot Foundation Hostel, Brixton.

16 July – Birmingham and Coventry.

22 July – Railton Road Youth and Community Centre, Brixton.

30 July – Stockwell Park Estate and Tulse Hill Estate, Brixton.

10 August – Wolverhampton and Handsworth.

  1 October – Brixton Police Station.

  1 October – Inner London Probation Service.

  7 October – South London Catholic Caribbean Chaplaincy.

  8 October – Tulse Hill School, Brixton.

14 October – Metropolitan Police Training Centre, Hendon.

16 October – Liverpool.

In addition Counsel for the Inquiry visited Brixton Police Station and three schools in the Brixton area: Priory Park School, Haselrigge Junior School and Dunraven Secondary School.

Immunity

6   In a letter of 16 April 1981, the Attorney General gave the following undertaking:

That any witness who appears before Lord Scarman's Inquiry can be assured that neither his evidence before the Inquiry nor any documents he is required to produce to the Inquiry will be used against him in any subsequent criminal proceedings, except in criminal proceedings in which he may be charged with having given false evidence before the Inquiry or having conspired with or procured others to do so.

Hearings

7   Lord Scarman held a preliminary public hearing in the Assembly Hall, Church House, Great Smith Street, Westminster, on 14 May 1981 at which he outlined various procedural aspects of the Inquiry and considered applications for representation before it. Although there were some attempts locally to mount a boycott of the Inquiry, nineteen applications for representation were made of which eleven were granted.

8   Phase 1 of the Inquiry was held in the Assembly Hall, Lambeth Town Hall, Brixton on twenty days between 15 June and 10 July 1981. Not all the parties to Phase 1 attended from the outset, but Lambeth Borough Council attended from the fourth day's hearing and the Brixton Legal Defence Group and the Rastafarian Collective from the fifth and sixth day's hearings respectively.

9   On the fifteenth day of the Inquiry hearings, 3 July, the Brixton Legal Defence Group notified the Inquiry that application was being made to the High Court for an order to prohibit Lord Scarman from hearing any further evidence or submissions in public or from making public any findings in relation to Phase 1 until the various criminal proceedings pending against the applicants arising from the disorders had been tried. Application was also made to prohibit the Home Secretary from making public any findings in relation to Phase 1 pending conclusion of the criminal proceedings. On 10 July Mr Justice Webster dismissed the application saying that 'it has not been established either that the continuance of the Inquiry in public or that the publication of the report which follows is in either case an act calculated to obstruct or interfere with the due course of justice'.

10   The hearings of the Inquiry continued during the determination of the application. Oral evidence was heard from fifty witnesses. Of these witnesses, twenty-one were police officers, three were journalists, three were members of the emergency services, and twenty-three were residents of the area and/or persons who had witnessed the course of events.

11   Phase 2 of the Inquiry was conducted mainly on the basis of written submissions, but public hearings on this Phase were held in the Hoare Memorial Hall, Church House, for six days between 2 September and 9 September 1981. Evidence was heard from eight witnesses called by the represented parties and the hearings concluded with closing addresses by the representatives of the parties and Counsel for the Inquiry.

12   Under the terms of his Warrant of Appointment, Lord Scarman had discretion to hear evidence in private. He considered it desirable to do so for parts of five days of the hearings in Phase 1 of the Inquiry.

Representation before the Inquiry

13   Counsel for the Inquiry were Mr R. Auld QC, Mr J. G. M. Laws, and Mr L. Crawford, instructed by the Treasury Solicitor. Nine parties were represented in both Phases of the Inquiry.

> The Commissioner of Police of the Metropolis and his Officers
>> Mr J. Hazan QC and Mr L. Marshall of Counsel, instructed by the Solicitor to the Metropolitan Police.
>
> Concern
>> Mr L. Blom-Cooper QC and Mr R. Drabble of Counsel, instructed by Messrs D. J. Freeman & Co.
>
> The Council for Community Relations in Lambeth
>> Mr M. Beloff QC and Mr M. A. Cottle of Counsel, and Mr A. Rose of Messrs Osmond, Gaunt & Rose.
>
> The London Borough of Lambeth
> Mr C. Whybrow of Counsel, instructed by Mr A. J. George of Lambeth Borough Council.

Brixton Neighbourhood Community Association
Brixton Domino and Social Club
The Melting Pot Foundation
    Jointly represented by Mr W. Hill QC (Jamaica) and Mr B.
    Bryan of Counsel, instructed by Messrs Sylvester Small &
    Co.
The Railton Road Youth and Community Centre
    Mr H. J. Simmonds of Messrs Wedlake Bell.
The Rastafarian Collective
    Mr L. Woodley of Counsel, instructed by Messrs Sylvester
    Small & Co.

14   In addition, the Brixton Legal Defence Group was represented at Phase 1 of the Inquiry by Mr R. Narayan and Mrs J. Gibbs
of Counsel, instructed by the Brixton Law Centre. The Commission
for Racial Equality was represented at Phase 2 by Mr S. Sedley and
Mr C. Abel of Counsel, instructed by Messrs Bindman and Part-
ners.

Costs

15   Under Section 32(5) of the Police Act 1964, the Home Secretary may direct that the whole or part of the costs incurred by any
person for the purposes of a local inquiry shall be defrayed out of the
police fund, subject to taxation. The Home Office invited Lord
Scarman to make recommendations to the Home Secretary on the
exercise of this power at the conclusion of the Inquiry.

16   Lord Scarman informed the parties concerned at the preliminary hearing that he intended to recommend to the Home
Secretary that the reasonable costs taxed on the common fund basis
of any party granted leave to be represented be met from the police
fund, except where he considered that the person representing the
party had wasted the time of the Inquiry. He would expect and hope
to be able to give a warning if and when he considered that point was
about to be reached and would not make any adverse recommendation as to costs without giving the party concerned an opportunity to
make representations to him.

17   At the conclusion of the Phase 2 hearings, Lord Scarman
indicated that he would recommend to the Home Secretary that the

reasonable costs of all the represented parties, taxed on the common fund basis, be met from the police fund save that in respect of the Commission for Racial Equality, who had attended only at Phase 2, and the Brixton Legal Defence Group, who had attended only at Phase 1, their costs would be limited to those Phases only.

Appendix B
VISITS

Melting Pot Foundation Hostel, Brixton
– 15 July 1981

Lord Scarman visited the hostel accompanied by Lady Scarman. The hostel normally accommodates ten homeless black girls between the ages of ten and eighteen; some eight girls were present during the visit. In informal discussions with the girls it was said that black and white schoolchildren did not generally mix once they had reached teenage, and that teachers tended to be biased against black children. The belief was that teachers misled them into believing they were doing better at school than was the case and, partly as a consequence, the search for employment proved a dispiriting and hopeless experience. As for the police, the girls knew the Home Beat Officer and thought well of him, but were critical of the behaviour of younger officers, particularly during the disorders. If the non-authoritarian approach of the Home Beat Officer was more widely adopted by others, they suggested, there would be a more harmonious relationship between the black community and the police.

Birmingham and Coventry
– 16 July 1981

1   The object of the visit was to enable Lord Scarman to explore, in a provincial setting, some of the issues arising under Phase 2 of his Inquiry. Discussions were held with local Councillors, police representatives and ethnic community leaders. There had been disorder involving black and white youths in a number of parts of the West Midlands during the preceding weekend. The general view put to Lord Scarman was that these disorders occurred essentially because of unemployment, frustration and in imitation of events elsewhere, rather than because of any deep-seated antipathy towards the police.

Some saw the media as bearing considerable responsibility for fostering expectations of violence among the young; but in general there had been little sign that recent disturbances had been racial in character.

(a) Birmingham

2   In discussion with representatives of the *West Midlands Police* it was emphasized that the force had for many years vigorously pursued a policy of community policing based on permanent beat officers. A particular effort had been made in Handsworth where police had, for example, taken the initiative in arranging the Handsworth Festival and in organizing discussion meetings between young police officers and young blacks and Asians. Some small groups within the community had on occasions tried to discredit such police initiatives. The force's approach, however, remained one based on community policing when normal times prevailed. When disorder broke out, the aim was a quick and positive response with the object of restoring normality speedily so that community-based policing could continue.

3   In discussion with the Leader and other Members of the *County Council* emphasis was placed on the effects of unemployment – felt particularly severely in areas like the West Midlands which had previously enjoyed considerable prosperity – and of urban decay. These twin evils, it was said, had combined to produce a feeling of hopelessness among the residents of the inner city. It was also believed that the media, in influencing young people's perception of a materialist society, and of violent behaviour, had, to some degree, contributed to the disorders. Although a general feeling of confidence in the Chief Constable and the police was expressed, the view that because the force was larger following reorganization the police were remoter from the community and from local leaders in particular was also expressed. It was felt that there was a greater need to establish channels of consultation between the police and community leaders at local level and to promote more community policing. Finally it was suggested that while more money for inner city areas could help reduce physical deprivation, there was also a

need for more sensitive and imaginative policies in the spending of funds.

4   In discussion with Members and Officials of the *Birmingham City Council* the Councillors endorsed the view that the recent disorders had been imitative and the product of unemployment and alienation from authority, rather than anti-police. Although relations between Councillors, local groups and the police were generally described as good, it was again suggested that the policy of community policing could be pursued still further. The lack of confidence in the police complaints procedure did not help the promotion of such police policies. Alienation, particularly among West Indian youths, unbalanced reporting by the media, and the difficulty of obtaining a prompt response to needs from local Government were other factors which combined to complicate the resolution of the community's difficulties.

5   The Chairman and Members of the *Community Relations Council* confirmed that, in their view, the structure of police/ community relations was generally sound: the problem was that the machinery was not used properly and effectively throughout the force hierarchy. The development of police liaison arrangements direct with the local community rather than through the offices of the Community Relations Council had not helped the Council's relationship with the police. Police operations sometimes ignored the role of the Police/Public Liaison Officer, who could help dispel unfounded anxieties in the community about such operations. Considerable emphasis was placed on the desirability of an independent element in the investigation of complaints against the police. The present system was criticized as being cumbersome and it was thought wrong that the police should investigate themselves. Once a complaint had been lodged, it was suggested that the police sometimes pressurized people to withdraw it. Where complaints were investigated, the outcome was generally unsatisfactory, while the response given to the complainant was stereotyped and unimaginative. In discussion on the recent disorders, unemployment, housing, the frustrations of youth, and the underlying prejudice in society against ethnic minorities were held to be important factors. The trivialization by politicians and the media of complex problems did not assist in their solution. Positive steps should be taken to

involve parents in coping with the difficulties of youth, through, for example, the development of community centres. Equally it was important that young people, especially police and probation officers, should be well informed about the nature of the multi-racial society in which they worked. There was, however, a reluctance on the part of ethnic minority leaders to urge black people to pursue a career in the police force, although there was less resistance to the possibility of black people becoming Special Constables. The criminal justice system as a whole was also criticized. It was said to discriminate against blacks: among other things, too few young people and too few blacks were appointed as Magistrates.

(b) Coventry

6   In his visit to *the police in Coventry*, Lord Scarman was informed of the particular difficulties that had arisen in the area following the murder of two Asians in the city, and of the steps which the police and community leaders had taken to try to reduce tension. The police had tried to respond to the tension by sustained contact with community leaders, doubling the number of permanent beat officers and promoting a mobile pattern of policing. Senior officers had also been ready to intervene personally where this was judged necessary in order to help defuse potential conflict. In the longer term, they were seeking to implement a positive system of community policing based on the permanent beat officer and a number of experimental schemes were under way. Although the Asian community had alleged the failure of the police to deal speedily with certain racist incidents in the city, the detection of racist crime had been generally successful, and from the police's point of view the relationship with the community was on the whole encouraging.

Railton Road Youth and Community Centre, Brixton – 22 July 1981

1   Lord Scarman visited the Centre accompanied by Lady Scarman. The Youth Club has some 200 registered members, mostly

black, although many more young people use it on an occasional basis. The Centre has a gymnasium, a games room and a chapel, and at the time of the visit a discotheque was in full session.

2   After touring the Centre, Lord Scarman had an informal discussion with black members of the Club. In the discussion the difficulty of finding and retaining a job was emphasized, as were the high job expectations which black youths had compared with their parents. Doubt was expressed that the schools were meeting the needs of young blacks and an added problem in employment was the prevalence of racial discrimination. Police behaviour was also criticized. Two of those present had been arrested under the 'sus' law and others said that they had been stopped and searched in a rough or rude manner. The possibility of blacks joining the police service was rejected, while at the same time it was thought that black people should be appointed as senior officers in the service. The intense suspicion of the police and the contrast between the aspirations and expectations of the young black people present and their hopes of fulfilling them emerged clearly from the discussion.

Stockwell Park Estate and Tulse Hill Estate – 30 July 1981

(a) Stockwell Park

1   The Estate, which is of a multi-racial character, houses some 1,050 families, about 40 per cent of them being single-parent families. The Tenants' Association described the Estate as one in which a combination of design faults and social problems had turned a planner's dream into a nightmare. The design of the Estate, with low-rise blocks of flats with exterior walk-ways and inter-connecting bridges, made the control of crime a problem. 'Muggings' and burglaries were of particular concern, although since the introduction of a Home Beat Officer with responsibility for the Estate, the overall level of crime had been reduced by about 50 per cent. High unemployment and the lack of social and recreational facilities in Brixton, however, provided a seed-bed for continuing problems among the youth of the Estate.

2   A tour of the Estate revealed the degree of environmental and social problems present. More hopeful signs were a social centre which was in the process of being built; the Neighbourhood Management Office, which was shared successfully by the Home Beat Officer and members of the Estate Management Team; and a section of the Estate housing pensioners with warden-controlled flats and its own Day Centre. The Tenants' Association emphasized, however, that funds for such improvements were severely curtailed and the need for them remained acute.

(b) Tulse Hill

3   The Estate comprised some 900 pre-war balcony flats in twenty-seven blocks. Two years earlier it had suffered from a high level of unused or squatted flats, a high rate of tenant turnover and high crime levels. In early 1980, a consultant from the Priority Estates Project had been appointed to try to improve this state of affairs. Environmental improvements included the establishment of a nature garden run by the tenants in association with the nearby Brockwell Park School, the establishment of a community hall and the development of an adventure playground and a summer play scheme. There was now an elected Tenants' Council on the Estate, which had made special efforts to ensure that ethnic minority groups were represented on it, and a Home Beat Officer had also been appointed.

4   Through the efforts of the tenants and the Home Beat Officer, crime on the Estate had been reduced. In 1979 reported break-ins had been averaging fifteen a week, but these were greatly reduced and there had been none between the end of April 1981 and the time of the visit. However, 'mugging' and the theft of motor vehicles remained a problem. The Tenants' Council was helping to tackle the problem of 'mugging', and a uniformed caretaker patrolled the Estate in the evening. In addition the posting of a Home Beat Officer to the Estate had been generally welcomed and the residents had expressed a desire for a still greater degree of community policing.

5   While improvements on the Estate had been achieved by concerted action, there were a number of underlying problems which made the task a continuing and difficult one. It was pointed

out that high unemployment with little prospect of change, coupled with society's emphasis on material acquisition, led to both material deprivation and a sense of hopelessness, particularly among the youth. Efforts to improve the environment were not helped by the adverse image of Brixton which had been projected by the media. Equally the background of hopelessness was reflected at an earlier age in school, where it was said that teachers' low expectations of children led to under-achievement and early school leaving, while teachers' failure to impose necessary discipline led to further problems.

Wolverhampton and Handsworth, Birmingham – 10 August 1981

1 The visit included discussions with police and community leaders in Wolverhampton and Handsworth and a meeting with the West Midlands County Probation and After-Care Service.

(a) Wolverhampton

2 In discussions with *the police* in Wolverhampton about the disturbances there on 10/12 July 1981, it was said that in the weeks preceding the disturbances, there had been a build-up of tension in the city, fed by rumours of imaginary incidents. When the disorders occurred they had not been racially motivated, nor had they been directed against the police, although the police became the target for attacks when they sought to restore order. The disturbances had, on the whole, been an expression of youthful hooliganism, urged on by a 'copy-cat' element for which, it was held, the media bore considerable responsibility. The activities had initially been uncoordinated, but as the disorder developed, there had been some evidence of organization, and in subsequent police inquiries some caches of petrol bombs had been uncovered. On more general matters, the police identified their relationship with black youths as the main area of friction. The permanent beat officers remained the backbone of the police's attempt to establish good relations with all sections of the community. The force's efforts had not been helped by the

withdrawal of the Wolverhampton Council for Community Relations from the Police/Community Liaison Committee. The police had, nevertheless, been able to liaise direct with many community groups and these contacts were continuing.

3   In discussions with *the Borough Council*, it was said that the disorders of 10/12 July 1981 and an ensuing incident in the Magistrates' Court had led to a deterioration in the relationship between the police and ethnic minority leaders. For its part, the Council had sought over the years to respond to the needs of ethnic minorities, and it had recently established a Race Relations Sub-Committee, and was in the process of employing its own Race Relations Adviser. The restraints on local authority expenditure had, however, seriously affected the authority's ability to maintain funding for ethnic minority projects. More generally, although it was said that the police and the Borough Council had on the whole managed community relations relatively well, there remained the longer-term problems of seeking to influence favourably majority attitudes towards the ethnic minorities and to encourage the minorities' participation in society's institutions. It was argued by one Councillor that positive discrimination was now necessary if progress was to be made. Improvement in education for ethnic minorities was also advocated by the Council and Lord Scarman was told that its policies included a scheme to cope with language problems among young children.

4   *Leaders of the ethnic minorities* suggested that, in essence, there were no real differences between the problems suffered by ethnic minorities in Brixton and those in Wolverhampton. Racial discrimination, urban decay, unemployment, inadequate education and insufficient funds to tackle the problems of ethnic minorities combined to provide a feeling of hopelessness, frustration and a foundation for civil disorder. To these factors were added the problems of policing and complaints about bias in the criminal justice system. It was said that the police were inadequately trained for their role in a multi-racial society. The police complaints system lacked public confidence and required the introduction of a genuinely independent element. The criminal justice system failed to take account of the special problems of ethnic minorities and it was suggested that custodial sentences were too readily handed out to these groups.

(b) West Midlands County Probation and After-Care Service

5   In discussions with the Chairman of the Probation and After-Care Committee, the Chief Probation Officer and other members of the Service about the immediate aftermath of the disturbances, it was suggested that more use might perhaps have been made of probation orders in sentencing people arrested during the disorders. More generally, young blacks were not receiving probation orders in proportion to their number in the offender population. This, it was said, reflected the cultural bias in Magistrates Courts' decisions which had been identified by recent studies conducted under the auspices of the Service. Attention was drawn to a Probation Service project in the Handsworth area where Probation Officers were involved in running a Cultural Centre. The aim was to prevent young people at risk from offending rather than to deal with those who had already offended. While it was recognized that, as a long-term aim, there were dangers in the Service undertaking such non-court work, such projects brought the Service nearer to the community and enabled the community to see the Probation Officer in a more positive light, and not simply as an agent of the Courts.

(c) Handsworth

6   At Handsworth, Lord Scarman met the Chief Constable of the West Midlands, Sir Philip Knights, Chief Superintendent Wilson, Superintendent David Webb and other *police officers*. They explained that the essence of policing there lay in close contact between the police and the community. The backbone of the police effort in the community was the permanent beat officer, who retained his identity as a police officer and was not merely a community worker in uniform. Police were, however, involved in many facets of community life, and such involvement was encouraged by senior officers. The overall approach had reduced crime levels to ones which were now generally in line with those in other parts of Birmingham and had made the police officers' task in Handsworth less difficult. While it would be wrong to suggest that problems never arose between the police and the ethnic minorities, the fact that the recent disorders there had been relatively short-lived was evidence of the progress made.

7   *The ethnic minority leaders* in Handsworth stressed that the recent disturbances had been neither racial nor directed against the police. The community enjoyed a good relationship with the police and the underlying reasons for the recent disturbances were considered to be essentially social and economic. The main problem lay with young people, who required jobs and facilities for recreation. Inevitably this meant more money: such funds should not be allocated only to those areas where relations were bad, but also to areas, like Handsworth, where they were good. While it was important that all groups within the community remained united, as such unity had been a foundation for the improvements in the area, additional resources were necessary if the remaining difficulties were to be readily overcome.

8   In a tour of some community centres in the area, the importance of providing more such centres within the community was emphasized as a means of providing a focus for the youth in the community, as well as a source of advice and help to them. The problems faced by youth in Great Britain were mirrored in other countries in Europe. Handsworth had been successful because the ethnic minorities had been accepted by and become part of the indigenous population without losing their group identity.

Brixton Police Station
– 1 October 1981

1   Lord Scarman spent the afternoon at Brixton Police Station, the headquarters both of 'L' District and of the Brixton Division. In the course of the visit, Lord Scarman met Commander Fairbairn and other senior officers, toured the Police Station and had a discussion with young officers about their experience of policing the area.

2   Among a number of points made in a wide-ranging discussion led by Commander Fairbairn, Lord Scarman was told that the crime situation in Brixton had deteriorated considerably since the April disorders. Although some progress had been made in re-building relations with community leaders, this had not been as rapid as the police would have liked, and there had been some evidence of

attempts to discredit leaders who had been prepared to cooperate with the police. Senior officers outlined a number of lessons they felt had emerged from the April disorders, including a number touching on the handling of disorderly crowds. The merits and demerits of introducing an up-dated Riot Act and of the procedure for considering complaints against the police were also discussed.

3   After a comprehensive tour of the Station, during which he spoke to a number of the officers on duty, Lord Scarman met a group of seven Police Constables (one of whom was black): senior officers were not present. The Constables described some of the problems they found in policing the area and the strains which these imposed. While few problems were found in dealing with members of the black community on an individual basis, hostility generally emerged quickly once a crowd grew. One officer spoke of the dissatisfaction he felt in being unable to develop, because of entrenched attitudes within the community and the strains which these entailed, the rapport with the community for which he would have wished. Another emphasized the deprived social and environmental context in which the police had to operate in Brixton. The importance of street crime and the difficulty of tackling it were also discussed. All the officers were agreed that younger officers had a role to play in communities like Brixton, though a more helpful response from the public of the area would assist them to discharge this.

Inner London Probation Service
– 1 October 1981

1   Lord Scarman met a group of seven members of the Inner London Probation Service, six of whom were officers working in the Brixton area and one the Assistant Chief Probation Officer with responsibility for Lambeth. The Probation Officers thought that the atmosphere in Brixton had generally been quieter since the disorders, although they suggested that the publication of the Inquiry's Report might provide a pretext for this to change.

2   In an exchange of views about the background to the disorders, complaints made by the Probation Officers' clients against

the police were referred to in general terms. These included alleged harassment and stereotyping of blacks as criminals, as well as violent police raids and the acceptance of a measure of police ill-treatment of black people as normal. Lack of confidence in the procedure for complaining against the police was said to be widespread.

3   At the same time, the difficulties of the police in coping with crime in the area were acknowledged and relations between the police and the Probation Service in Brixton were described as generally good. Railton Road was a social centre for the black community, not simply in Brixton but far beyond, and as such was inevitably a magnet for criminals. Social and cultural circumstances also made the police task difficult: not merely the generation gap between West Indian parents and their children, the lack of any extended family to help unmarried mothers cope with their children and the cultural gap between young black people and young white police officers, but the deprived social and physical environment in which the black community had to live. Among the specific problems mentioned – apart from unemployment which seriously affected both the white and the black communities – were racism in prisons and alleged difficulty in obtaining social security benefits. It was suggested that the procedure for securing benefits was lengthy and demoralizing and that social security offices in the Lambeth area were marked by their impersonal design and the poor conditions they offered both for staff and their clients. The present scale of unemployment threatened, it was said, to overwhelm the system.

4   Finally, in a discussion on schooling, it was suggested that secondary schools were too large and that as a result children with problems were lost in them. The House system into which schools were often divided was largely an administrative device. Many West Indian parents claimed that there was a lack of discipline in the schools but there was generally little contact between parents and schools, a defect for which both shared some responsibility.

South London Catholic Caribbean Chaplaincy – 7 October 1981

1   Accompanied by Lady Scarman, Lord Scarman visited the Chaplaincy, where he met a group of adult black members of the Catholic community in South London and a group of younger black members. The visit was arranged by the Archbishop of Southwark's Chaplain to the West Indian community in South London, Father Charles Walker.

2   The older members formed part of a Group set up within the archdiocese of Southwark to continue the work of the Coordinating Congress which had recently brought Catholic lay-people and clergy together to discuss issues facing the Church. The Group identified social factors as the most significant source of the disorders. Homelessness, family breakdown, unemployment and racial discrimination were features of an unjust society in which white people were reluctant genuinely to accept black, and in which black people had no stake. Young black people in particular found themselves in conflict with white institutions, with the police and even with their own parents, and were therefore inclined to reject society as a whole. Rastafarianism, for example, provided both an opportunity of obtaining a new identity and of protesting against white society. Problems between young black people and the police – the allegedly abrasive approach of the Special Patrol Group was said to be a particular problem – had to be seen against this wider social background.

3   The Group identified a number of areas where positive action to improve the situation was necessary, with particular emphasis on education and employment. On education, the Group felt that teachers were inclined to stereotype and discriminate against black pupils and that this was the reason why pupils under-achieved. The natural reluctance of parents to become involved in schools must be overcome. Asian members of the Group mentioned the importance of a curriculum which reflected the diverse cultural backgrounds of pupils in a multi-racial society and the desirability of mother-tongue teaching, although proficiency in the English language was also essential. Smaller classes for immigrant children might be a solution. On employment, the problem of discrimination was men-

tioned as particularly important, along with the need to train unemployed youngsters. Finally, the Group emphasized the leading role the Christian Church must play in overcoming discrimination and working for a more just society.

4   The discussion with the younger Church members further exposed some of the cultural and social factors mentioned by the adult Group. The generation gap between West Indian parents and children, the differences in disciplinary approach between home and school, and the limitations of the educational system were referred to: on schools, the young people thought that they were so geared on an examination basis that they did not develop the natural skills of pupils or prepare them satisfactorily for work. They noted that black and white children seemed to become conscious of their different colour on reaching secondary school. The media were felt to be partly responsible for the continued ignorance and prejudice among white people about black people, a prejudice which resulted in many black people lacking any sense of belonging to British society.

5   The group of young people suggested that the disorders had sprung from a combination of resentment and frustration which had been manipulated to some extent by external influences. As for the police, most of the young people present said that they had been stopped and questioned at some time. They suggested that one reason why black people resented being stopped was that they did not know why they were being questioned. They felt that the police operated on the basis of an unwritten assumption that black youths were criminals and that this reflected wider assumptions among white people about the inferiority of blacks.

Tulse Hill School, Brixton
– 8 October 1981

1   The School was built in the 1950s and at the time of the visit had just under 1,000 boys of mixed ethnic origin with some seventy staff giving a pupil/teacher ratio of 14:1. The average class size was in the lower twenties. A wide curriculum and facilities are offered to cater for the needs and abilities of all pupils. The relationship

between the various ethnic groups in the School was described as good.

2   Two members of the Inner London Educational Authority's Multi-Ethnic Inspectorate were present. They explained that the Inspectorate aimed to meet the special needs of ethnic minorities, promote equality of opportunity in education and make all pupils aware of the cultural origins and diversity of a multi-racial society. To this end improvements were being made in the curriculum content, and ethnic minorities were being encouraged to make full use of the whole curriculum. The teaching of standard English was a vital element in this. It was stressed, however, that the programme of education was not one for schools alone, and that considerable attention was being given to involving parents in the work of schools.

3   In discussions with some members of the staff, the approach to teaching in the School was considered. The aim was to provide a broad education in a wide curriculum and encourage a questioning approach to the subjects. It was emphasized that motivating the pupils in their work and inculcating the basic disciplines of work and organization were important. The flexible and personal approach to the teaching in the School aimed to achieve this and fit the pupils for adult life. The School had a School/Work Liaison Officer whose task was both to assist in finding work for the pupils and to inform the School of employers' needs with the aim of adapting the curriculum to meet them.

4   Lord Scarman concluded his visit with a tour of classrooms where he was able to see work in progress and talk to the pupils.

Metropolitan Police Training Centre, Hendon – 14 October 1981

1   Lord Scarman visited the Training Centre, where he was met by Deputy Assistant Commissioner G. J. Dear, responsible for all training matters in the Metropolitan Police, Commander M. Taylor and other senior officers. Lord Scarman discussed with Mr Dear and his colleagues the training undertaken by a police constable during the probationary period, i.e. the first two years of his service.

Discussion focused in particular on that part of the training which was designed to develop skills in human interaction, including the proposed introduction of human awareness training and of a more precise system for continuous assessment of a Probationer's progress. Lord Scarman was told that having looked closely at initial recruit training recently, the final course for Probationers and the continuation training they received were to be future subjects of review, and the effectiveness of the recently introduced 'street duties course' would be assessed next year.

2   Public Order training and the development of tactical skills to meet new public order problems were also discussed, as was the management training given to supervisory officers, including Inspectors and Sergeants. Following his discussions with senior officers, Lord Scarman was able to sit in on a group of recruits learning about crowd behaviour and the development of disorder. At the end of the class, Lord Scarman had an opportunity to speak to the recruits.

Liverpool
– 16 October 1981

1   The visit took place in part in response to an invitation from the Merseyside Police Committee, in part so that Lord Scarman might see for himself the background to the written evidence he had received from organizations and individuals in Liverpool. During the visit, he toured Liverpool 8 (Toxteth) and met the Police Committee, City Councillors, the Chief Constable and his officers, and religious and community leaders.

2   Opening the discussion with the *Police Committee*, the Chairman, Councillor Margaret B. Simey, explained that the Committee had detected in the causation of the disorders in Toxteth a serious gap between the police and certain sections of the Liverpool community. It had accordingly set up a Working Party which had taken evidence from various community organizations in Liverpool 8, the Merseyside Community Relations Council, the Merseyside Probation and After-Care Committee, and the Police Representative organizations on Merseyside. The Working Party's Interim Report,

shortly to be considered formally by the Police Committee, identified a number of possible ways in which this gap might be bridged. In the discussion which ensued, reference was made to a number of the Working Party's conclusions: the theme of the discussion was how a relationship of mutual trust between the police and all elements of the community might be established. Improved training, consultation with local communities, a more sensitive approach by the police, the status of community liaison officers, policing methods, and lack of confidence in the police complaints procedure were among the issues discussed. Members of the Committee also referred to the concern they felt about the issues of police accountability, the operational independence of the Chief Constable and the role of the Police Authority; and about the serious financial burden which the present arrangements for riot compensation (which were based on the Riot [Damages] Act 1886) threatened to impose on the Authority. None of the Committee members indicated any desire to become involved in decisions about prosecution or the day-to-day management of the police force: many of the elected members, however, did indicate a desire for a greater say in the development of policing policies.

3   In the course of the discussion with the Police Committee the importance of social conditions, especially unemployment, as a factor in the background to the disorders had been mentioned. The vitiating effect of unemployment was again mentioned when Lord Scarman met the Leader of *Liverpool City Council*, Sir Trevor Jones, and the Leader of the Labour and Deputy Leader of the Conservative Groups on the Council, together with its Chief Executive and Community Relations Officer. The Council representatives pointed out that very substantial local authority resources had been spent in Liverpool 8 over the years: it would not therefore be correct, in their view, to describe the area as substantially more deprived than certain other parts of Liverpool. Nor had the disorders been racial: both black and white youths had been involved. Rather, they had been a revolt against authority, particularly the police, fuelled by the central problem of unemployment. Sir Trevor Jones described the steps which the City Council was taking to ensure that a proper proportion of members of ethnic minority communities were recruited to its work-force, and to an exercise the Council had

conducted to consult local opinion by means of a questionnaire; the answers to large-scale unemployment, however, lay in central government's hands. As for the police, none of the political leaders wished to see support for law and order in any way impaired, but they believed steps to improve the relationship between the police and the community in Liverpool 8 were essential. The Police Committee was felt to be remote and emasculated: it was suggested that the Metropolitan Boroughs should have more of a say in policing, perhaps by the Police Committee being constituted of representatives of the Boroughs on a proportional basis rather than, as at present, of County Councillors and Magistrates.

4   Following a tour of Toxteth during which he briefly visited the local police station, Lord Scarman went to the Headquarters of the *Merseyside Police*, where he met the Chief Constable, Mr Kenneth Oxford, senior officers, and representatives of the Merseyside branches of the Police Superintendents' Association and the Police Federation. Among the issues discussed were the impact of the disorders on the force, including its younger officers, the law on disorder, police training and the police complaints system. The Chief Constable indicated that he was currently considering proposals he was to put to his Police Committee which he hoped would, over time, improve substantially the relations between the police and the Liverpool 8 community. At the same time, he pointed out that while manpower and other resources remained limited, any changes in the policing of Liverpool 8 would have an effect on the policing he was able to provide in other parts of the County.

5   Lord Scarman then visited *Church House*, where he met the Anglican Bishop of Liverpool, the Right Reverend David Sheppard, and the Roman Catholic Archbishop of Liverpool, the Most Reverend Derek Worlock. In an informal conversation, the two religious leaders spoke of the constructive role the Church had tried to play before, during and since the disorders. The two leaders referred to the long-standing relative deprivation of the Liverpool 8 area, particularly the extent to which it suffered from unemployment, and to the problem of relations between the police and the community. The importance of a community policing approach, of neighbourhood police stations, of recruitment procedures, of police

236

training, of the procedure for considering complaints against the police, and of a recognition of the role played by racial discrimination in the lives of black people were among the issues discussed. The Church leaders also emphasized the importance of involving communities – particularly the black community – in important decisions which would affect their members' life.

6   Lord Scarman next travelled to the offices of the *Merseyside Community Relations Council*, where he met the Chairman of the Committee, Mr Wally Brown, and other officers, Committee members and staff of the Council. Mr Brown began by pointing out a number of what the Council regarded as important omissions or errors in the written evidence of the Chief Constable of Merseyside to the Inquiry. Having clarified these points, Mr Brown went on to say that the Council was unhappy that the use by the police of CS gas in controlling the disorders in Toxteth on 6 July 1981 had not been investigated by an outside agency. There was, he said, room for doubt as to whether the Chief Constable had correctly assessed the likely degree of risk to the Town Centre from the rioting crowds, and there was evidence that the police had fired the gas directly at rioters. Police relations with the community had been unsatisfactory for some time and were one of the main causes of the disorders. Lack of confidence in the police complaints procedure, the juvenile caution system, and harassment of young people by police officers were among the factors mentioned as tending to undermine this relationship. Improvements in training and the complaints procedure were essential if this was to be overcome. The widespread existence of racial prejudice and the small number of posts black people occupied in important social institutions were also mentioned. Central and local government action was urgently needed to overcome these problems.

7   Finally, Lord Scarman visited the Charles Wootton Centre, in Upper Parliament Street, Liverpool 8, where he met members of the *Liverpool 8 Defence Committee*. The Defence Committee Members emphasized the status of the well-established black members of the Liverpool 8 community as black Britons, not immigrants. In their view, police harassment over a long period, not unemployment, was the main cause of the disorders. The Committee cited various examples of alleged harassment, criticized the Chief Con-

stable's report to his Police Committee on the disorders, and said
that the enforced resignation of the Chief Constable was essential if
police/community relations in Liverpool 8 were to be restored.
They accepted the need for law and order to be preserved and for an
effective police force; they objected, however, to police action
during the riots, particularly in the use of CS gas, and to the heavy
and abrasive way in which Liverpool 8 was policed. If this did not
alter, the community as a whole, it was said, would oppose it. A
change in the attitude of police officers was desirable, along with
improvements in police training and a move towards community
policing. Finally, the members of the Committee referred to a
recent picket they had conducted of a Crown Court at which a youth
arrested during the disorders was to be tried, and asked Lord
Scarman about the law on contempt of court. Lord Scarman
explained that simply standing outside court was not a contempt,
although it might raise other questions such as obstruction of the
highway. If leaflets were handed out to potential jurors or placards
were displayed in such a way as to influence them, however,
contempt would arise. He advised the Committee to avoid the
possibility of laying itself open to contempt proceedings in future.

Appendix C
EVIDENCE RECEIVED BY THE INQUIRY

(1) List of those who gave
Oral Evidence to Phase 1 of the Inquiry

Commander L. Adams
Mr R. C. L. Baker
Mr W. A. Ball
Chief Superintendent R. Boyling
Mr D. W. Brettle
Police Constable J. A. Brown
Police Constable M. P. Bullen
Deputy Assistant Chief Fire Officer B. W. Butler
Police Constable M. J. Cameron
Mr H. Y. Chin
Mr J. R. Clare
Mr P. R. Costello
Mr D. D. Currie
Mr J. G. Ellis
Commander B. K. Fairbairn
Commander M. Ferguson
Mr J. D. Fraser MP
Miss M. E. Fudger
Police Constable R. S. Fuller
Police Constable R. G. Garrett
Mr M. P. Girdler
Mr W. H. Hall
Mr D. Hoffman
Mr W. Jackson
Police Constable R. Jones
Reverend G. R. Kent
Councillor E. R. Knight
Councillor S. Lansley
Mr C. A. H. Laws
Mr L. A. Leon

Mr H. Lindo
Police Constable S. T. Lock
Superintendent F. MacLennan
Mr I. S. Madray
Police Constable S. P. Margiotta
Mr A. Morgan
Assistant Chief Ambulance Officer J. E. Moss
Reverend R. W. H. Nind
Reverend D. Petersen
Chief Superintendent W. G. Phillips
Detective Chief Superintendent J. J. Plowman
Chief Superintendent J. P. Robinson
Inspector P. H. Scotchford
Chief Superintendent R. M. Sillence
Mr S. J. Smith
Police Constable R. J. Timperley
Miss C. Tisdall
Police Constable P. F. Thornton
Deputy Assistant Commissioner L. F. J. Walker
Mr R. S. Webb

(2) List of those who gave
Oral Evidence to Phase 2 of the Inquiry

Mr J. Bones
Dr C. Cross
Deputy Assistant Commissioner G. J. Dear
Mr J. J. Figueroa
Assistant Commissioner W. H. Gibson
Mr G. Greaves
Mr D. Lane
Mr O. Sylvestre

(3) List of Organizations and Individuals who submitted Written Evidence to Phase 2 of the Inquiry

Amongst those submitting evidence were:

Action Learning Trust
Acton, Dr T. A.
African Advisory Committee
Aldrich, Professor Howard
All Faiths for one Race (AFFOR)
Argent, Reverend Alan
Armitage, Reverend Michael
Ashton, D. L. W.
Aspinall, Dr R.
*Association of Chief Police Officers of England, Wales and Northern Ireland
Association of Jamaicans (UK) Trust
Avebury, Lord
*Avon and Somerset Constabulary
Bailey, Ian, and Reeves, Mark
Baker, Roger C. L.
Bakhshi, Dr S. S.
Banton, Professor Michael
Barker, A.
Battersea Community Action Group
Bays, Councillor Anthony W.
Bean, June
Bennun, Mervyn Edward
Bensted, A. F.
Bertram, G. C. L.
Bex, Reverend A. A.
*Bing, Inigo, and others
*Birmingham Community Relations Council
Black, Bernard
Board of Deputies of British Jews, The
*Bones, Jah
Boxer, Charles

*Asterisks denote that the evidence was circulated to represented parties.

Bradford Metropolitan Council, City of
Bramwell, D. R. and A. C.
Branton, A.
Brent, London Borough of
Bristol, City of
Bristol Council for Racial Equality
Bristol Resource Centre
British Association of Settlements and Social Action Centres
British Overseas Optical Missions
British Resistance, The (Chelmsford Pride)
Brixton Advice Centre
Brixton Community Arts Centre
Brixton Council of Churches
*Brixton Domino and Social Club, The
*Brixton Neighbourhood Community Association
Brixton Residents and Traders Association
*Brixton Society, The
Brixton Workshop
Brockett, R. A.
*Brown, John
Brown, Michael
Bryce-Smith, Professor D.
Bull, Ray
Butler, M.
Cain, Maureen
*Caribbean House Group
Catholic Commission for Racial Justice
Centre for Contemporary Studies
Chandhrey, G. A.
Chapman, R. P.
Circle Trust, The
Clapham Park East Tenants' Association
Clark, Edmund P.
*Cocking, V. J.
Coggins, Palma
Cohen-Dunkley, Mabel
Colchester, Reverend John C. W.
Colman, Andrew M., and Gorman, L. Paul

Commission for Racial Equality
*Concern
*Council for Community Relations in Lambeth
Cramp, H. W.
Crawford, Jeff
Crisp, Dorothy
Croydon Council for Community Relations
Davison, C. N.
*Deakin, Professor Nicholas
Dellar, D.
*Devon and Cornwall Constabulary
Disablement Income Group
Ealing, London Borough of
Ealing – Southall Labour Party
Economic League, The
*Education and Science, Department of
Effra Neighbourhood Council
*Employment, Department of
Ende, T. A.
Endicott, Grattan
*Environment, Department of
Evans, D. L.
Evelegh, Colonel J. R. G. N.
Families Need Fathers
Fire Brigades Union
*Fraser, John, MP
Friends of Blair Peach Committee, The
Gaskell, George, and Smith, Patten
Ghodsian, M.
Goan Association (UK)
Gould, Professor S. Julius
Greater Manchester Council – Hytner Report
Greater Manchester Police
Grey, Thomas R.
Griffith, Albert R.
Guildford, Bishop of
Gumper, George E.
Gupta, Councillor S. D.

Hackney Council for Racial Equality
Hackney, London Borough of
Hamilton, David
Hansford-Miller, Dr Frank
*Hastie, Tom
Haye, Linda B.
*Health and Social Security, Department of
Heaton, Phil
Hewitt, Stanley E. K.
Holdaway, Dr Simon D.
*Home Office
Inglewood, Lord
*Inner London Education Authority
*Inner London Probation and After-Care Service
International Committee on Race Relations
Iqbal, Dr Muhammad
Jamaican High Commission
Jeffries, A.
Jenkins, J. F.
Jenkyns, Patricia
John, B. A.
Justices' Clerks' Society
*Kingston, Bishop of, and the Borough Dean of Lambeth
Kirklees Metropolitan Council
Knibb, John Gordon
Kyle, T.
*Kyriacou, Mrs H.
Lambeth Federation of Tenants
*Lambeth Institute
*Lambeth, London Borough of
*Lambeth Youth Committee
Laughton, Janet
Lee, Catherine
Legal Action Group
Legalise Cannabis Campaign
Leonard, J. E.
*Lewisham, London Borough of
Little, Professor A. N.

Liverpool, City of
London and Counties Tenants' Federation
*London Voluntary Service Council
Lyell, Nicholas MP
Lyon, Michael
McKay, Sheila
Mackesy, Patricia
Maclachlan, T. K.
Magna Carta Campaign for the Protection of the Ethos of
    Britain
Manchester, City of
*Manpower Services Commission
Martin, Gloria
*Melting Pot Foundation, The
Merseyside Community Relations Council
Merseyside County Council
Merseyside Police
Merseyside Probation and After-Care Service
Methodist Centre, The – Princes Park, Liverpool 8
*Methodist Church – Division of Social Responsibility
*Metropolitan Housing Trust
*Metropolitan Police
Moberly, Dr Patience
Monahan, Jennifer
Mookerjee, Saura Prasad
Moore, George
Moore, Professor Robert, and Wallace Dr C. C.
Morgan, I.
*Morris, Professor Terence
Morrison, A.
Muller, L. W.
National Association for Asian Youth
National Association for Multi-Racial Education
National Association of Probation Officers
National Association of Probation Officers – Merseyside
    Branch
*National Council for Civil Liberties
National Union of Licensed Victuallers

*National Union of Teachers
National Viewers' and Listeners' Association
National Youth Bureau
Nelson, Reverend Vernon
New Bridge, The
Nind, Reverend Robert W. H.
Nottingham, City of
Nottinghamshire Probation and After-Care Service
O'Connell-Kotalawela, Maureen
Oxley, Charles
Pal, Sumil Kumar
*Parkinson, Astel
Payne, Ronald
Pearce, Andrew, MEP
Percival, Arthur
*Perry, Reverend Cecil
Petersen, Reverend Dennis
Philipson, Major A. T.
Pick, Ulrich
Pitt, Councillor Robin
*Police Federation, The
*Police Superintendents' Association of England and Wales,
   The
Portman, Mrs M., JP
Powell, John
Price, Miss K. E.
Princes Park and Granby Community Council (Liverpool 8)
Priority Estates Project
Pritchard, Dr R. John
Railton-Mayall Residents Action Group
*Railton Road Youth and Community Centre
Rampton, Anthony
*Rastafarian Collective
Rasta International HQ
Revell, Anna
*Rex, Professor John
Rickcord, Ronald G. W.
Roberts, K. and others

Rowe, Andrew
Royal Town Planning Institute, The – North-West Branch
*Runnymede Trust
SRI International
St Andrew's Primary School, Stockwell
Sanders, R.
Sandole, Dr Dennis J. D.
Scott, Reverend G. Michael
*Scott, Mary
Scrimshaw, Peter
Shah, R. K. D.
Shaw, John, and Luckham, Bryan
Shaw, L. W.
Shelton, William J. M., MP
Sheth, Pranlal, and Wainwright, David
Simey, Lady Margaret B.
Simmonds, Reverend Paul R.
Smith, Reverend Graham
South London Catholic Caribbean Chaplaincy
South London Islamic Centre
Southwark, Archdiocese of – Coordinating Congress Continuation Group
*Sports Council
Stephens, Reverend Peter J.
Sterling, George
Stickland, Charles A.
Stockwell Park Estate Tenants' Association
Stoke Newington Community Association
Stroud, C. Eric, and Pollak, Margaret
*Sylvestre, Owen
Tavistock Clinic, The
Tayler, Reverend Robert
Taylor, Maxwell
Thomas, Mivart G. W.
Thompson, Councillor A.
Thompson, Thomas
*Tilley, John, MP
*Timms, Peter

*Trades Union Congress
Tuckman, Patricia C.
Turton, Timothy R. S.
Vassall Neighbourhood Council
Vetta, Atam
Wade, Dr C. M., and others
Waitman, Philip
Walker, Kenneth M.
Warren, Peter M.
Watt, Rebecca
Watt, Tom
*Wegg-Prosser, Charles
Westbury, Jack
West Indian Ex-Servicemen's Association UK
*West Indian Standing Conference
*West Midlands County Council
West Midlands County Probation and After-Care Service
*West Midlands Police
West Yorkshire Metropolitan County Council
*West Yorkshire Metropolitan Police
Wilding, Dr J. M.
Will, Ian M.
Williams, G. M. J.
Willis, Mrs F. C.
Wojlas, B. J.
Woodward, Roger
Woolf, Bernard F.
World Order for Cultural Exchange, The – and the World
    Council of Ideologies
YMCA National Centre, Lakeside, Cumbria

In addition, some 450 letters were received from members of the public giving their views on the issues before the Inquiry.

Appendix D
BIBLIOGRAPHY

Amongst the Publications available to the Inquiry were:

Alderson, John, *Policing Freedom*, MacDonald and Evans, 1979

Anderton, Bill, 'Police and Community: A Review Article', *New Community*, Vol. III, No. 3, Summer 1974

Banton, Michael, *Police Community Relations*, Collins, 1973

Banton, Michael, 'The Definition of the Police Role', *New Community*, Vol. III, No. 3, Summer 1974

Boot, Adrian, and Thomas, Michael, *Jamaica: Babylon on a Thin Wire*, Thames and Hudson, 1976

Bristol TUC, *Slumbering Volcano? Report of an Enquiry into the Origins of the Eruption in St Paul's, Bristol on 2nd April 1980*, Bristol, 1981

Brown, John, *Shades of Grey; Police/West Indian Relations in Handsworth*, Cranfield Police Studies, 1977

Chase, Louis, 'West Indians and the Police', *New Community*, Vol. III, No. 3, Summer 1974

Clarke, and others, 'The Selection of Evidence and the Avoidance of Racism: a Critique of the Parliamentary Select Committee on Race Relations and Immigration', *New Community*, Vol. III, No. 3, Summer 1974

Clarke, Edith, *My Mother Who Fathered Me: A Study of the Family in Three Selected Communities in Jamaica*, George Allen and Unwin, 2nd Edition, 1966

Commission for Racial Equality, *Youth in Multi-Racial Society: The Urgent Need for New Policies*, March 1980

Craig, Dennis, *Language Identity and the West Indian Child*, West Indian Concern, London

Dade County Citizens' Committee, *Report of the Governor's Committee into the Disorders in Dade County (Miami), May 1980*, Florida, 1980

Demuth, Clare, *Sus; A Report on Section 4 of the Vagrancy Act 1824*, Runnymede Trust, 1978

Dodd, D., 'Police and Thieves on the Streets of Brixton', *New Society*, 16 March 1978

Field, and others, *Ethnic Minorities in Britain: A Study of Trends in Their Position Since 1961*, Home Office Research Unit Report No. 68, HMSO, 1981

Gibson, Ashton, *Pregnancy Among Unmarried West Indian Teenagers*, West Indian Concern, London

Hain (ed), Kettle, Campbell and Rollo, *Policing the Police: Volume 2*, John Calder, 1980

Hall, and others, *Policing the Crisis: Mugging, the State and Law and Order*, Macmillan, 1978

HM Chief Inspector of Constabulary, *Report for 1980*, HMSO, HC 409, 1981

Holdaway, Simon, 'The Reality of Police/Race Relations', *New Community*, Summer 1978

House of Commons – Home Affairs Committee, *Race Relations and the 'Sus' Law*, Session 1979–80, Second Report, HMSO, HC 559

House of Commons – Home Affairs Committee, *Racial Disadvantage, Volume I – Report With Minutes of Proceedings*, Session 1980–81, Fifth Report, HMSO, HC 424–1

Humphrey, Derek, *Police Power and Black People*, Panther, 1972

Institute of Race Relations, *Police Against Black People*, Evidence submitted to the Royal Commission on Criminal Procedure, IRR, 1979

James, David, 'Police/Black Relations: The Professional Solution', *The British Police*, edited by Simon Holdaway, Arnold, 1979

John, Augustine, *Race in the Inner City*, Runnymede Trust, 2nd edition, 1972

Judge, Anthony, 'The Police and the Coloured Communities', *New Community*, Vol. III, No. 3, Summer 1974

Lago and Troyna, 'Black and Bitter', *Youth and Society*, No. 29, June 1978

Lambert, J. R., *Crime, Police and Race Relations*, OUP/IRR, 1970

Lambeth, London Borough of, *Final Report of the Working Party into Community/Police Relations in Lambeth*, January 1981

Manning, Mary, 'At the Roots of a Black Riot', *Community Care*, 13 October 1976

Bibliography

Mansfield, C. P., 'New Role for Women Police', *Police Review*, 11 May 1979

Marshall, Commander Peter, 'Policing: The Community Relations Aspect', *New Community*, Vol. III, No. 3, Summer 1974

Miami, City Police Department, *Miami Riots, May 1980 – After-action Report*

National Advisory Commission on Civil Disorders, Report, Washington DC, 1968 (The Kerner Report)

National Advisory Committee on Criminal Justice Standards and Goals, *Disorder and Terrorism*. Report of the Task Force on Disorders and Terrorism, 1976

National Commission on the Causes and Prevention of Violence, *To Establish Justice, To Insure Domestic Tranquility*. Final Report of the Commission, Washington DC, December 1969

Rights in Concord – The Response to Counter-inaugural Protest Activities in Washington DC, January 18–20. (A special staff study submitted by the Task Force on law and law enforcement)

Law and Order Reconsidered. (A staff report to the Commission)

Rights in Conflict – The Violent Confrontation of Demonstrators and Police in the Parks and Streets of Chicago during the Week of the Democratic National Convention of 1968. (A report by Daniel Walker, Director of the Chicago Study Team)

National Council for Civil Liberties, *Southall, 23 April 1979*. Report of the Unofficial Committee of Inquiry, London, 1980

The Death of Blair Peach. The supplementary report of the Unofficial Committee of Inquiry, London, 1980

Nettlefold, Rex M., *Mirror, Mirror – Identity, Race and Protest in Jamaica*, William Collins and Sangster (Jamaica) Ltd, 1970

New Jersey, State of: Governor's Select Commission on Civil Disorder, *Report for Action*, February 1980

Parks, Genn and Dodd, *Surveying Victims*, John Wiley and Sons, 1977

Parry, J. H., and Sherlock, P., *A Short History of the West Indies*, Macmillan Press, 3rd Edition, 1971

Patterson, Sheila, *Dark Strangers*, Tavistock, 1963

Phillips, Melanie, 'Brixton and Crime', *New Society*, 8 July 1976

Police Complaints Board, *Triennial Review Report, 1980*, HMSO, Cmnd 7966

Police Foundation, *Newark Foot Patrol Experiment*, Washington DC, 1981

Police – Immigrant Relations in England and Wales, *Observations on the Report of the Select Committee on Race Relations and Immigration*, HMSO, Cmnd 5438, 1973

Policy for the Inner Cities (White Paper), HMSO, Cmnd 6845, June 1977

Pryce, Kenneth, 'The Life-Styles of West Indians in Britain; A Study of Bristol', *New Community*, Vol. VI, No. 3, Summer 1978.

Pulle, Dr Stanislaus, *Police-Immigrant Relations in Ealing*, Runnymede Trust, 1973

Race Today, Vol. 5, No. 11, December 1973. (The entire issue)

Race Today, Vol. 8, Nos. 7/8, July/August 1976.(The entire issue)

Racial Discrimination, HMSO, Cmnd 6234, 1975

Review of the Public Order Act 1936 and Related Legislation, HMSO, Cmnd 7891, 1980

Roberts, Duggan and Noble, *Unregistered Youth Employment and Outreach Careers Work: The Final Report – Part I, Non-Registration*, Department of Employment. (To be published)

Robinson, Clive, 'Police/Immigrant Relations: the Community Relations Commission's Involvement', *New Community*, Vol. III, No. 3, Summer 1974

Rose, E. J. B., and Associates, *Colour and Citizenship – A Report on British Race Relations*, Oxford University Press, 1969

Royal Commission on Criminal Procedure, *Report*, HMSO, Cmnd 8092, January 1981

The Investigation and Prosecution of Criminal Offences in England and Wales: The Law and Procedure, HMSO, 8092-1, January 1981

Select Committee on Race Relations and Immigration, *Report on Police/Immigrant Relations*, HMSO, HC 471–I, 1971–72

Report on the West Indian Community, HMSO, HC 180–I, 1976–77

Short, Clare, *Talking Blues*, All Faiths for One Race, Birmingham, 1978

Bibliography

Stevens, P., and Willis, C. F., *Race, Crime and Arrests*, Home Office Research Study No. 58, HMSO, 1979

Troyna, Barry, 'The Reggae War', *New Society*, 10 March 1977

US Department of Justice, Law Enforcement Assistance Administration, *Prevention and Control of Urban Disorders: Issues for the 1980s*, Washington DC, August 1980

Whitaker, Ben, *The Police in Society*, Eyre Methuen, 1979

Williams, K. M., *The Rastafarians*, Ward Lock Educational, 1981

Working Party on the Establishment of an Independent Element in the Investigation of Complaints against the Police, *Report*, HMSO, Cmnd 8193, March 1981

Wyndham Place Trust, *Violence in Britain*, 1980

Youth in Society, No. 31, October 1978. (The entire issue)

Appendix E
MAP

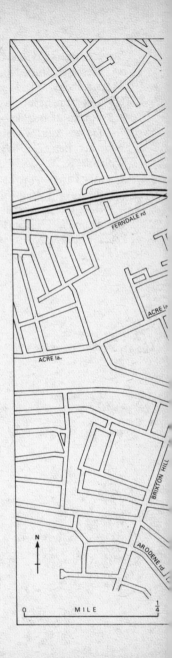

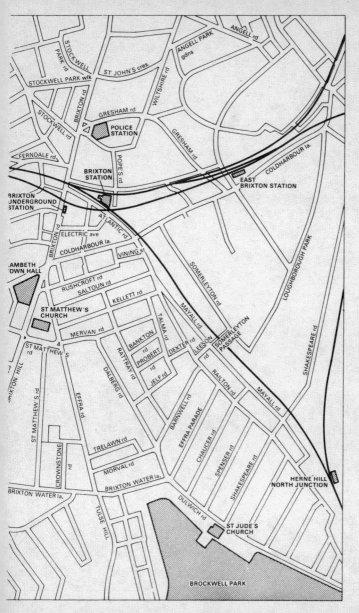

MORE ABOUT PENGUINS, PELICANS, PEREGRINES AND PUFFINS

For further information about books available from Penguins please write to Dept EP, Penguin Books Ltd, Harmondsworth, Middlesex UB7 0DA.

In the U.S.A.: For a complete list of books available from Penguins in the United States write to Dept DG, Penguin Books, 299 Murray Hill Parkway, East Rutherford, New Jersey 07073.

In Canada: For a complete list of books available from Penguins in Canada write to Penguin Books Canada Ltd, 2801 John Street, Markham, Ontario L3R 1B4.

In Australia: For a complete list of books available from Penguins in Australia write to the Marketing Department, Penguin Books Australia Ltd, P.O. Box 257, Ringwood, Victoria 3134.

In New Zealand: For a complete list of books available from Penguins in New Zealand write to the Marketing Department, Penguin Books (N.Z.) Ltd, Private Bag, Takapuna, Auckland 9.

In India: For a complete list of books available from Penguins in India write to Penguin Overseas Ltd, 706 Eros Apartments, 56 Nehru Place, New Delhi 110019.

A CHOICE OF
PELICANS AND PEREGRINES

☐ *The Knight, the Lady and the Priest*
Georges Duby   £5.95

The acclaimed study of the making of modern marriage in medieval France. 'He has traced this story – sometimes amusing, often horrifying, always startling – in a series of brilliant vignettes' – *Observer*

☐ *The Limits of Soviet Power* **Jonathan Steele**   £3.50

The Kremlin's foreign policy – Brezhnev to Chernenko, is discussed in this informed, informative 'wholly invaluable and extraordinarily timely study' – *Guardian*

☐ *Understanding Organizations* **Charles B. Handy**   £4.95

Third Edition. Designed as a practical source-book for managers, this Pelican looks at the concepts, key issues and current fashions in tackling organizational problems.

☐ *The Pelican Freud Library: Volume 12*   £4.95

Containing the major essays: *Civilization, Society and Religion, Group Psychology* and *Civilization and Its Discontents*, plus other works.

☐ *Windows on the Mind* **Erich Harth**   £4.95

Is there a physical explanation for the various phenomena that we call 'mind'? Professor Harth takes in age-old philosophers as well as the latest neuroscientific theories in his masterly study of memory, perception, free will, selfhood, sensation and other richly controversial fields.

☐ *The Pelican History of the World*
J. M. Roberts   £5.95

'A stupendous achievement . . . This is the unrivalled World History for our day' – A. J. P. Taylor

A CHOICE OF
PELICANS AND PEREGRINES

☐ *A Question of Economics* **Peter Donaldson** £4.95

Twenty key issues – from the City and big business to trades unions – clarified and discussed by Peter Donaldson, author of *10 × Economics* and one of our greatest popularizers of economics.

☐ *Inside the Inner City* **Paul Harrison** £4.50

A report on urban poverty and conflict by the author of *Inside the Third World*. 'A major piece of evidence' – *Sunday Times*. 'A classic: it tells us what it is really like to be poor, and why' – *Time Out*

☐ *What Philosophy Is* **Anthony O'Hear** £3.95

What are human beings? How should people act? How do our thoughts and words relate to reality? Contemporary attitudes to these age-old questions are discussed in this new study, an eloquent and brilliant introduction to philosophy today.

☐ *The Arabs* **Peter Mansfield** £4.95

New Edition. 'Should be studied by anyone who wants to know about the Arab world and how the Arabs have become what they are today' – *Sunday Times*

☐ *Religion and the Rise of Capitalism*
   R. H. Tawney £3.95

The classic study of religious thought of social and economic issues from the later middle ages to the early eighteenth century.

☐ *The Mathematical Experience*
   Philip J. Davis and Reuben Hersh £6.95

Not since *Gödel, Escher, Bach* has such an entertaining book been written on the relationship of mathematics to the arts and sciences. 'It deserves to be read by everyone . . . an instant classic' – *New Scientist*

PENGUIN TRAVEL BOOKS

☐ **Arabian Sands** **Wilfred Thesiger** £3.50

'In the tradition of Burton, Doughty, Lawrence, Philby and Thomas, it is, very likely, the book about Arabia to end all books about Arabia' – *Daily Telegraph*

☐ **The Flight of Ikaros** **Kevin Andrews** £3.50

'He also is in love with the country . . . but he sees the other side of that dazzling medal or moon . . . If you want some truth about Greece, here it is' – Louis MacNeice in the *Observer*

☐ **D. H. Lawrence and Italy** £4.95

In *Twilight in Italy, Sea and Sardinia* and *Etruscan Places,* Lawrence recorded his impressions while living, writing and travelling in 'one of the most beautiful countries in the world'.

☐ **Maiden Voyage** **Denton Welch** £3.50

Opening during his last term at public school, from which the author absconded, *Maiden Voyage* turns into a brilliantly idiosyncratic account of China in the 1930s.

☐ **The Grand Irish Tour** **Peter Somerville-Large** £4.95

The account of a year's journey round Ireland. 'Marvellous . . . describes to me afresh a landscape I thought I knew' – Edna O'Brien in the *Observer*

☐ **Slow Boats to China** **Gavin Young** £3.95

On an ancient steamer, a cargo dhow, a Filipino kumpit and twenty more agreeably cranky boats, Gavin Young sailed from Piraeus to Canton in seven crowded and colourful months. 'A pleasure to read' – Paul Theroux

PENGUIN TRAVEL BOOKS

☐ *The Kingdom by the Sea* **Paul Theroux**   £2.50

1982, the year of the Falklands War and the Royal Baby, was the ideal time, Theroux found, to travel round the coast of Britain and surprise the British into talking about themselves. 'He describes it all brilliantly and honestly' – Anthony Burgess

☐ *One's Company* **Peter Fleming**   £2.95

His journey to China as special correspondent to *The Times* in 1933. 'One reads him for literary delight . . . But, he is also an observer of penetrating intellect' – Vita Sackville West

☐ *The Traveller's Tree* **Patrick Leigh Fermor**   £3.95

'A picture of the Indies more penetrating and original than any that has been presented before' – *Observer*

☐ *The Path to Rome* **Hilaire Belloc**   £3.95

'The only book I ever wrote for love,' is how Belloc described the wonderful blend of anecdote, humour and reflection that makes up the story of his pilgrimage to Rome.

☐ *The Light Garden of the Angel King* **Peter Levi**   £2.95

Afghanistan has been a wild rocky highway for nomads and merchants, Alexander the Great, Buddhist monks, great Moghul conquerors and the armies of the Raj. Here, quite brilliantly, Levi writes about their journeys and his own.

☐ *Among the Russians* **Colin Thubron**   £2.95

'The Thubron approach to travelling has an integrity that belongs to another age' – Dervla Murphy in the *Irish Times*. 'A magnificent achievement' – Nikolai Tolstoy

PENGUIN REFERENCE BOOKS

☐ *The Penguin Map of the World* £2.50

Clear, colourful, crammed with information and fully up-to-date, this is a useful map to stick on your wall at home, at school or in the office.

☐ *The Penguin Map of Europe* £2.95

Covers all land eastwards to the Urals, southwards to North Africa and up to Syria, Iraq and Iran * Scale = 1:5,500,000 * 4-colour artwork * Features main roads, railways, oil and gas pipelines, plus extra information including national flags, currencies and populations.

☐ *The Penguin Map of the British Isles* £1.95

Including the Orkneys, the Shetlands, the Channel Islands and much of Normandy, this excellent map is ideal for planning routes and touring holidays, or as a study aid.

☐ *The Penguin Dictionary of Quotations* £3.95

A treasure-trove of over 12,000 new gems and old favourites, from Aesop and Matthew Arnold to Xenophon and Zola.

☐ *The Penguin Dictionary of Art and Artists* £3.95

Fifth Edition. 'A vast amount of information intelligently presented, carefully detailed, abreast of current thought and scholarship and easy to read' – *The Times Literary Supplement*

☐ *The Penguin Pocket Thesaurus* £1.95

A pocket-sized version of Roget's classic, and an essential companion for all commuters, crossword addicts, students, journalists and the stuck-for-words.